Construction Defect Litigation

THE COMMUNITY ASSOCIATION'S GUIDE
TO THE LEGAL PROCESS

With immense gratitude for the love, support, and many teachings of my beloved parents, Dr. and Mrs. Sherwood E. Feinberg.

Construction Defect Litigation

THE COMMUNITY ASSOCIATION'S GUIDE TO THE LEGAL PROCESS

By Ross W. Feinberg, ESQ.
& Ronald L. Perl, ESQ.

Community Associations Press®
Alexandria, VA

ISBN 978-1-59618-005-5
© 2006 Community Associations Press,® a division of Community Associations Institute.

Community Associations Press
A Division of Community Associations Institute
225 Reinekers Lane, Ste. 300
Alexandria, VA 22314

To order additional copies of this book, please write to the publisher at the address above or call
(888) 224-4321. You can also order online at *www.caionline.org/bookstore.cfm.*

*This publication is designed to provide accurate and authoritative information in regard to the subject matter covered.
It is sold with the understanding that the publisher is not engaged in rendering legal, accounting, or other professional
services. If legal advice or other expert assistance is required, the services of a competent professional should be sought.*
—From a Declaration of Principles, jointly adopted by a Committee of the American Bar
Association and a Committee of Publishers

Printed in the United States of America

Library of Congress Cataloging in Publication

Feinberg, Ross, 1958–
    Construction defect litigation : the community association's guide to the legal process /
    By Ross Feinberg & Ronald L. Perl.
        p. cm.
    Includes index.
    ISBN-13: 978-1-59618-005-5
    1. Construction contracts—United States. 2. Liability (Law)—United
States. 3. Construction industry—Law and legislation—United States.
4. Actions and defenses—United States. 5. Homeowners'
associations—United States. 6. Condominium associations—United
States. I. Perl, Ronald L., 1951– II. Community Associations Institute.
III. Title.
    KF902.F45 2006
    343.73'07869—dc22
                                2006006439

Contents

Acknowledgments vii

Part I—Fundamentals 1
  Introduction 3
  Chapter 1: Overview 5
  Chapter 2: Communicating with the Attorney and Members 15
  Chapter 3: Attorney-Client Privilege 23

Part II—The Investigation 27
  Chapter 4: Checking the Statutes of Limitations 29
  Chapter 5: Hiring the Construction Defect Attorney 33
  Chapter 6: Assembling the Expert Team 37
  Chapter 7: How Experts Identify Defects 45
  Chapter 8: Invasive Testing 53

Part III—Before Filing a Lawsuit 57
  Chapter 9: Builder's Right-to-Repair Laws 59
  Chapter 10: A Builder's Right-to-Repair: Step-by-Step 69
  Chapter 11: Other Steps before Litigation 73

Part IV— The Lawsuit 81
  Chapter 12: Who Files Suit—Association or Owners? 83
  Chapter 13: Legal Theories of Recovery 91
  Chapter 14: Construction Defect Litigation Step by Step.............................111

Part V— Alternative Dispute Resolution 125
  Chapter 15: Mediation...127
  Chapter 16: Arbitration, Judicial Reference, & Private Judges 135

Part VI—Finances 141
  Chapter 17: The Finances of Litigation..143
  Chapter 18: Recoverable Damages..149

Part VII—The Morning After 155
  Chapter 19: Reconstruction 157

Part VIII—Special Considerations 169
  Chapter 20: High-Rise Building Claims 171

Part IX—Appendices...177
  1. State Standing-to-Sue Statutes 178

Contents (continued)

2. Construction Defect Statutes of Limitations for the 50 States and the District of Columbia 179
3. Commercial General Liability Insurance Triggers of Coverage 206
4. Reconstruction Contract Term Definitions 217
5. Investigating and Remediating Mold...220

Index..224

About the Authors 226

About CAI 231

Acknowledgments

I would like to give special thanks to my colleague Ronald Perl, ESQ., for his many contributions to this text and for supporting me as a contributing author. Additionally, this text would not be possible without the support of Community Associations Institute, its chief executive officer, Thomas Skiba, and the director of Community Associations Press, Debra Lewin.

Special appreciation is also due to my partners at Feinberg Grant Mayfield Kaneda & Litt, LLP, our staff, and especially my long-time paralegal, Kim Daley, and our office administrator, Sonia Ariss, each of whom put countless hours into organizing, interpreting and finalizing the manuscript. The text could not have been completed without the encouragement and support of my partners and the other professionals within the firm.

Finally, I would like to thank my family for being ever so patient with me while I put this book together. While this text has been a vision of mine for many years, it was my wife, Kimberly, who made me believe that I could complete the project and my precious children, Caroline and Rocky, who somehow gave me the time away from them to complete the task.

It is my sincere hope that you find the book educational and informative whether you are an attorney, forensic expert, community manager, board member, homeowner, or simply an individual interested in the construction defect process.
—*Ross Feinberg*

Community Associations Press is grateful to Scott B. Carpenter, ESQ., G. Douglas White, P.E., Benjamin Dutton, RS, Nico F. March, CFM, Lauren Lee, CMCA, AMS, and board member Patty Kawakami for reviewing this manuscript and providing valuable feedback. Their expertise and time are greatly appreciated.

PART ONE

Fundamentals

Introduction

Developers and contractors are professionals whose businesses are challenging under even the most ideal conditions. Residential development and construction are made all the more complex by fierce competition for resources, a shortage of qualified labor, an erratic economy, and incessant market demands.

Developers and contractors dislike construction defect litigation as much as homeowners do, and most will make genuine efforts to resolve problems quickly and efficiently—if you let them.

Whether a defect is severe enough to warrant legal action depends on which side of the contract you signed. For the homeowner, understandably, all defects are serious; but, from a practical standpoint, most probably aren't serious enough to require a lawsuit. Constructive negotiations with the developer, builder, or contractor nearly always lead to resolution. In fact, most construction defects are resolved without legal action—and for good reason. Litigation is extremely costly. Associations and homeowners must compare the cost to repair construction defects against the cost to argue about them.

Although we are attorneys, we're not encouraging readers to rush to the courthouse at the first sign of damage. On the contrary, we encourage you to pursue friendly resolution with your developer or contractor, let them make repairs, and consider all non-legal options seriously before you file suit. However, for the unfortunate minority who find themselves faced with litigation, we intend this book to provide enough guidance to make the process as productive and positive as possible—not only for homeowners and associations, but also for developers, contractors, and others involved in the process.

For common-interest developments, also known as community associations, an already complex process can be aggravated by added layers of governance and operation. Thus, the association's manager and its board become key players in the litigation process. It's a complicated, time-consuming process they generally know little about. For self-managed associations, board members also serve as managers who not only aren't experts on litigation, but also may not have a firm grasp on governing *and* operating their associations.

In some cases, association boards consist of developer directors (because as owner of the unsold homes, the developer has a vested interest in governing the association) and homeowner directors. These are associations in transition. The balance of governance gradually shifts toward homeowner directors as properties sell, but resolving construction defects during the transition stage presents unique challenges because developers and homeowners are likely to have different interests. Addressing the specifics of the transition process is beyond the scope of this book; however, the process for resolving defect claims described here applies to those in transition and should prove very useful.

Construction defect litigation is complex, time consuming, and staggeringly expensive. If you're embarking on this process, we believe this book will simplify many of its complexities, save you a lot of time, and, ultimately, cost you less money.

CHAPTER 1

Overview

Resolving construction defect claims is a legal process; so, of necessity, this is a book in part about law. But, it isn't a legal book or a book written just for lawyers. It's a national construction defect guide written for managers, board members, homeowners, and others in (and working for) community associations who need to participate in and understand the construction defect litigation process.

The manager and the board will play the central roles in this process that will be directed by the association's general counsel and the construction defect attorney. Communication and teamwork will be essential.

The Main Players

The community manager plays a central role in the construction defect litigation process. For self-managed associations this important role is filled by board members. Therefore, wherever this text speaks directly to managers, it's also intended for those board members who are also managing their associations.

Assisting an association or group of homeowners with defect claims can be challenging and rewarding for a manager; but, board members, homeowners, and others need to understand the manager's role, their own roles, and the importance of communication and teamwork to everyone's success.

Coordinating a defect suit will increase the manager's activities—likely beyond the scope of the management contract. Boards should expect to sign an addendum to the contract listing additional services, responsibilities, and fees. The defect attorney should work with the manager from the beginning to determine the scope of these responsibilities. For self-managed boards, the increase in activities should be supported by a defect committee, if possible.

A construction defect case will require that boards make many decisions that can affect possibly hundreds of homeowners and usually millions of dollars. Despite the advice of attorneys, managers, and experts, these decisions will be very difficult and often have no apparent right or wrong approach. This is a huge responsibility for a group of homeowner volunteers. Fortunately, boards are protected by a legal concept called the business judgment rule. Therefore, one of the objectives of this book is to assist boards to make decisions about their construction defect case that satisfies the business judgment rule.

The Business Judgment Rule

Making informed decisions is at the heart of what is referred to as the business judgment rule.

The business judgment rule exists in one form or another in every state in the union.[1] Generally, the rule provides that courts will defer to—and not second guess—the business judgment of directors, if the directors act in good faith, with loyalty to the corporation (the association), and on an informed basis.[2]

The business judgment rule is critically important to directors and managers because the association is usually responsible for the repair and maintenance of the common areas,[3] and board decisions about these areas—particularly when a community is faced with construction defects—may be controversial. Members may have different views on whether to pursue developers for defects, how to investigate defects, and how to make repairs. Some members may sue to overturn a board's decisions on construction defects. This is where the business judgment rule comes into play.

The business judgment rule immunizes directors from personal liability, if they follow it. Stated another way, a director who follows the rule cannot be sued successfully. Also, courts cannot overturn decisions made by directors who act in good faith and in what they believed was the association's best interests.[4] A hallmark of the business judgment rule is that, when the rule's requirements are met, a court will not substitute its judgment for that of the board.[5]

CASE NOTE: A case in Florida illustrates how the business judgment rule was applied in a construction defects suit. In *P.S. Farrington v. Casa Solana Condominium Association, Inc.,** water leaked through cracks on the outside of a condominium building, making it necessary to repair the exterior, replace windows, and repair interior units. Unfortunately, the association had no recourse against the developer, so it had to pay for the repairs itself with a special assessment.

The association's governing documents authorized the board to levy a special assessment for immediate or emergency needs. However, before doing so, the board hired architects and engineers to investigate the damage and recommend the best methods to address the problems. After reviewing the reports of the architects and engineers, the board determined that in "its business judgment," there was an immediate need for the repairs and levied the special assessment.

The owners filed an injunction to stop the board from contracting for the repairs and collecting the special assessment alleging, that the problems had existed for several years, so there was no immediate need—as required by the governing documents. The trial court, invoking the business judgment rule, declined to issue the injunction. The owners appealed, but the court of appeals upheld the first decision finding that the board had acted reasonably because it had relied on the architects and engineers to provide sufficient information to make an informed decision. If the board had not relied on the professionals, it could have exposed itself to liability, and its actions could have been second-guessed by the courts. *517 S.2d 70 (Fla. 3d DCA 1987).

The concepts underlying the business judgment rule derive from the realities of doing business in a community association. The rule has been justified on two grounds. First, directors should be given wide latitude to handle corporate affairs because hindsight by a court is a poor way to evaluate business decisions. Second, owners voluntarily undertake the risk of bad business judgment since they aren't required to purchase in a common-interest development.[6]

What is a Construction Defect?

Does the association have a routine maintenance problem or a construction defect that should generate a claim? Defects fall into several categories, and the manager who understands the differences will be able to identify whether defects exist and who should investigate them.

Violation of Industry Standards

Construction methods and materials that fail to meet industry standards are subject to defect claims. Standards vary from one area to another depending on a number of factors. For example, a construction technique that is appropriate in the dry Southwest may violate industry standards in the humid Northeast. Standards aren't compiled in a single reference in most states, so whether they have been violated is the subject of expert opinion. Unlike most states, California has comprehensive building standards that provide useful examples of defects nationwide.[7]

Violation of Building Codes

Violation of laws and local ordinances is another category of construction defect claims. Most local governments (such as cities and counties) have adopted the Uniform Building Code, the Uniform Plumbing Code, the Uniform Fire Code, and other similar codes designed for nationwide application. Additionally, local jurisdictions frequently enact ordinances relating to construction practices apart from the uniform codes. Violation of these uniform codes and other laws also give rise to construction defect claims.[8]

Failure to Follow Plans and Specifications

Another category of defect claim results from a builder's failure to follow the plans and specifications prepared by architects, geotechnical engineers, structural engineers, civil engineers, mechanical engineers, and other design professionals.

Design Deficiencies

Defects can relate to design as well as violation of industry standards, building codes, and failure to follow plans and specifications. A case in point is *Del Mar Beach Club Owners Assn v. Imperial Contracting Co.*,[9] in which a developer built condominiums on an unstable bluff overlooking the Pacific Ocean. The California Court of Appeal held that placing buildings on the bluff was a design defect sufficient for the developer to be held liable for construction defects.

Product Failures

Many products are manufactured specifically to be built into residential structures

What is a Construction Defect Claim?

California first defined a construction defect claim in 1998:
Any civil action that seeks monetary recovery against a developer, builder, design professional, general contractor, material supplier, or subcontractor of any residential dwelling based on a claim for alleged defects in the design or construction of a residential dwelling unit. *California Code of Civil Procedure Section 664.7.*

Then Nevada broadened the definition:
"Constructional defect" means a defect in the design, construction, manufacture, repair or landscaping of a new residence, or an alteration of or addition to an existing residence, or an appurtenance and includes, without limitation, the design, construction, manufacture, repair or landscaping of a new residence, of an alteration of or addition to an existing residence, or of an appurtenance:

1. Which is done in violation of law, including, without limitation, in violation of local codes or ordinances;

2. Which proximately causes physical damage to the residence, an appurtenance or the real property to which the residence or appurtenance is affixed;

3. Which is not completed in a good and workmanlike manner in accordance with the general accepted standard of care in the industry for that type of design, construction, manufacture, repair or landscaping; or

4. Which presents an unreasonable risk of injury to a person or property. *Nevada Revised Statutes 40.615.*

And Washington state contributed further to the definition:
"Action" means any civil lawsuit or action in contract or tort for damages or indemnity brought against a construction professional to assert a claim, whether by complaint, counterclaim, or cross-claim, for damage to or the loss of use of real or personal property caused by a defect in the construction of a residence or in the substantial remodel of a residence. "Action" does not include any civil action in tort alleging personal injury or wrongful death to a person or persons resulting from a construction defect. *Revised Code of Washington, Title 64, Section 2(1).*

While Arizona limited its definition to actions against sellers:
Homeowners' Association Dwelling Action" means any action filed by a homeowners' association against the seller of a dwelling arising out of or related to the design, construction, condition or sale of the dwelling (emphasis added). *Arizona Revised Statutes Section 33-1901.*

—roofs; siding; windows; sliding glass doors; and heating, ventilation, and air conditioning (HVAC) systems. If these products fail because they were designed poorly or manufactured with improper materials or faulty techniques, they can give rise to construction defect claims.

HISTORICAL PERSPECTIVE: Disputes over defective construction have been around for decades, but only recently has construction defect litigation evolved into separate area of practice. Construction defect cases in California increased significantly during the 1980s as a natural consequence of a booming construction industry and a lack of skilled labor. By the mid-1990s, defect litigation had become a separate area of practice in California and other states, like Arizona and Nevada, where building was also booming. Today, most states have attorneys who specialize in construction defect claims.

State legislatures responded to the increase in defect litigation by enacting laws that were either pro-homeowner or pro-builder. Many states have passed various builders' right-to-repair laws establishing steps that associations and homeowners must take before filing a lawsuit. California led the way in 1995 with what is commonly called the Calderon Legislation.* Presently 21 states now give developers the right to make repairs under certain circumstances before construction defect actions can be filed. **California Civil Code Section 1375, part of the Davis-Sterling Common Interest Development Act.*

Other Categories of Defects

Other examples of construction defect categories include: improper soil compacting and landfill operations,[10] improper irrigation and landscaping,[11] and using poor building materials.[12]

Gather Evidence

The community manager—whether a professional community manager or a board member of a self-managed association—invariably is the first person to hear about defects from homeowners: the roof is leaking, there's no hot water, the HVAC system isn't cooling enough, the street has a new pothole or the sidewalks have cracked, and there's a swamp of standing water in the tot lot. The community manager must document each complaint and solve each problem. Recognizing these problems as potential construction defects, investigating them, and gathering evidence is the beginning of the manager's pivotal role in the process.

Document Complaints

The manager should document all complaints from homeowners concerning potential defects and report them to the association board. If the manager doesn't already have standard procedures and reporting forms for communicating construction defect issues to the board, he or she should develop them.

Make Temporary Repairs

The community manager must not only report complaints to the board, but also recommend how to resolve them. First, the manager must decide whether a particular complaint is a maintenance issue or a potential defect. If it's a potential defect, the manager will recommend to the board temporary repairs that will limit further damage and forestall personal injuries.

The manager should maintain separate records for each temporary repair, and the contractors doing the work should thoroughly document each repair with photographs and detailed field notes. If defect claims are eventually made, the costs of temporary repairs should be recoverable at trial. Generally, only temporary repairs should be made at this early stage since permanent repairs may destroy key evidence if claims are pursued.

Inspect the Defects

Community managers and boards generally get their first indication that potential construction defects exist from patterns of resident complaints or temporary repairs. A single complaint of a leaking roof or blocked plumbing may not suggest a defect, but multiple reports of the same problem indicate that it's time to investigate.

Some management companies have working relationships with construction companies that perform forensic investigations. If the manager doesn't know of qualified investigators, the association attorney probably does. Therefore, it's quite common for boards or managers to contact an attorney at this early stage. One advantage of bringing the attorney into the investigation at an early stage is that the law firm, rather than the homeowners or their association, can retain the necessary experts to conduct an investigation. If the experts are retained by the law firm, the results of their investigation can be protected from early disclosure by the attorney work-product privilege—under which the opinions and written reports of experts working at the direction of the attorney are protected from disclosure until the case reaches a certain stage in trial preparations.

At this stage, the investigation is informal—primarily visual inspections give the experts an idea of the potential for real problems.

Investigate the Responsible Parties

Information and evidence also needs to be gathered concerning the potential parties to be pursued in any construction defect claim, including the developer, general contractor, design professionals (such as architects and engineers), subcontractors, and material suppliers.

Assemble Documents

The community manager should assemble and preserve all documentation that will later be used if the association pursues a claim against the developer or others. Numerous categories of documents need to be collected: HOA organizational documents, project plans and specifications, homeowner complaint records, temporary repair records, and communications with the builder.

Survey the Homeowners

If complaints are increasing or patterns are emerging, surveying all homeowners might be a useful means of gathering early evidence of potential defect claims. If the board and manager prepare the survey, they should seek advice about its contents from the association attorney. Preferably, the attorney should prepare and distribute the survey and receive the responses directly. Otherwise, the results may not be protected by attorney-client privilege.

DEVELOPER'S PERSPECTIVE: Sometimes the developer or consultants can't find some of the defects or understand why the association's consultants think that a certain condition constitutes a defect. A joint walkthrough provides the developer with an opportunity to fully understand the claimed deficiencies and to discuss solutions with the association's experts. To encourage the free exchange of ideas and information, these walkthroughs are usually conducted without attorneys or board members, and whatever occurs during the walkthrough cannot be used later as evidence. In a successful walkthrough, knowledgeable professionals work together toward solutions in a non-adversarial context; they don't make decisions, they make recommendations upon which the decision makers can act.

Hire a Construction Defect Attorney

The board needs to consider the extent and severity of the defects, and the opinion and recommendations of the manager, and decide whether to hire an attorney who specializes in construction defects. The manager will be invaluable in the search process.

Assemble a Team of Experts

At some point soon after defects have been identified, the association will need to hire experts qualified to evaluate them and recommend necessary repairs. These experts may be hired before the construction defect attorney, but it's best to hire the attorney first and get his or her help with hiring the experts.

Investigate the Defects Again

The experts will visually inspect the property, working closely with the community manager who will schedule inspections with homeowners. They will also work with the attorney who will be closely involved with the board and the manager.

Steps Before Filing a Lawsuit

As the investigation progresses, the association or owners may be required to take formal steps before they can file a lawsuit against the developer or others. Since the mid-1990s, many states have enacted various forms of pre-litigation legislation designed to resolve defect claims without formal legal action. These steps generally include notifying the developer of possible defects in writing, identifying the defects, allowing the developer to inspect them, and participating in mediation in an attempt to resolve the claims. At least 21 states have gone one step further, giving developers the right to make repairs before litigation.

During this time, the attorney and community manager will coordinate the necessary inspections and testing between the association and the investigators for the homeowners and for the developer. Throughout the process, the attorney should maintain accurate records of units or areas inspected, tested, and temporarily repaired and should provide copies to the association manager or board at least monthly.

Filing the Lawsuit

In most cases, these pre-litigation steps resolve the problem. But in the few instances when they don't, actual litigation begins when the association files a complaint against the developer and other defendants. The association's or homeowner's attorney can name just the developer in the complaint, or may also include subcontractors, material suppliers, and design professionals who were implicated during the preliminary investigation. If the suit names only the developer, and subcontractors, material suppliers, or design professionals are involved, the developer will file cross claims against them.

Construction defect cases are by their nature complex litigation. It isn't uncommon for 30 or more parties to be involved in a construction defect lawsuit and for the damages to range in the millions of dollars. Tens of thousands of documents will be generated, and if the case isn't settled early, dozens of depositions may be taken. If the case proceeds to trial, testimony generally will last for weeks or months.

There are two approaches to a construction defect case. First is the traditional approach, which follows the rules of civil procedure: discovery, which includes interrogatories and requests for admissions and documents, filing and arguing discovery motions, taking depositions, pretrial conferences, settlement conferences, and if the case is not resolved, a full-blown trial. The traditional approach slows the process and drives up costs. For instance, every party could serve interrogatories on every other party, resulting in a huge duplication of effort and needless expense.

The second, and more enlightened, approach is the case management order (CMO). With a CMO, everyone agrees to suspend the normal rules of discovery and instead follow a road map that's been tailored for construction defect cases. It conserves resources and expedites the process by establishing deadlines.

The community manager plays an important role in executing a CMO. He or she keeps the lines of communication open constantly among individual unit owners, the board, the expert team, and defect attorney, and ensures that the attorney-client privilege is protected. The manager facilitates communication especially between the defect attorney and the board, ensuring that the board receives written litigation status reports at least monthly and meets with the attorney at least quarterly to discuss the progress of the defect claims. The community manager also keeps the board and attorney informed about new homeowner complaints, requests for temporary repairs, or other activities that may have a bearing on the litigation.

If defect litigation proceeds to trial, present and past community managers become material witnesses. They are frequently among the first witnesses to be deposed. The defendants are looking for testimony that establishes when defects were first identified because that may bolster their statute-of-limitations defenses.

Resolution and Reconstruction

Although the process typically takes two years or more, construction defect cases are eventually resolved either by settlement or a trial judgment. While no nationwide study is available, it is estimated that at least 95 percent of construction defect cases are resolved by settlement.

The manager, board, and experts work together to decide what repairs to make with the available settlement proceeds. The funds available for repair are the net funds—what's left after deducting attorneys' fees, expert fees, and other costs of the investigation. The board may also hire a reconstruction consulting firm to help set repair priorities.

The association will next select and hire a reconstruction contractor with the help of the manager who will identify prospective candidates, check their references, and arrange interviews.

Reconstruction can take anywhere from a few weeks to a year or more, depending on the size of the project and the scope of the repairs. The community manager will be very busy during this time, serving as liaison among individual owners, the reconstruction contractor, the project manager, and the board. This is a particularly challenging time for a community manager: reconstruction frequently brings traffic delays, noise, safety concerns, and frayed homeowner nerves. Managers who keep everyone informed about what's happening and when greatly ease the disruption.

When the reconstruction is completed, the managers and board should be able to look back with pride on a successful claims resolution.

This is a broad overview of what's in store for community associations facing a construction defect case. The following chapters will explore each aspect in more depth.

Endnotes

1. 3A Fletcher, Cyclopedia of the Law of Practice Corporations (Perm. Ed. 1986) sec. 1039.

2. *Id.*

3. *See,* for example, California Civil Code section 1364.

4. Lee v. Interinsurance Exchange, 50 Cal.App.4th 694, 57 Cal. Rptr.2d 798 (1996).

5. Katz v. Chevron Corp., 22 Cal.App.4th 1352, 27 Cal.Rptr.2d 681 (1994).

6. 18B American Jurisprudence Second, Corporations, section 1704 (1985).

7. California Civil Code Section 896.

8. *See, for example,* Nevada Revised Statutes Section 40.615(1).

9. 123 Cal.App.3d 898, 176 Cal. Rptr. 886 (1981).

10. Avner v. Longridge Estates, 272 Cal.App.2d 607, 77 Cal.Rptr. 688 (1969).

11. Raven's Cove Townhomes, Inc. v. Knuppe Development Co., 114 Cal.App.3d 783, 171 Cal.Rptr.334 (1981).

12. Kreiger v. Eichler Homes, Inc., 269 Cal.App.2d 224, 74 Cal.Rptr. 749 (1969).

CHAPTER 2

Communicating with the Attorney and Members

A ny legal action, and especially a construction defect case, is an involved and detailed undertaking involving many people. As with so many other aspects of community association governance and management, continuous and open communication will be the key to success in a defect case. Board members and especially managers should strive for effective communication among the members, the attorney, and the association's expert team. The level and nature of communications with the association attorney, especially, will change as he or she assumes the role of coordinator in the legal case.

Attorney Communications with the Board
Written Reports
It's common for attorneys handling defect claims to prepare written status reports for the board either monthly or quarterly. The manager should discuss the timing and manner of reporting with the board and then convey the board's preferences to the attorney in writing.

Important topics that should be covered in each written status report include:

1. Recent developments: The attorney should report on developments in the case since the last report, such as inspections, exchange of documents, expert investigations, formal discovery, mediations, pretrial conferences, and the assigned trial date.

2. Evaluation: As soon as possible in the claims-resolution process, the manager should ask the attorney to evaluate the association's case, including the best legal theories for recovery, defenses available to the developer and subcontractor, and the potential range of recovery. The attorney should constantly update this evaluation as the case proceeds toward trial.

3. Status of costs and fees advanced: Defect cases are generally handled on a contingency fee basis. Costs associated with the claims (filing fees, court reporting fees, reproducing plans, and other expenses) and expert fees are financed in a number of ways. Except in the rare case where an association can cover these costs from current revenues, it must repay the costs and fees when the claims are resolved. The association may repay a reserve fund, a lender, or an attorney who advanced costs and fees.

Repaying costs will reduce the funds available for reconstruction. Therefore, the board must achieve a delicate balance between conducting a thorough investigation to prepare a case for trial, without allowing the investigation's costs to consume too large a portion of the settlement proceeds. To make proper decisions, the board must be kept informed of the costs that have been advanced and must be repaid.

4. Upcoming events: The attorney should advise the board of upcoming key events that may involve them or the homeowners. Examples of key events are inspections, testing, depositions, mediations, and trial.

Board Meetings

The board will undoubtedly want to meet periodically with the construction-defect attorney. The community manager should let the attorney know when and how often the board wishes to meet, and the meetings should be conducted in executive session. In addition, board members, manager, and attorney should communicate freely by letter, phone, fax, or e-mail—particularly as claims near possible resolution or preparations for trial are underway because as developments occur, decisions need to be made.

The community manager must vigilantly maintain the attorney-client privilege when handling these communications. Keeping all privileged documentation in separate files marked "Privileged & Confidential—Attorney-Client Communications" becomes more challenging—and more important—as the frequency and level of communication increases.

Attorney Communications with Members

While the association is the client and the attorney reports to the board, there are many occasions when the attorney communicates directly with the owners.

Homeowner Surveys

Surveys are frequently used to gather information during the course of a defect investigation—particularly at the outset—from individual owners concerning defects they're aware of and problems they've experienced. Surveys are generally prepared by, or with the assistance of, the attorney and circulated by the board, the manager, or the attorney. A cover letter from the attorney typically accompanies the survey that explains its purpose, provides contact information for members who have questions, and specifies the deadline for returning it directly to the attorney.

Completed surveys should always be returned to the association attorney to protect attorney-client privilege. Experienced attorneys who represent homeowners in defect claims maintain that the owners' responses to surveys are protected. Defendants, on the other hand, frequently take the position that the survey responses are not privileged. Judges are split. However, there is no privilege if the survey responses are not sent by the members directly to the attorney.

Disclosure Statements

Most states require homeowners to make certain written disclosures when they sell their homes.[1] Homeowners who have knowledge of construction defects or pending construction-defect litigation are required to disclose that information.

To assist homeowners to meet these requirements, many attorneys who handle defect claims prepare disclosure statements and periodically—perhaps quarterly—distribute them to members. The attorney may distribute them directly to homeowners or provide them to the community manager or board for distribution with invoices or newsletters.

Disclosure statements are intended for dissemination to third parties such as realtors and prospective purchasers. They are not privileged communications and do not contain attorney-client material.

What's In a Disclosure Statement?

- When and where a lawsuit for construction defects was filed.
- The parties to the lawsuit.
- The present status of the case.
- The anticipated trial date.
- A list of defects revealed by the investigation to date.
- A statement that the law firm represents the homeowners association, and does not represent individual homeowners.
- A request that owners refrain, if at all possible, from making alterations or repairs (including painting and new floor coverings) until the defect claims are resolved.

Developments in the Claims Process

Although the attorney will be communicating primarily with the board as defect claims progress toward resolution, sometimes direct communication with the members is in order. Remember, when a common interest development is the plaintiff, the defect attorney doesn't represent the individual unit owners; therefore, communications with individual owners are not privileged, and the attorney will omit sensitive information that should only be shared with the board.

Special Membership Meeting Notice

In many states, before lawsuits can be filed, the association must convene a membership meeting. Giving members adequate notice of these meetings is also mandated. For example, in California, the attorney must notify all members that:[2]

1. A meeting will take place to discuss problems that may lead to a civil action against the developer.

2. The time and place of the meeting.

3. The options that are available to address the problems, including filing a civil action, alternatives to pay for those options, and whether payments will be made from reserve funds, or regular, special, or emergency assessments.

4. The complete text of any written settlement offer and a concise explanation

of the specific reasons for the terms of the settlement offer.

Even in states that don't require a meeting, notice still must be sent to the members. Typically, the notices must include the following:[3]

1. The nature of the action to be filed and the relief sought.

2. The expenses and fees the board anticipates incurring to prosecute the action.

Membership Meetings

During the course of defect claims resolution, the association attorney will periodically attend annual or special membership meetings to brief members and residents on the steps taken in the claims process, the steps remaining before trial, and the general progress made toward resolution.

As is the case in correspondence to members, the attorney should not discuss privileged information at such meetings. Invariably owners ask the attorney how the lawsuit will turn out; however, he or she must walk a thin line—being open and frank with the members, while at the same time not conveying privileged information.

Sometimes it will be useful for the experts involved in the case to participate in annual or special member meetings, along with the attorney. They may give presentations on their findings using slides, diagrams, and other visual aides.

The attorney must explain some realities of the defect claims resolution process to members whether at annual meetings or otherwise. Chief among the realities is that there is never enough money from a resolution to repair all the defects. However, as part of their services, the attorney and experts will help the board prioritize the repairs. The first priority is to repair defects that threaten life safety, such as electrical deficiencies that pose fire hazards. The second priority is to repair defects that are damaging the structures by water intrusion through the roofs, walls, windows, doors, and other openings. The lowest priority is typically to repair items that pose no threat to people or structures, such as landscaping.

Owners often mistakenly believe that they will receive a distribution from the settlement to use as they see fit. Therefore, another reality that the attorney must communicate to members is that all settlement funds (less attorneys' fees, expert fees, and costs) will be used only for repairs that are the obligation of the association. Such repairs involve common-area deficiencies as well as defects within individual units that are integrally related to the common area.

Notice of Inspections and Testing

During construction defect lawsuits, claims invariably are investigated by visual inspections and invasive testing. The attorney must manage all communications with the members during this process.

During visual inspections, the attorneys and experts for the various parties examine the interiors and exteriors of a select number of individual units. The evidence gathered during visual inspections and invasive testing is critical to proving an association's case and equally critical for the developer or builder in defending against it. It's therefore of paramount importance that each unit owner who is asked to make his or her unit available for inspections or testing do so. Owners will get a stronger sense of the importance of cooperating if they receive a letter from the association's attorney describing the inspections, testing, dates, schedule, and a statement about the importance of participating.

Preparing for Trial

When the pretrial discovery phase begins, the defect attorney communicates frequently with members. Depositions begin at this point, and can last for months. The people most knowledgeable about the claims for each party will be deposed. For community associations, those most knowledgeable include past and present managers, board members, and owners. Even in an average size defect case, it isn't uncommon for dozens of owners to be deposed.

The attorney will send letters to the members bringing them up to date on the general status of the case and advising them that their depositions will be taken soon. Rarely are all owners deposed. Typically, the association's attorney and the developer's attorney agree on how many and which units will be represented and the schedule for the depositions. Staff in the attorney's office schedule depositions by phoning the owners using contact information provided by the association manager.

To achieve the best possible settlement, it's very important for the association to be prepared for a trial, regardless of the odds against it. Therefore, as the trial date approaches, the association's attorney must communicate frequently with association members and keep them ready to participate in a trial.

If a defect case does go to trial, the association's attorney will call many witnesses including present and former community managers and board members, a few owners, and the association's expert witnesses. While not all owners will be called as witnesses, the attorney will generally send a letter to all owners advising them of the date and location of the trial and encourage them to attend. It isn't necessary or practical for all owners to attend, but a strong show of interest by owners attending the trial will impress the judge and the jury, if there is one.

The community manager plays a vital role in preparing for trial by assisting the attorney to select and locate owners to be witnesses and convincing owners to attend the trial in support of the association's cause.

Settlement

Once the claims are settled, either the board or defect counsel will communicate the facts of the settlement to the members; however the attorney will probably be more effective explaining the important provisions of a settlement. Members need to know as much as possible about the terms of the settlement, including terms that are confidential and the consequences of violating them—monetary penalties or exposure to subsequent claims and lawsuits.

Generally, the role of the association's defect attorney ends when the case is concluded by settlement or by judgment—for those rare cases that go to trial. But prior to settlement, the attorney frequently provides information to the board on reconstruction issues—potential contractors or repair priorities.

Tools for Member Communications

Maintaining excellent communications with the members throughout the defect claims resolution process must be a top priority for community managers and board members.

Newsletters

Most associations have monthly or quarterly newsletters they can use to keep members updated on the defect claims resolution. While claims are in progress, the association can run a column such as, "What's New in Our Defect Litigation?" where recent developments can be summarized without disclosing privileged information.

The attorney will send progress reports to the board periodically; and, although they can't be shared with the members, the manager can extract non privileged information from these reports to pass along to members in the newsletter. For example, the attorney's progress report might describe the invasive testing that recently took place and also evaluate the test results based on information received from the association's experts. The newsletter, by contrast, would report on the testing, but not the evaluation.

Newsletters can also notify members of key dates in the claims resolution process, such as upcoming inspections, testing, depositions, mediations, and the trial date.

While settlements will be the subject of special communications to the members from the board or attorney, they can be announced in newsletters as well. The newsletter must, of course, omit the confidential details of the settlement.

Flyers

Posting flyers on bulletin boards, mail kiosks, and other locations throughout the community will remind members about events already announced in the newsletter or at a meeting. Flyers can also be used to solicit last minute assistance from members. For instance, members will resist invasive testing for a number of reasons, and flyers appealing for participation can be helpful.

Frequently Asked Questions with Answers

As defect cases near resolution, members have many questions: How much is the developer paying in settlement? How much are the subcontractors paying? How much of the settlement is going to the lawyers? How much is going to the experts? How much will be left to make repairs? Do the individual homeowners get any money? When will the settlement funds be available? When will repairs begin? How long will it take? What happens if money is left over?

At this point the manager should prepare a list of frequently asked questions with answers. These FAQs can be printed in the newsletter, made into a handout to distribute at or before meetings, mailed to nonresident owners, and posted on the association's website

Written FAQs have several advantages. First, members receive consistent answers to commonly asked questions. Second, board members and community managers won't be plagued by owners asking the same questions repeatedly. Third, homeowner meetings—where these questions are routinely asked—will be shorter if owners have the information they need on a handout going into the meeting.

Walk the Community; Talk to the Members

Face-to-face communications are invariably the best. Community managers and board members should walk through the community at least monthly. Such walks are particularly helpful when defect claims resolution is in progress.

While board members and managers frequently walk the community to identify common area maintenance problems and violations of association rules, they should also consider the walk a forum in which to simply talk to owners they meet along the way. Owners are always interested in hearing directly from the manager and board members about the status of the claims and airing their specific concerns face-to-face.

Endnotes

1. *See, for example,* Nevada Revised Statutes Section 40.688.

2. California Civil Code Section 1365(k).

3. *See, for example,* Section 5, Title 64, Revised Washington Statutes and Colorado Revised Statutes Section 38-33.3-303.5.

CHAPTER 3

Privileged Communications

I t's very important for the manager and board to understand the nature of privileged communications so that they can protect those privileges during defect litigation. At the same time, it's important for the manager to keep the members well informed of all key developments during the claims resolution process without compromising privileged information. This being said, it's up to the attorney, not the manager, to report regularly to the members either in newsletter articles or letters.

Attorney-Client Privilege

Communications between attorneys and clients are privileged; this means that no oral or written communications between the attorney and the client can be discovered by other parties—or any third parties—to the claims or litigation. The privilege is very broad: it covers all communication concerning the investigation of construction defects, the legal theories of recovery, the strengths and weaknesses of the opposing party and its experts, evaluations of the likelihood and possible amount of recovery, and the options for reconstruction. The purpose of the privilege is to promote full, candid discussion of all pertinent facts and legal issues, both favorable and adverse, and to assist the client in evaluating options and making decisions.

But who is the client? Community managers and boards must understand this question. In common interest developments, generally the association is the client because it's responsible for the maintenance and repair of common areas, which are defined in the association's governing documents, including the CC&Rs. Invariably, the areas that require repair or replacement when defective construction has taken place are the common areas—roofs, exterior siding, stucco, exterior doors and windows, decks, balconies, porches and landscaping, and other elements. Associations act by and through their boards; and, the manager, in turn, acts as agent to the board.

It's important for owners to understand that they aren't the clients, and it's critical that the manager understand this as well. The association's attorney should lay down guidelines at the outset of the process that clarify this distinction and explain how to protect privileged communications from disclosure. The manager must diligently ensure that the guidelines are implemented and maintained—especially the guideline that privileged communication between the attorney and the board is not to be disseminated to the members.

Work-Product Privilege

Related to, but separate from, the attorney-client privilege is the work-product privilege or work-product doctrine. This privilege is, like the attorney-client privilege, recognized in virtually all states. "Work product" can generally be described as the thoughts, efforts, and strategies of the attorney while working on a particular client's case. Like communications between an attorney and a client, an attorney's work product is protected from discovery by opposing, or any third, parties to litigation. Work product also extends to communications between attorneys and other professionals who investigate and document defects—construction consultants, architects, and engineers.

Reports, field notes, photographs, and other documents prepared by these professionals for the attorney are subject to the work-product privilege, and they cannot be discovered by opposing parties until such time as the professional is formally declared an expert who will be a witness at trial. Thus, the work-product privilege permits the attorney to consult with different professionals without fear of discovery.

Attorneys may provide their clients with written reports, studies, and evaluations prepared by consultants who have not yet been designated as trial witnesses without waiving the work-product privilege. Again, attorneys and board members must ensure that the privilege is not waived by disseminating information to those who are not the client, i.e., the association members.

Invoices for legal or professional services are privileged communications, and they're frequently overlooked when filed. These documents may be reviewed and approved by the board, but they are then typically routed by the community manager to accounting personnel for payment. Thus, they tend to end up in accounting department files, rather than legal files. If these documents are to remain in accounting files, they must be segregated as "Privileged & Confidential —Attorney-Client Communications" files. The privilege applies to these documents because they frequently describe legal issues, investigations by consultants, and activities of counsel that divulge privileged information.

Board Meeting Packets

When defect claims resolution is in progress, the manager will provide key documents relating to the pending claims—status reports from counsel, expert reports, invoices for legal and expert fees, and temporary repair invoices—in the board meeting packet. These should be segregated and placed in a separate section of the board packet clearly labeled with words such as, "Executive Session Materials —Defect Litigation—Privileged and Confidential."

The manager and board members must keep executive-session materials separate from the other non-privileged documents, even after the board meeting. All too frequently, managers or board members file packets without segregating executive-session materials. These files may remain in storage for years before a request is made in pending defect litigation for all board packets.

Rules to Safeguard Attorney-Client Privilege

- Ensure that all privileged communications are routed only to board members—not to any member of the association.
- File all attorney-client communications (whether generated by the attorney, the board, or the community manager) in separate files clearly marked "Privileged & Confidential—Attorney-Client Communications."
- If some members of the board are employed by or closely aligned with the developer, establish a separate defect-litigation subcommittee composed only of homeowner directors, and route privileged communications to this subcommittee, rather than to the full board.
- Establish separate files for the subcommittee and each of its members that will contain privileged communications from counsel; reports, studies, and subcommittee members' meeting notes.
- If financial documents relating the claims—such as invoices from attorneys, experts, or consultants—are to remain in the association's accounting files, segregate and mark them "Privileged & Confidential—Attorney-Client Communications."
- Do not attach privileged communications, such as reports from the attorney or experts, to board meeting minutes or to communications to homeowners.
- Discuss defect-resolution issues in executive session.
- Advise owners not to communicate directly with the developer or its representatives. Instead, homeowners should communicate with the defect subcommittee, through the community manager. The defect subcommittee, in turn, can communicate with the developer until a construction defect attorney is hired.
- Ensure that homeowner responses to surveys are sent directly to the attorney.

At that point, unless the manager or defect attorney carefully reviews the contents of the packets, privileged documents may be reproduced inadvertently. This disclosure of privileged materials can lead to a blanket waiver of the attorney-client privilege. The best insurance against this type of inadvertent disclosure is to segregate all executive session materials from the outset.

Waiving Privileges

The community manager has perhaps the greatest responsibility to preserve the attorney-client privilege and the work-product privilege because he or she passes all privileged communications between the attorney and the board.

The client owns the privilege, which may be waived in one of several ways. First, the privilege is waived if the client voluntarily discloses attorney-client communications to third parties. Second, and more importantly, the privilege may be waived by a totally inadvertent disclosure to third parties. Inadvertent disclosures are by far the most common in construction defect litigation.

CONSTRUCTION DEFECT LITIGATION

Whether disclosure is deliberate or inadvertent, the consequences may be the same. In some jurisdictions, waiver of the privilege by the inadvertent disclosure of a single privileged communication can open up all other privileged communications to discovery by the opposing party.

PART TWO

The Investigation

CHAPTER 4

Checking the Statutes of Limitations

Athorough investigation of potential construction defects forms the backbone of an association's claims against the developers, builders, and others involved in a construction project. As soon as the community manager begins to receive multiple homeowner complaints, he or she should report the issues to the board. At this point, the board and manager should determine whether to undertake a preliminary investigation.

Obviously, one of the first steps in any investigation is ensuring that the statutes of limitations have not expired. This is a particular concern for community associations as prior boards may have been aware of construction issues yet not taken any action. Put simply, though time frames differ across the country, the statute of limitation establishes a number of years in which a homeowner or association may, in fact, file the lawsuit. If the statute has expired and no argument for an extension can be made, the association can't file a lawsuit no matter how damaged the property may be. Appendix 2 provides an analysis of statutes of limitations across the country.

Statute-of-Limitations Overview

Construction defect investigations can become extremely expensive. It isn't unusual for defect investigations in communities with 200 or more homes to cost from $500,000 to more than $1 million over the course of the several years it takes to resolve all claims. Therefore, it's extremely important for the board to undertake a preliminary statute analysis as soon as potential construction defects are detected and an investigation is begun.

A statute-of-limitations analysis requires an in-depth understanding of the state's statutes related to construction defects. Although the association's regular attorney can assist with the preliminary analysis of statute defenses, the more prudent approach is for the board or community manager to seek an attorney who specializes in construction defect claims. Many such attorneys will perform a preliminary statute-of-limitations analysis for an association without charging a fee, and associations should take advantage of these services.

Recently, many states have adopted builders' right-to-repair legislation in which the statute-of-limitations periods have been shortened—thus making the analysis even more important for associations.[1] For instance, in California, actions to recover for defective irrigation systems, drainage, and inter-unit noise all must be brought within one year of closing.[2]

Construction defects can be either patent or latent. A patent defect typically is defined as a "deficiency that is apparent by reasonable inspection"[3]—it's clearly visible. Examples of patent defects are sagging roofs, cracking sidewalks, cracking exterior stucco, interior drywall cracking, and broken water pipes. By contrast, a latent defect is one that is not apparent by reasonable inspection.[4] The Wyoming Supreme Court eloquently explained the latent defect concept in the case of *Tavares v. Horstman:* "The ordinary home buyer is not in a position, by skill or training, to discover defects lurking in plumbing, the electrical wiring, [or] the structure itself, all of which is usually covered and not open for inspection."[5]

Some states have different statutes for patent defects and latent defects, making the distinction between the two extremely important. For instance, in California, an action arising from patent defects must begin within four years of completing the work.

There are exceptions, however. If an injury to property or person occurs during the fourth year, the period is extended for a year.[6] Furthermore, the patent defect statute of limitation does not apply to owner-occupied, single-family homes.[7]

Statutes of limitations for latent defects are generally longer—frequently as long as 10 years[8]—than those for patent defects since latent defects aren't obvious and, generally, are only identified by experts. However, statutes of limitation may be different in actions for personal injury or wrongful death caused by latent construction defects.[9]

The Preliminary Statute Analysis

The community manager initiates the preliminary statute-of-limitations analysis by gathering the association documents that show when the statute began. Documentation varies from state to state, depending on particular triggering points in the state's legislation. For example:

In Arizona, the statutes of limitation begin when improvement to real property is substantially complete.[10] Substantial completion means when the following events first occur:

1. The property is used by the owner or occupant.

2. The property is first available for use after having been completed according to the contract, including changes.

3. Final inspection, if required, is conducted by the governmental body that issued the building permit.

California defines substantial completion differently. It is the date not later than one of the following, whichever occurs first:[11]

1. The date of final inspection by the applicable public agency.

2. The date a valid Notice of Completion is recorded.

3. The date the improvement is used or occupied.

4. One year after termination or cessation of work on the improvement.

In states like Arizona and California where the date depends on action by public agencies, the community manager or the defect attorney must obtain the records from the public agencies.

Notices of completion and final building permits are seldom located among the association's records, but the manager can have a title company retrieve them based on property descriptions contained in the association's governing documents—plot plans and legal descriptions attached to the CC&Rs. The manager should compare the notices of completion to the association's documents to ensure that they match the association's property descriptions.

Copies of building permits are easier to obtain than notices of completion. The community manager should contact the city or county department that has jurisdiction over construction.

Other documents can trigger statutes of limitations. For instance, in California, for homes first sold on or after January 1, 2003, the date for certain types of claims is not the date of substantial completion, but rather the closing escrow date.[12] This can be problematic for community associations, where there is no single escrow closing date because individual units close on different dates over extended periods.

When the community manager and the board have determined when the statute of limitations commenced, they should confer with the association attorney. In some cases, it may be obvious that the association cannot pursue defect claims. For example, if the association's property was substantially completed on January 1, 1993, and the longest possible limitation period is ten years, the association would be barred from taking action after January 2003. Under these circumstances, there's no point pursuing an expensive and time consuming expert investigation to build a case against a developer. However, the defects still need to be repaired; the manager and board should conduct an abbreviated investigation to determine what repairs are appropriate and how to pay for them.

The preliminary statute-of-limitation analysis must consider factors—other than the mere passage of time—that can only be identified by an experienced defects claims attorney. For instance, in some states, statutes of limitation do not begin as long as the developer controls the board. In others, the statute may be "tolled," or stopped, until the homeowners association discovers the defects or while the developer attempts to repair the defects. And the developer may be prohibited from asserting a statute defense if the developer caused an association to delay filing a lawsuit by promising repairs.[13]

If the association's claims are not barred by the statutes of limitations, the community manager, board, and defect attorney should determine the steps to take next. In almost all instances, the association should continue its investigation.

Endnotes

1. California Civil Code Section 896.

2. California Civil Code Section 896(g)(6), (g)(7).

3. California Code of Civil Procedure Section 337.1(e).

4. California Code of Civil Procedure Section 337.15(b).

5. 542 P.2d. 1275, 1279 (Wyo. 1975).

6. California Code of Civil Procedure Section 337.1(c).

7. California Code of Civil Procedure Section 337.1(f).

8. *See, for example,* California Code of Civil Procedure Section 337.15.

9. *Id.*

10. Arizona Revised Statutes Section 12-552.

11. California Code of Civil Procedure Section 337.15(g).

12. California Civil Code Section 896(g)(1),(g)(6), (g)(7), (g)(8), (g)(9), (g)(10), (g)(12) and (g)(13).

13. Lantzy v. Centex Homes, 31 Cal.4th 363, 2 Cal.Rptr.3d 655 (2003).

CHAPTER 5

Hiring a Construction Defect Attorney

B ased on the evidence that's been gathered, should the association attempt to work directly with the developer to resolve the claims, or should it hire an attorney who specializes in construction defects?

Associations that elect to negotiate a settlement with the developer themselves must bear in mind two important considerations. First, the statute of limitations for filing a claim may be as short as one year from the date the project was finished. If negotiations with the developer last longer, the association's right to file a legal action is lost. Second, the board may not be aware of all claims that should be made. If a settlement is reached, the developer will insist on a full release, which will eliminate the association's right to file claims that may be discovered in the future.

Construction defect law is complex and differs from state to state. Even for trained attorneys, construction defect claims are among their most difficult cases. Millions of dollars are usually at stake, so if the association has viable construction defect claims, hiring a construction defect attorney is probably a wise decision.

Why Two Attorneys?

The association likely has an attorney with expertise in community association law—sometimes referred to as general counsel. But, this is not the person to handle the association's construction defect claims—even if he or she specializes in this area of the law. The reason is simple: the association's general attorney and a defect attorney play different and separate roles in a defect case.

Not only is general counsel handling the association's day-to-day legal matters, but during a defect case, he or she will be very busy as the association's construction defects watch dog. He or she will:

- Help the board select the defect attorney.
- Advise the board about defect counsel's fee structure.
- Advise the board about financing necessary expert investigations.
- Oversee elections relating to loans.
- Assist the board to implement special assessments if needed to pay for expert investigations.
- Assist the board to select reconstruction contractors.

- Advise the board how best to invest any funds that might be recovered until reconstruction gets underway.

How does the association board find the right attorney or law firm to handle its construction defect case?

Begin by creating a list of potential candidates. Ask the community manager for recommendations based on his or her experience, references from peers, and endorsements from local chapters of professional organizations like Community Associations Institute. Also ask the association's general counsel to recommend viable candidates. Do *not* include names of attorneys who are board members or close relatives or friends of board members.

Requests for Proposals

The community manager should prepare a draft request for proposal (RFP) (for the board's review and input) that can be sent to the candidates on the list. The RFP ensures that the information submitted by all candidates is comparable.

The RFP should provide the following background information so that candidates can assess their suitability for your case:

- A comprehensive description of the association property: location, number and type of units, date of incorporation, age, amenities and facilities, and any other property information relating to the case.
- A list of all potential adverse parties: developer, general contractor, etc.

The RFP should request that the candidates provide the following information in the proposal:

- A description of the legal services the law firm will offer: expert investigation; pre-litigation; and, if necessary, litigation through trial.
- A description of the law firm: number of partners and associates, age of firm, and practice areas covered.
- A description of the firm's experience in handling construction defect claims: number of associations represented, number of individual homeowners represented, track record in settlement and trial, and insurance coverage expertise.
- Homeowner association references.
- Proposed fee structure.
- Law firm's ability to finance the expert investigation, and at what cost to the association.

Mail the RFP to all candidates and include a deadline for returning proposals, the address where proposals should be sent, and a contact name and phone if candidates have questions.

Interviews and Reference Checks

Once all proposals are received, the board, manager, and general counsel should meet and select two or three finalists. (Large associations may want to delegate either the selection process or the entire defect claim process to a subcommittee.) The board or subcommittee should then meet with the managing partner and the lead defect counsel for each finalist firm to ascertain their knowledge of construction defect law, community association law in general, mediation and trial experience in defect cases, track record, and fee structure.

Just as the association does when hiring any person or firm, it will want to do a background check before retaining a law firm for its defect case. The manager should talk to homeowner references and inquire within his or her professional circle about the firm.

The association now has the candidates' proposals, data gathered during the interviews, and information from references; but, there will still be questions. The board, manager, and general counsel should meet again to further evaluate the candidates. The key considerations should be the firms' reputation, experience, and track record.

Fees and Fee Structures

Fees are always an important factor in making decisions; however, boards should remember that fees are negotiable, and the fees listed in the proposal are simply the opening bid. This is an area where the association's attorney can provide valuable assistance. Most states require that fee agreements be in writing, and even if they don't, it's always advisable.

Contingency Fees

Most construction defect cases are handled under a contingency fee structure—the fees are a percentage of the ultimate recovery. No recovery, no fee.

Some cases are handled under a sliding, or tiered, contingency fee structure —at various points in the process certain fees apply. For example, in a three-tier structure, if a settlement is achieved early in the process (tier one), the contingency percentage would be low. If a settlement is achieved a set number of days before going to trial (tier two), the contingency percentage would be a little higher. For instance, the second-tier fee might apply to settlement 60 days or more before trial. The highest (tier three) contingency percentage would apply if a settlement is achieved 60 days or fewer before trial.

This is only one example of a contingency fee. Variations are common and a straight coningency fee is preferable.

Most construction defect cases are settled with a cash payout before they go to trial. However, there are cases where the developer agrees to make repairs instead of cash payments or a combination of cash payments and repairs. And, in a limited number of cases, damages from defects have been so severe (such as in landslide cases) that the developer and its insurance companies have actually bought back the property in return for cash payments.

How are fees determined in these cases where settlement is based on something other than cash? Generally, they're based on the fair market value of repairs or of the property—if the developer buys it back. However, fair market value depends on which side of the case you're on, so the fee agreement should specify that mediation and arbitration will be used to resolve any disputes that might result when arriving at this number.

Should fee percentages be based on gross or net settlement amounts? Compare: if the fee percentage is 30 percent and the gross settlement is $3 million, the gross fee is $900,000. Whereas, if the fee percentage is 30 percent, the gross settlement is $3 million, and the expert fees and costs that must be subtracted are $500,000, the net fee is $750,000—$3 million minus $500,000 times 30 percent.

Retainer

Should community associations ever consider retaining a defect attorney at an hourly rate? This may be cost effective *if* the claims are likely to be resolved quickly, however this is very hard to predict. In general, paying by the hour has several downsides: First, making a regular monthly payment to the defect attorney often puts a strain on an association's cash flow. Indeed, it's unlikely that the operating budget includes funds for this expense. Second, by the time the case concludes, the fees may consume the entire settlement and leave no funds for repairs. Third, there's little motivation for attorneys to achieve a prompt settlement if they're being paid by the hour.

CHAPTER 6

Assembling the Expert Team

The community manager frequently uses the same contractors who perform the association's routine maintenance and temporary repairs to investigate potential construction defects. An experienced general contractor can identify whether a problem is a maintenance issue or a potential construction defect. In large communities where many common-interest developments exist, general contracting companies can be found that not only provide contracting services but also work with attorneys to provide forensic investigation services. These companies can be particularly helpful and cost effective in the initial investigation to identify potential construction defects.

Community managers should give the general contractors who are conducting temporary repairs specific instructions about identifying potential construction defects. The manager should require contractors to document all temporary repairs fully with photographs, field notes, and videotape, if possible, and to deliver documentation promptly. The manager should review the documentation and forward it to the board if appropriate.

An experienced general contractor making the repairs or conducting the preliminary investigation may be able to identify the specific defects. In other instances, the contractor may recognize potential defects, but may not be able to identify them in any detail. In either event, a common thread of repairs or reports of potential defects from the contractor is an indication to the manager and board that its time to hire experienced experts for the next step of the investigation—starting with a construction defect attorney.

Because the attorney is such a key figure in the entire process, hiring and working with the right one is covered in detail in Chapter 5. Many attorneys who handle construction defect cases have assembled teams of experts that they will make available to associations for a preliminary investigation at no charge.

The Architect

In most instances, the first expert the association or attorney should hire is an architect. An architect's training and experience typically covers many of a building's major components, including roofs, exterior finishes, walls, wall openings, decks, balconies, waterproofing, foundations, and all the other features that make up what is generally referred to as the building envelope. The architect will recognize defects that may require further investigation by other specialists, such as soils engineers, structural engineers, civil engineers, mechanical engineers, electrical engineers, industrial hygienists, or landscape architects.

The community manager should provide the architect with documents such as project plans, specifications, maps, correspondence with the developer, and records of repairs completed to date. The architect will conduct a preliminary visual inspection of the association's property, focusing on the potential defects reported by the community manager and the contractors who performed the temporary repairs.

DEVELOPER'S PERSPECTIVE: If the association has made claims of design deficiencies, the claims should be reviewed and evaluated by the designer. If the association claims that construction deviated from code or standards, improper materials were used, design drawings lacked sufficient detail, or the proper inspections weren't conducted, the architect and engineer are uniquely situated to evaluate and respond. If the association claims that work deviated from the plans and specifications or design intent, the architect and engineer can also assist in evaluating those claims. Besides inspecting the property, they will carefully review shop drawings, responses to requests for interpretation, job meeting minutes, and other documents to determine whether a given condition actually constitutes a defect and, if so, who might be responsible for it.

Design professionals can be very helpful in correcting deficiencies properly, delineating corrections, and defining their scope—essential information when determining their costs.

Following the architect's review of project documents and visual inspections, the community manager should arrange for the architect, community manager, board members, association attorney, and a defect attorney (if one has been retained) to meet so that the architect can present his or her observations.

After this meeting, the board should decide whether to proceed with a full investigation of potential defects. If at all possible, the board should consult with an experienced defect attorney when making this decision. If the board decides on a full investigation, the architect and defect attorney can recommend which disciplines should be represented on the expert team. In addition to architects, the following experts are typically needed:

Engineers
Engineers evaluate whether various elements of an association's complex comply with building codes, plans, and specifications:
- **Structural engineer**: evaluates structural elements.
- **Electrical engineer**: evaluates electrical components.
- **Civil engineer**: evaluates components—other than the actual structures— curbs, gutters, and sidewalks—called "hardscape"—and roadways, site grading, drainage, and water and sanitation facilities.

- **Mechanical engineer**: evaluates plumbing; sewer; heating, ventilation, and air conditioning (HVAC); and fire safety systems.
- **Soils engineer**: evaluates soil conditions, mass grading, fine grading, groundwater, and potential earth movement.
- **Landscape architect**: evaluates—together with the civil engineer—landscaping, irrigation, and drainage.

Construction Industry Specialists

Generally, the architect will evaluate roofing defects, waterproofing issues, stucco defects, and windows. However, there are circumstances in which specialists in these areas will be needed:

- **Roofing**: a roofing specialist might be needed in large complexes, those with unique roofing systems, or when potential defects require investigation by a specialist.
- **Waterproofing**: a waterproofing specialist is needed when there are serious defects associated with below-grade waterproofing, decks, balconies, and other building components.
- **Stucco**: stucco consultants are needed when widespread stucco defects exist, such as cracking, spalling, and discoloration.
- **Windows**: window consultants are needed when it appears that windows and sliding glass doors have been defectively manufactured or designed.

Other Experts

In addition to the construction-industry related specialists and consultants listed above, experts in other areas are sometimes needed.

- **Statistical consultants**: When it isn't feasible to evaluate every unit in a large complex, a statistician may be needed to identify a few representative units to inspect and test based on scientifically-accepted random sampling methods.
- **Industrial hygiene consultants**: Industrial hygienists and toxicologists determine whether mold and other toxic substances are present in structures, specify how to eliminate them, and follow up with tests to ensure they're gone.
- **Appraisers**: Appraisers are needed when the value of the overall project and individual units with and without defects are at issue, frequently in connection with the damage phase of a construction defect case.

Licensed General Contractors

Once the other experts have prepared their reports, and made their repair recommendations, an experienced local reconstruction contractor prepares a detailed cost-of-repair estimate.

Finding the Right Expert

Managers and boards should consider a combination of educational credentials and construction-industry experience when selecting experts. Experts should have forensic experience, but that experience should not be 100 percent defect investigation. Ask the expert for a detailed resume, fee schedule, and industry references; review them carefully; and check references. Review the firm's website, and talk to attorneys who have worked with them in the past—on either side of litigation.

It's particularly important for the manager or board to verify that the prospective experts have sufficient experience with the specific type of construction in which the association is having problems. Also, as the association is selecting its experts, potential or actual conflicts of interest should be ruled out by the defect attorney by verifying that the candidates have never worked on the project or for the developer of the association. Furthermore, the association's contract should require experts to avoid conflicts of interest while they're under contract with the association and to report potential conflicts if they arise during the process. For example, a conflict would exist if, in the middle of the association's investigation, its drainage expert was hired to also work on a new project by the same surveying firm that once worked for the developer the association is now pursuing.

DEVELOPER'S PERSPECTIVE: In contrast to associations, developers can rely on their staff design teams to address design- and code-compliance issues. Sometimes, however, association reports raise issues that can only be resolved by independent experts. Window consultants, stucco consultants, or soils engineers may be needed to evaluate complex claims. Obviously, the developer will take longer to respond to a claim if he has to hire outside consultants.

Fees and Contracts

The association should establish a budget for each expert, and require them to adhere to it. Expert fees can be controlled by closely defining the scope of work and monitoring actual fees. Budgeting these fees allows the association to conduct a thorough investigation, while reserving the maximum portion of any recovery for reconstruction.

The association should execute a retainer agreement with each of its experts that addresses, at least, the following points:

1. **Names of the key parties:** the homeowners association, developer, community manager, and attorney.

2. **A description of the project:** number of units and stories; and types of siding, roofs, doors, and windows.

3. **Scope of services to be rendered:** visual inspections, invasive testing, presentation of claims, expert meetings, and mediations.

4. **Schedule of hourly rates.**

5. **Expense reimbursement parameters.**

6. **Insurance:** certification of workers' compensation, comprehensive general liability, and errors and omissions coverage.

7. **Indemnity:** expert agrees to indemnify, defend, and hold the association harmless in claims arising from and relating to the work.

8. **Licenses**: professional licenses and contractors licenses held by the expert.

9. **Conflicts of interest**: lack of conflicts at the time the expert is hired and agreement to disclose potential conflicts that may arise during the work.

The community manager should maintain a file of all fully-executed agreements.

How to Find the Right Experts

- **Construction defect attorney.** Experienced construction defect attorneys maintain their own lists of specialists, consultants, and experts.

- **Industry organizations.** Community Associations Institute (CAI), and similar organizations have chapters throughout the country that maintain rosters of attorneys and experts who practice in the field of construction defect litigation.

- **Construction industry trade groups.** The American Institute of Architects and the American Society of Civil Engineers provide regional data on industry experts.

- **Legal organizations.** The Defense Research Institute and local trial lawyers' associations maintain databases of experts.

- **Consulting firms.** Some states have human-resource firms that specialize in locating experts.

Monitor Expert's Fees

Throughout the course of construction defect litigation, the defect attorney must keep the board fully advised of expert fees and other investigative costs. Preferably, the attorney should send a status-of-claims report to the board via the manager—either monthly or quarterly—that includes summaries of expert fees and costs incurred to date. These regular reports are the board's and manager's only means of monitoring expense levels—an important task considering that expert fees and other investigative costs can ultimately consume a significant portion of a settlement, thereby reducing the funds available for reconstruction.

The Expert's Reports

Because defect investigations are time consuming and extremely expensive, all experts must fully understand from the outset that the goals of a defect investigation are for the experts to investigate and report their findings, which will be used by a cost estimator to prepare a detailed cost-of-repair analysis. The cost-of-repair then becomes part of the association's settlement demand, which is the starting point for resolving claims.

To achieve these goals, each expert's report must contain the following information for each defect. These reports are privileged up to a certain point in the resolution process; they should not be disclosed to the developer, subcontractors, or other third parties until the appropriate time.

CONSTRUCTION DEFECT LITIGATION

1. Defect identification. Reports begin by identifying each defect listed by category. For instance, an architect's report, would group defects in categories that would include roofing, entry decks, balconies, exterior stairs and landings, exterior stucco, exterior doors, windows, concrete, fire-resistant construction, wallboard, interior stairs, fireplaces, flooring, and countertops.

2. Defect location. Each expert report describes the location of each defect, indicates the number of affected units, and provides their specific street address or unit number. This information is cross referenced to the supporting documentation including photographs and field notes.

3. Inspected areas. Each report lists the number of units or areas investigated for each specific defect. The addresses and unit numbers are noted for further investigation and verification.

4. Percentage of defective units. Each report states the percentage of units where each defect was observed. This is a simple calculation in which the number of units with defects is divided by the number of units that were inspected.

5. Violation of plans, code, standard, or warranty. Each report lists the expert's opinions of the causes of the problems.

- Was the defect caused by a deviation from the plans and specifications?
- Was the defect caused by errors, omissions, or deficiencies in the design?
- Did the structure comply with building codes and local ordinances that were in effect at the time of design and construction?
- Was the defect caused by the builder's failure to follow industry standards?
- Did the builder and subcontractors comply with manufacturer's recommendations for installing roofing, flashing, doors, windows, and sliding glass doors?
- Was the defect caused by defective manufactured products? (While defects most frequently result from using the wrong product or installing it improperly, sometimes the product itself is defective. Examples include roofing membranes, siding, and insulated dual-pane windows and sliding glass doors.)

6. Damages. Each report describes the damages that result from each defect. For example, during the initial inspection, the architect noted stains around the interior windowsills, trim, and drywall indicating water intrusion. It seems the flashing around the windows was not installed in the proper sequence. While the stains are part of the resulting damages, invasive testing will show that, in fact, a number of building components have been damaged—exterior siding or stucco, plywood underlayment, studs, structural hold-downs, insulation, interior drywall, trim, and the HVAC ducts adjacent to the windows.

Other types of damages can result from defects. Some defects, such as defective wiring, present a threat to safety and need to be addressed immediately. Others include the inability to maintain the structure in its present state, the need to move residents out while repairs are made, and decreasing the expected life of various building components.

The damages component of each report becomes very important during settlement negotiations. Most construction defect claims are resolved when the developer's or contractor's insurance company pays; however, in many instances, insurance coverage is only available when there is resulting property damage.

7. **Repair recommendations**. The final section of each report contains the expert's detailed repair recommendations. These are step-by-step instructions for repairing defects, beginning with removing defective components and ending with the various steps necessary to accomplish the repair. The repair recommendations are used by the cost estimator to prepare the detailed cost estimate that will be used in settlement negotiations and at trial.

DEVELOPER'S PERSPECTIVE: When a developer is notified about a construction defect claim, he may ask the project manager to investigate. This is a mistake. Asking a person to evaluate his or her own work in the face of a defect claim isn't likely to elicit an objective response. A number of major developers have recognized this problem, and they now assign investigations to employees who have no stake in the outcome or to outside consultants. Some developers have adopted more aggressive risk-control programs in which they inspect the property as construction progresses.

The developer begins the investigation by reviewing the association's expert reports. The developer will also ask those in his organization who will respond to the claims to review the reports. This will normally include field personnel and supervisors who are included in the developer's transition team.

Responsible developers take claims very seriously and will make sure that they're evaluated by knowledgeable and qualified representatives. Initially, the developer will inspect the site—using the association's report as a guide—to get an idea of the types, number, and severity of the deficiencies. The developer will also try to determine whether any subcontractor may be responsible for the defective work.

Often, when associations claim that finished construction deviates from the original plans, the developer has only to review the change orders or approved amendments to show that job requirements were altered.

Similarly, when associations claim that construction deviates from building codes, the developer will review the codes. Construction codes are subject to interpretation, and there are circumstances in which the developer's consultants and the association's consultants genuinely disagree about how codes should be applied to the project.

At some point the developer may need a more in-depth evaluation and find it necessary to conduct invasive testing and/or to hire outside consultants.

Clearly the association must have sufficient information to make legitimate claims, and developers must have equally complete information to make intelligent and meaningful responses.

CHAPTER 7

How Experts
Identify Defects

The association's experts will use various benchmarks when conducting their investigations, including building codes, local ordinances, manufacturer's installation directions and specifications, and industry standards. Industry standards are frequently the most important component. They are generally not found in reference books such as the Uniform Building Code; rather they are the collective requirements by which residential housing is constructed. The standards vary from region to region, depending on weather, soil conditions, and the availability of building materials. The association's experts will include applicable building standards in their reports and in their testimony in depositions and at trial.

In an unusual move, the California Legislature enacted a comprehensive set of industry standards as part of its builder's right-to-repair legislation in 2002. While the standards only apply to homes in California, they are nonetheless useful in understanding how experienced experts conduct their investigations. Clearly, nationwide industry standards are beyond the scope of this book; however, the California standards provide a good overview.[1]

Industry Standards for Water Intrusion

In most parts of the country, defective construction that results in water intrusion is the most common category of defect encountered.

California's standards relating to water intrusion include:[2]

1. A door shall not allow unintended water to pass beyond, around, or through the doors or its designed or actual moisture barriers, if any.

2. Windows, patio doors, deck doors, and their systems shall not allow water to pass beyond, around, or through the window, patio door, or deck door or its designed or actual moisture barriers, including internal barriers within the systems themselves.

3. Windows, patio doors, deck doors and their systems shall not allow excessive condensation to enter the structure and cause damage to another component.

4. Roofs, roofing systems, chimney caps, and ventilation components shall not allow water to enter the structure or to pass beyond, around, or through the designed or actual moisture barriers, including internal barriers located within the systems themselves.

5. Decks, deck systems, balconies, balcony systems, exterior stairs, and stair systems shall not allow water to pass into the adjacent structure.

6. Decks, deck systems, balconies, balcony systems, exterior stairs, and stair systems shall not allow unintended water to pass within the systems themselves and cause damage to the systems.

7. Foundation systems and slabs shall not allow water or vapor to enter into the structure so as to cause damage to another building component.

8. Foundation systems and slabs shall not allow water or vapor to enter into the structure so as to limit the installation of the type of flooring materials typically used for the particular application.

9. Hardscape, including paths and patios, irrigation systems, landscaping systems, and drainage systems that are installed as part of the original construction shall not be installed in such a way as to cause water or soil erosion to enter into or come in contact with the structure so as to cause damage to another building component.

10. Stucco, exterior siding, exterior walls, including exterior framing, and other exterior wall finishes and fixtures and the systems of those components and fixtures, including pot shelves, horizontal surfaces, columns, and plant-ons, shall be installed in such a way so as not to allow unintended water to pass into the structure or to pass beyond, around, or through the designed or actual moisture barriers of the system, including any internal barriers located within the system itself.

11. Stucco, exterior siding, and exterior walls shall not allow excessive condensation to enter the structure and cause damage to another component.

12. Retaining and site walls and their associated drainage systems shall not allow unintended water to pass beyond, around, or through their designed or actual moisture barriers including any internal barriers so as to cause damage. This standard does not apply to those portions of any wall or drainage system that are designed to have water flow beyond, around, or through them.

13. Retaining walls and site walls, and their associated drainage systems, shall only allow water to flow beyond, around, or through the areas designated by design.

14. The lines and components of the plumbing system, sewer system, and utility systems shall not leak.

15. Plumbing lines, sewer lines, and utility lines shall not corrode so as to impede the useful life of the systems.

16. Sewer systems shall be installed in such a way as to allow the designated amount of sewage to flow through the system.

17. Shower and bath enclosures shall not leak water into the interior of walls, flooring systems, or the interior of other components.

18. Ceramic tile and tile countertops shall not allow water into the interior of walls, flooring systems, or other components so as to cause damage.

Investigation Techniques for Water Intrusion

Several experts investigate water intrusion, including the architect, structural engineer, civil engineer, mechanical engineer, roofing consultant, waterproofing consultant, and stucco consultant. During visual inspection, the association's experts will look for violations of the industry standards relating to water intrusion in the following ways:

1. The architect will look for water intrusion through and around doors, windows, sliding glass doors, decks, balconies, and exterior stairs. The most visible

signs of water intrusion are stains on ceilings, walls, window frames, doorframes, baseboard, and flooring. The architect or roofing consultant will look for water intrusion through and around roofing systems, chimney caps, and ventilation components. Visible signs of water intrusion through the roof are stains on the ceiling and in the attic.

2. Architects or waterproofing consultants will visually inspect and test decks, balconies, and below-grade walls for evidence of water intrusion. Signs of water intrusion on decks and balconies are stains on ceilings, walls, and floors; and signs of water intrusion through below-grade walls are stains, peeling paint, or degraded concrete wall blocks.

3. The civil engineer will determine whether common area drainage, landscaping, irrigation, and hardscape—including streets, curbs, gutters, and sidewalks—are allowing water to intrude on structures or cause damage to building components. The civil engineer will also determine whether unintended water is passing beyond, around, or through privacy walls between units and retaining walls in violation of industry standards.

4. The architect and stucco consultant will determine whether the stucco violates industry standards by allowing water into structures through cracks or improper interface with windows, doors, decks, balconies, flashing, exterior trim, and utility outlets.

5. The association's mechanical expert will visually inspect the accessible portions of the plumbing, sewer, and utility systems to determine if they leak and inspect them to determine if they're corroded.

The mechanical engineer will test the sewer systems to determine whether they allow the designated amount of sewage to flow through them. He or she will also inspect and test shower and bath enclosures, ceramic tile, and tile countertops for signs of water leakage into interior walls, flooring systems, or other interior components.

If the architect detects mold or other toxic substances resulting from water intrusion or excessive moisture, an industrial hygienist or toxicologist will generally be brought in to investigate in detail. Most construction defect cases include water intrusion issues and related moisture entrapment. As mold often results from excessive moisture, more and more construction defect cases involve claims of mold. See Appendix 5 for detailed information about mold.

Industry Standards for Structural Issues

California's industry standards relating to structural issues include:[3]

1. Foundations, load bearing components, and slabs shall not contain significant cracks or significant vertical displacement.

2. Foundations, load bearing components and slabs shall not cause the structure, in whole or in part, to be structurally unsafe.

3. Foundations, load bearing components, slabs and underlying soils shall be constructed so as to materially comply with the design criteria set by applicable government building codes, regulations and ordinances for chemical deterioration or corrosion resistance in effect at the time of original construction.

4. A structure shall be constructed so as to materially comply with the design

criteria for earthquake and wind load resistance, as set forth in the applicable government building codes, regulations, and ordinances in effect at the time of original construction.

Investigation Techniques for Structural Issues

Evidence of violation of structural building standards is difficult to gather during visual inspections. However, the structural engineer can inspect for a limited number of structural problems. Cracking—exterior stucco, interior drywall, foundations, slabs—may be evidence of potential structural problems. Additionally, sloping floors, uneven ceilings, and out-of-plumb walls may again be warning signs of structural problems within the buildings.

The structural engineer will conduct most of his or her investigation during invasive or destructive testing when various building components are removed to gain access to concealed areas.

Industry Standards for Soils Issues

California's building industry standards relating to soils issues include:[4]

1. Soils and engineered retaining walls shall not cause, in whole or in part, damage to the structure built upon the soils or engineered retaining walls.

2. Soils and engineered retaining walls shall not cause, in whole or in part, the structure to be structurally unsafe.

3. Soils shall not cause, in whole or in part, the land upon which no structure is built to become unusable for the purpose represented at the time of original sale by the builder or for the purpose for which that land is commonly used.

Investigation Techniques for Soils Issues

Like the structural engineer, the soils engineer will conduct only a limited investigation during visual inspections. The soils engineer will walk through the entire community and look for unusual soil conditions—settlement, expansive soil, proper grading, excessive erosion, slope creep, and corrosive soil.

The soils engineer will examine retaining walls for obvious cracks, tilting, or separation, and also examine garage floor slabs, curbs, gutters, walkways, and other concrete elements in the common areas for excessive cracking or separation. Questionable conditions will be tested by excavation, soils sampling, and other techniques.

Industry Standards for Fire Protection

The California industry standards for fire protection include:[5]

1. A structure shall be constructed so as to materially comply with the design criteria of the applicable government building codes, regulations and ordinances for fire protection of the occupants in effect at the time of the original construction.

2. Fireplaces, chimneys, chimney structures, and chimney termination caps shall be constructed and installed in such a way so as not to cause unreasonable risk of fire outside the fireplace enclosure or chimney.

3. Electrical and mechanical systems shall be constructed and installed in such a way so as not to cause an unreasonable risk of fire.

Investigation Techniques for Fire Protection

The mechanical engineer or a fire protection consultant will examine the fire protection system; fireplaces, chimneys, and chimney termination caps, and the mechanical systems and structures, including HVAC systems, to determine whether they comply with building codes and local fire regulations and ordinances. The mechanical engineer will also consider the location of fire sprinklers within units and the possible interference of ceiling light fixtures and fans with the sprinklers. The number, location, and operation of smoke detectors will also be analyzed.

Industry Standards for Plumbing and Sewer Issues

California's industry standard for these systems is simple: "Plumbing and sewer systems shall be installed to operate properly and shall not materially impair the use of the structure by its inhabitants."[6]

Investigation Techniques for Plumbing and Sewer Issues

The mechanical engineer will visually inspect and test, when necessary, all appliances in the units such as hot water heaters, HVAC units, washing machines, dryers, dishwashers, stoves, and refrigerators. Building codes and local ordinances spell out specific procedures for installing appliances, and the mechanical engineer will be looking for code violation and safety issues. Common defects include: lack of hold-downs for water heaters and stoves, improper appliance venting, and inaccessible appliance shut-off valves.

Industry Standards for Electrical Systems

Here again, the California standard is brief: "Electrical systems must operate properly and must not materially impair the use of the structure by its occupants."[7]

Investigation Techniques for Electrical Systems

The architect, an electrical engineer, or an electrical consultant will visually inspect all exposed electrical components including the main circuit breaker panels, subpanels, wiring, grounding, conduit, and fixtures. Each of these will be judged against the National Electric Code, as adopted in the local jurisdiction, together with local regulations and ordinances. Common defects include: improper sizing of circuit breakers and wire, failure to protect wire from driven screws or nails, and improper grounding.

Industry Standards for Other Areas of Construction

California rounded out its list of industry standards by covering the following additional areas:[8]

1. Exterior pathways, driveways, hardscape, sidewalks, and patios installed by the original builder shall not contain cracks that display significant vertical displacement or that are excessive.

2. Stucco, exterior siding, and other exterior wall finishes and fixtures, including but not limited to, pot shelves, horizontal surfaces, columns, and plant-ons, shall not contain significant cracks or separations.

3. To the extent not otherwise covered by these standards, manufactured products, including but not limited to windows, doors, roofs, plumbing products and fixtures, fireplaces, electrical fixtures, HVAC units, countertops, cabinets, paint and appliances shall be installed so as not to interfere with the products' use life, if any.

4. Heating, if any, shall be installed so as to be capable of maintaining a room temperature of 70 degrees Fahrenheit at a point three feet above the floor in any living space.

5. Living space air-conditioning, if any, shall be provided in a manner consistent with the size and efficiency design criteria specified in the California Code of Regulations.

6. Attached structures shall be constructed to comply with inter-unit noise transmission standards set by the applicable government building codes, ordinances or regulations in effect at the time of original construction.

7. Irrigation systems and drainage shall operate properly so as not to damage landscaping or other external improvements.

8. Untreated wood posts shall not be installed in contact with soil so as to cause unreasonable decay to the wood based upon the finish grade at the time of original construction.

9. Untreated steel fences and adjacent components shall be installed so as to prevent unreasonable corrosion.

10. Paint and stains shall be applied in such a manner so as not to cause deterioration of the building surfaces for the length of time specified by the paint or stain manufacturers' representations, if any.

11. Roofing materials shall be installed so as to avoid materials falling off the roof.

12. The landscaping systems shall be installed in such a manner so as to survive for not less than one year.

13. Ceramic tile and tile backing shall be installed in such a manner that the tile does not detach.

14. Dryer ducts shall be installed and terminated pursuant to manufacturer installation requirements.

15. Structures shall be constructed in such a manner so as not to impair the occupants' safety because they contain public health hazards as determined by a duly authorized public health official, health agency, or governmental entity having jurisdiction.

Investigation Techniques for Other Areas of Construction

Various members of the association's expert team will visually inspect these other areas of construction. For instance, both the civil engineer and the soils engineer will inspect the exterior pathways, driveways, hardscape, sidewalks, and patios for excessive cracks or significant vertical displacement. The architect and stucco consultants will inspect stucco, exterior siding, and other exterior wall details, such as potshells and columns, for significant cracks, spalling, or separation. The architect or specialty consultants will inspect the manufactured products, such as windows, doors, roofs, and fireplaces to determine whether installation interferes with the products' useful life.

The mechanical engineer will inspect the manufactured products in the HVAC systems and determine whether the heating system is capable of maintaining the required room temperature and whether the air conditioning system meets the required design criteria.

The architect or an acoustical consultant will determine whether attached structures comply with inter-unit noise transmission standards.

The civil engineer and landscape architect will determine whether drainage and irrigation systems operate properly and whether the landscaping will survive for at least one year.

The architect will inspect paint, stain, wood posts, and steel fences for compliance with the building standards.

The architect or roofing consultant will examine roofing materials and installation to determine whether they are properly installed.

Similarly, the architect will determine whether ceramic tile and tile backing comply with industry standards.

The mechanical engineer will inspect dryer ducts and terminations for proper installation.

Finally, the architect will determine whether construction violates public health standards or poses a threat to safety.

The California legislature intended that these standards address every function or component of a structure. However, to the extent that a function or component is not addressed, the legislature provided that it will be actionable if it causes damage.[9] Experts frequently find violations not specifically addressed in the standards, and they'll testify to these violations as needed.

Endnotes

1. California Civil Code Section 896.
2. California Civil Code Section 896(a).
3. California Civil Code Section 896(b).
4. California Civil Code Section 896(c).
5. California Civil Code Section 896(d).
6. California Civil Code Section 896(e).
7. California Civil Code Section 896(f).
8. California Civil Code Section 896(g).
9. California Civil Code Section 897.

CHAPTER 8

Invasive Testing

V isual inspections are the important first step to identify potential construction defects. However, in most instances, finding the cause of a defect requires testing, and testing requires removing building components to expose wall cavities, subterranean spaces, and other portions of the structure. This is referred to as invasive or destructive testing.

Establishing the Testing Protocol

After each expert has visually inspected the property and reviewed the project plans and specifications, he or she recommends what testing is necessary to determine the cause of the potential defects. Each expert communicates his or her recommendations to the association's defect attorney in a privileged document. The defect attorney will review the recommendations and discuss them with each expert as necessary until they agree on a testing protocol.

The attorney may call a meeting with all experts to review the testing recommendations and to reach final agreement on the scope of the testing. This is important at this stage for several reasons:

- Overlaps or gaps in testing can be eliminated.
- Testing can be sequenced to minimize the time and expense of the process.
- More than one expert can take advantage of a particular testing operation.

For example, if a drywall cut between two units is made in the proper place, it can be used by the architect and the structural, mechanical, and electrical engineers. The architect can observe insulation and party walls; the structural engineer can observe structural tie-downs, fire blocking, shear walls, and nailing patterns; the mechanical engineer can observe HVAC ducts and piping; and the electrical engineer can determine if wiring is properly sized and protected from nails and screws.

A general contractor opens wall cavities and other areas for invasive testing. This contractor must be licensed, insured, bonded, and have experience conducting invasive testing. The contractor should participate in the meetings with experts and the attorney in preparation for the testing. The experts are like the directors of a motion picture, and members of the contractor's team are the actors. Each has an important role, and each must understand the role of the others.

The Cost of Invasive Testing

Invasive testing can be very expensive—sometimes exceeding $5,000 per unit for the general contractor's services alone. In a 200-unit common-interest development, it would not be unusual for 10 percent or more of the units to be subject to invasive testing. At a conservative $5,000 per unit, the cost of the contractor's services for testing 20 units could easily exceed $100,000. When the experts' fees are added, the total cost of testing 20 units easily exceeds $150,000.

Once the number of units to be tested and the scope of testing have been established, each expert and the general contractor should submit a testing budget to the defect attorney who will review each one, discuss any necessary changes with the expert, and forward them to the association board via the community manager for review and approval. Absent some significant change of circumstance, the experts and each contractor should be required to stay within their own budgets. If there is a change, the contractor and experts should contact the attorney immediately to discuss and adjust the budget, if necessary.

The Homeowner's Role

Invasive testing can be very traumatic for owners—it's like open-heart surgery on a house. Homeowners must be forewarned with the details of the testing process so they aren't surprised as it unfolds. They must also understand the importance of the tests to the association's case. It's the manager's responsibility to ensure that members are informed. In many cases, CC&Rs give the association—and, by extension, it's attorney and experts—the right to enter units for inspections and maintenance. The manager may need to remind owners about these provisions; and, if necessary, remind them that the association can go to court to force them to cooperate.

The Steps in Invasive Testing

Generally, the steps in a typical community association testing program are as follows:

1. The general contractor places protective tarps on floors and furniture in each residence.

2. The expert team tours the residence with the contractor's foreman to mark areas of the walls, ceilings, and other components that will be opened for testing.

3. Experts for the all participants photograph the areas to be tested before the work begins—a step called "pre-shots."

4. All experts leave the residence so testing can begin.

5. The general contractor protects the contents of the residence by moving furniture and artwork, covering belongings and clothing, and tenting areas to be tested to reduce the spread of construction dust. Experienced contractors photograph these spaces so everything can be returned properly when testing is complete.

6. The general contractor exposes wall cavities and other designated interior and exterior building components by removing drywall, trim, and other interior features according to the approved protocol. Similarly, stucco, siding, trim, deck coating, and other exterior components are removed to expose underlying conditions such as the sequence of flashings around windows, doors, and at decks.

Roofing is frequently removed, as well, to expose underlayment, flashing, and nailing patterns.

7. Experts for all parties return to the unit to observe conditions, conduct tests, make field notes, and take photographs. For example, windows and doors are tested by the contractor spraying water against them to simulate actual weather conditions while experts inside observe water intrusion and other conditions. Bathtubs and showers are also tested for leaks.

8. In some instances, testing is accomplished in stages. For instance, building codes and project plans may call for multiple layers of drywall and plywood on walls between units to comply with fire and structural codes. The general contractor may remove these components one layer at a time, making it necessary for experts for all parties to return after each layer of material is removed to document the conditions.

9. When the experts finish documenting their observations, the testing is concluded, and all experts are asked to leave the unit.

10. The general contractor returns to the residence and patches the openings in the walls and elsewhere. Existing drywall is replaced or new drywall installed, texture is applied, and trim is reinstalled. Carpet is reinstalled and stretched. On the outside of the residence openings in decks, patios, and stucco are waterproofed.

11. The general contractor removes protective covers, re-hangs artwork and drapes, repositions furniture, and cleans the inside of the unit.

12. The general contractor makes appointments with the homeowners to paint the interior patches and restore decks, patios, and stucco to their original conditions. Frequently, the general contractor will need to make several appointments to restore components like stucco and decking.

The community manager should closely monitor the patching and restoration to ensure that the general contractor's work satisfies the board and the owners. This requires that the manager contact each homeowner whose residence was tested to confirm that they are satisfied with the restoration work. If they aren't, the manager should prepare a punch list of deficient restoration work and provide it to the general contractor, the board, and the defect attorney. Once the general contractor has completed the punch list items, the community manager should inspect the restoration work again. With proper restoration work, residences should look just as they did before the testing began.

The Cost-of-Repair Report

Following invasive testing, each expert will update his or her preliminary report with the results of the testing and forward it to the defect attorney. The attorney reviews and forwards the reports to the construction contractor or cost-estimating consultant who will prepare a detailed cost-of-repair report for the association. The cost estimator's report covers all repair recommendations made by each expert. When completed, the cost-of-repair report is sent to the defect attorney who will forward copies to other appropriate parties like the developer's attorney. The cost-of-repair report is used to formulate the association's initial settlement demand.

DEVELOPER'S PERSPECTIVE: Visual inspection may confirm the presence of a defect, but it usually isn't sufficient to determine its cause. Therefore, when invasive testing is needed, the association's and the developer's interests will be best served by joint testing. With joint testing, the developer's subcontractors may perform the work—opening walls, removing bricks, or similar tasks, and restoring the area. This can be less expensive than if the association hires its own contractors, especially in larger projects where construction is ongoing. Thus, joint testing saves money for both parties, eliminates a second round of inspections by the developer, and minimizes disruption for residents.

Joint inspections also ensure that all parties are looking at the same conditions. While there still may be disagreement about a remedy, at least both sides will be considering the same facts and circumstances. The more cooperation and good faith offered by each party, the greater the opportunity for early resolution without litigation.

Joint invasive testing should be coordinated by the association's attorney with the association's and the developer's representatives and consultants. Careful planning is needed since, even with joint testing, it isn't always necessary for all consultants to be present at the same time. For example, the contractor can expose a particular area for testing during a specific time period—usually one day—and all parties can conduct their tests that day. In other situations all consultants should be present at the same time. For example, if the association claimed a component had been assembled incorrectly, all parties would want to witness its disassembly—a destructive process that would only happen once.

After everyone has analyzed their test results, they should meet, discuss their findings, and attempt to find a mutually satisfactory solution. The information shared in these meetings and the resulting discussions cannot be used later as evidence if the case goes to trial. This encourages a candid discussion because no one fears that any information will be used against them. Nevertheless, the association and the developer should agree in writing—before the joint inspections—how they can use the resulting information and how they can't.

PART THREE

Before Filing a Lawsuit

CHAPTER 9

Builders' Right-to-Repair Laws

From California to Pennsylvania, numerous states have enacted right-to-repair legislation that provides community association developers with an opportunity to investigate and repair building defects before litigation begins.

Right-to-repair laws contain traps for the unwary like very short statutes of limitation on certain types of claims. For this reason, the community manager should recommend that the board retain an attorney experienced in resolving defect claims to guide them through the right-to-repair process.

Pennsylvania's Residential Construction Dispute Resolution Act (PRCDRA) provides a good example of the now-common right-to-repair law.[1] Over the past few years, right-to-repair bills like the PRCDRA have been passed by legislatures in 21 states, including Alaska, Arizona, California, Colorado, Florida, Indiana, Kansas, Kentucky, Michigan, Montana, Nevada, Ohio, Oregon, Pennsylvania, South Carolina, South Dakota, Washington, and West Virginia. Right-to-repair laws have also been on record for several years in other states including Louisiana and Virginia.

The predecessor to and model for the various state bills was California's Davis-Sterling Common Interest Development Act.[2] This has since been supplemented by the California Civil Code, which applies to associations and single family homes alike and lays down a mandatory procedure for construction defect claims.[3]

These bills are the state's response to the growing number of residential construction-defect lawsuits filed in the past two decades. States have attempted to stall the litigation trend with statutory reform. In particular, right-to-repair legislation has been seen as a way to promote negotiation and settlement as alternatives to civil litigation.

Typically, these laws require a homeowner to give the builder written notice of a defect claim. The builder then inspects the alleged defect and offers to make a repair, settle the claim with cash, or reject the claim. The homeowner retains the right to sue if the builder rejects the defect claim. This procedure is intended to promote settlement without a long, drawn-out lawsuit.

State legislators consider several factors when constructing right-to-repair laws, but apply them differently in various states. For example, statutes of limitations specific to construction defects vary among states; definitions of key terms vary from state to state, giving rise to confusion in interpreting the statutes; and pre-litigation procedures, including cooling off periods and other time limits, vary between states and often are not clearly defined in the statutes. Nevertheless, these state laws all promote negotiation and settlement.

DEVELOPER'S PERSPECTIVE: Developers don't enjoy being sued—it's expensive and time consuming. They much prefer to find and remedy legitimate construction defects. In fact, their right to repair is a source of tension with attorneys. Developers complain that associations and their attorneys are quick to sue, seek windfall damages, and fail to let developers simply repair or replace defective work. That's why the National Association of Home Builders (NAHB) is promoting legislation that would require associations to let builders make corrections and not let them sue if they fail to do so.

Defining Terms

The definitions section of the PRCDRA includes several fundamental terms that are fairly uniform throughout all state laws. In particular, *action* is defined as "[a] civil lawsuit, judicial action or arbitration proceeding asserting a claim, in whole or in part, for damages or other relief in connection with a dwelling, caused by a construction defect."[4] In some states, action includes a civil action for damages resulting from personal injury or wrongful death, while in other states personal injuries are specifically excluded.[5] Additionally, the PRCDRA specifically states that "[t]his act shall not apply to any claim for personal injury or death."[6]

The term for the potential defendant also differs among the right-to-repair statutes. In some states, the construction professional is the party who must receive notice and has the right of repair.[7] In other states, a claimant must provide notice to the builder or contractor, subcontractor, or other similar party.[8] For simplicity, in this chapter, contractor, builder, and construction professional will be used interchangeably.

The bill defines a "claimant" as "[a]ny person who asserts a claim concerning a construction defect."[9] The bill states that "[i]f a claimant files an action without first complying with the requirements of this act, on application by a party to the action, the court or arbitrator shall enforce the terms of this act."[10] Thus, the claimant must follow the statutory procedures before filing a civil action or "the court or arbitrator shall enforce the terms…."[11] In West Virginia, the statute is very explicit in stating that the court must dismiss a civil action alleging a construction defect if the provisions of the right-to-repair statutes are not complied with before the filing.[12] Additionally, the action cannot be re-filed until the statute's requirements are fulfilled.[13]

Required Procedures

Virtually all right-to-repair legislation contains similar procedural requirements that a claimant must follow prior to filing any action against a contractor. Some state statutes even explicitly state that the procedures outlined in the right-to-repair bill are "exclusive and required prerequisites."[14]

Giving Notice

In the PRCDRA, a claimant *must* provide written notice of the claim to the contractor at least 90 days before initiating an action.[15] This notice provision varies among the states; in California, for example, the statute merely says that the claimant must provide notice, and does not explicitly list a time limit.[16] Contrarily, in Florida, the requisite notice must be given at least 60 days before filing a suit.[17] In Washington, the statute requires notice "no later than forty-five days before filing an action."[18] In none of the right-to-repair states is the listed time more than 90 days. Although the length of the notice varies, all states require that the notice be in writing.[19]

In the PRCDRA, for example, the owner must provide notice only to the contractor.[20] (Indeed, the Pennsylvania statutes don't even define subcontractor.[21]) Whereas, in Indiana, owners must provide notice to a construction professional, which includes subcontractors.[22]

The notice of the claim must include several statements to fulfill the statutory requirements. In the PRCDRA, the notice must state that the claimant asserts a construction defect and is providing notice pursuant to the act.[23] The notice must "describe the claim in detail sufficient to explain the nature of the construction defect and the result of the defect."[24] Under the Pennsylvania bill, the notice must "include any reports that describe the construction defect that would be discoverable under the law and that the claimant possesses."[25] Pennsylvania's key language seems to be that the notice must provide "reasonable detail" of the alleged construction defect, and a majority of the states include a similar provision.[26]

Other states have slight variations: In Colorado, claimants must file an "initial list of construction defects" with the court or arbitrator[27] in addition to the notice of claim. Oregon requires claimants to delineate "[t]he remediation the owner believes is necessary" (along with the other general information)[28] and to include "[a]ny report or other document evidencing the existence of the defects"[29] in the notice. And, Nevada's statute requires claimants to "describe in reasonable detail the cause of the defects if the cause is known."[30]

The Contractor's Response

Once notice has been given, the contractor has a specific amount of time to respond to the alleged claim. For example, in California, the builder "shall acknowledge, in writing, receipt of the notice of the claim."[31] How long a contractor (or builder) has to respond varies from state to state.[32] In the PRCDRA, the contractor must respond within 30 days of receiving the notice.[33] In California, the builder must acknowledge receipt within 14 days.[34] If a builder fails to acknowledge receipt of the notice within the prescribed time, the right-to-repair statute may impose sanctions and even relieve the homeowners from the requirements of the statute.[35]

The contractor's response to a notice of a claim usually includes the following elements: 1. an offer to settle the claim by monetary payment, 2. an election to repair the defect, 3. a proposal to inspect the dwelling, or 4. a denial or rejection of the claim.[36] A common provision in right-to-repair statutes is that once notice has been received by a contractor, the claimant must provide the contractor "complete access to inspect the dwelling."[37]

The contractor's inspection provides a way for the contractor to evaluate the strength of a claim—if it's weak, the contractor can reject it; if it's strong, the contractor may negotiate a settlement or offer to repair the defect.

State statutes specify the timeframe in which contractors should inspect a claimant's dwelling, and they require homeowners to make the dwelling available for the inspection. For example, the PRCDRA requires claimant's to allow the contractor (and any consultants) to view the residence[38] within 21 days of the contractor's request and to provide "reasonable access to the residence" for the inspection.[39] The inspection "may include any reasonable measures, including testing, for determining the nature, cause and extent of the defects described in the notice of effect...."[40] Additionally, some states specifically require the claimant to allow the contractor access during "normal working hours."[41]

Builders in California who want to inspect a dwelling must complete the inspection within 14 days of acknowledging receipt of the notice.[42] The 14-day inspection period is fairly standard among the states; however, the Florida statute provides contractors 30 days after receiving notice if a claim involves a single-family home or homeowner's association representing 20 or fewer homes.[43] For associations representing more than 20 homes, the inspection must take place within 50 days of receiving notice.[44] This wasn't always the case in Florida: prior to 2004, the inspection had to occur within five business days of service of the notice of claim.[45]

Fourteen days may be insufficient for a contractor to inspect, investigate, and evaluate a defect claim. Indeed, one critic of the California right-to-repair statute has said:

> Because the builder has only fourteen days to complete testing and investigations, the right-to-repair elements of the statute will likely benefit the homeowner because the builder will have less time to evaluate the severity and intricacies of defect claims. Although the builder may request a time extension for additional testing, the pressure will remain on the builder to meet the time limits or lose the right to repair. In some cases, it may simply be easier for the builder to offer to repair, even if the extent of the defect is questionable, than risk losing the right to repair.[46]

Both the PRCDRA and California statutes explicitly state that if the builder conducts any testing on the claimant's property, the builder must restore the property to its pretest condition after the testing has been completed.[47] If the builder fails to inspect or test the property within the specific time frame, California law releases the claimant from the requirements of the right to repair statute.[48] The California statute also includes an important provision stating that "if a builder intends to hold a subcontractor...responsible for its contribution" then notice must be provided by the builder so that the subcontractor can attend the inspection.[49] This type of provision is a standard provision within the state statutes in that it requires notice to any party by the property owner or builder that may be liable for a defect.

Under the PRCDRA, within 14 days of the inspection, the contractor may serve a written response to the claimant that offers to settle, repair, or deny the claim.[50] If the offer is to repair the defect, the contractor must specify a timetable for the repairs in the response.[51]

According to the PRCDRA, the claimant must accept or reject the contractor's offer within 30 days of receiving it.[52] If the claimant rejects the offer, he or she must explain in writing to the contactor the reasons for the rejection.[53] The contractor then has 10 days to make a supplemental offer.[54] If the claimant fails to respond to the offer, it will be deemed accepted.[55] Under Indiana law, to accept the construction professional's offer, a claimant must serve a written acceptance letter within 60 days of receipt of the offer.[56] Among the states, the timeframe for accepting an offer differs; in Kansas, for example, the claimant must accept by written notice no later than 30 days after receiving an offer.[57] If the claimant rejects the contractor's offer to remedy the construction defect, the claimant may then bring an action against the contractor for the construction defect claim.[58] In the event the contractor disputes the claim or does not respond to the claimant's notice of claim within the appropriate time, the claimant may then bring an action against the contractor.[59]

Some states specifically prohibit claimants from rejecting reasonable offers from contractors. In Nevada, for example, if a claimant rejects a reasonable offer for settlement, a court may deny the claimant's attorney's fees and costs and award fees and costs to the contractor.[60] The PRCDRA provides that if a claimant rejects a reasonable monetary offer or refuses to allow a contractor to make an accepted repair, the claimant may not recover an amount in excess of "the fair market value of an offer to repair the construction defect or the actual cost of the repairs," or the amount of the offer of settlement.[61] Moreover, under the PRCDRA, what's "reasonable"—whether in dollars or in repairs—will be determined by a judge or jury.[62] Similar to the Nevada statute, the Pennsylvania statute provides that, if the claimant rejects a reasonable monetary offer or offer to repair, the claimant may not recover costs or attorney's fees incurred after rejection.[63]

How Statutes of Limitations Affect Right-to-Repair Laws

Another fundamental aspect of the typical right-to-repair statute is how it interacts with and affects applicable statutes-of-limitations periods. The statutes generally include a provision tolling (temporarily suspending) the applicable statutes of limitations; however, these provisions differ from state to state. In the PRCDRA, the legislation states "[s]ervice under this subsection shall toll all applicable statutes of limitations until 90 days after the receipt of the notice of claim."[64] In Colorado, when a construction professional is notified of a claim, the statute of limitations is suspended until 60 days after the notice-of-claim process is completed.[65]

In Oregon, if a contractor has been notified of a defect claim within the required time and responds to the owner in writing denying the claim, the time to commence an action is extended 120 days.[66] Similarly, if the contractor makes a written offer to repair or pay for the defects and the owner rejects that offer, the time to commence an action is extended 120 days.[67] If the owner accepts the contractor's written offer, the contractor has 30 days after the "date specified in an accepted written offer by which the offering contractor...is to complete the remediation...."[68]

Under Kansas law, the claimant's notice of claim suspends the statute of limitations for 180 days after the latest of three dates: 1. the date the claimant personally serves or mails the notice; 2. the date agreed on for the contractor to make payments, or 3. the date agreed on for the contractor to completely remedy the construction defect.[69]

In Florida, receipt of the notice of claim suspends the statute of limitation until the later of 90 days or 120 days, as applicable; or, if the claimant has accepted the offer, 30 days "after the end of the repair period stated in the offer. By stipulation of the parties, the period may be extended and the statute of limitations is tolled during the extension."[70]

California law provides a very detailed statute-of-limitations provision: the applicable statute of limitations is extended from the time of the claimant's original claim to 100 days after the repair is completed.[71] In the event the builder fails to acknowledge the claim, elects to avoid the statutory procedure, or fails to request an inspection within the prescribed time, the time to file an action is extended to 45 days after the time for the builder to respond to the notice of claim.[72] If a builder attempts a non-adversarial procedure in lieu of the statutory procedure, the time for filing a complaint is extended to 100 days after completing the alternative procedure or 100 days after the non-adversarial procedure is deemed unenforceable, whichever is later.[73]

An Emphasis on Negotiation and Settlement

Negotiation and settlement are recurring themes throughout the various right-to-repair statutes. For example, the California Code specifies that "[t]his chapter establishes a *nonadversarial* procedure...."[74] Along the same lines, California law also provides that a builder may make an offer to *mediate* the dispute with a homeowner.[75] West Virginia legislators made it clear by stating in their right-to-repair statute that "[t]his article is intended to establish procedures for the *negotiation* of a claim...."[76] Additionally, parties are "encouraged to resolve any disagreement concerning the contract short of litigation."[77] In Florida, legislators believe "that it is beneficial to have an *alternative method* to resolve construction disputes that would reduce the need for litigation as well as protect the rights of homeowners."[78]

Because right-to-repair laws are relatively new, and many people don't know they exist, some legislators have included specific provisions in their statutes requiring contractors and construction professionals to notify homeowners[79] that there are specific requirements that must be followed before they can file a lawsuit for construction defects.[80] Contractors and construction professionals must provide notice "[u]pon entering a contract for sale, construction, or substantial remodeling of a residence..."[81] that he has a right to correct construction defects before a homeowner sues. Additionally, the notice must be "conspicuous and may be included as part of the underlying contract signed by the home owner."[82] Some state statutes, like Pennsylvania's PRCDRA, do not include any such notice provision in the statutes.[83]

Right-to-repair statutes may differ from state to state on procedural requirements, but they all agree that negotiation and settlement are preferred over litigation. Indeed, many states have made negotiation and settlement mandatory, and individuals who attempt to bypass them are subject to sanctions. By allowing construction professionals the right to repair or financially compensate homeowners for alleged defects, states have created non-adversarial environments in which disputes can be resolved expeditiously.

Endnotes

1. H.R. 2761, 187th Gen. Assem., Reg. Sess. (Pa. 2003).

2. *See* California Civil Code Section 1375, *et seq.* (2004).

3. *See* California Civil Code Section 895, *et seq.* (2004).

4. H.R. 2761, 187th Gen. Assem., Reg. Sess. (Pa. 2003).

5. *Compare* California Civil Code Section 931 (holding that personal injury actions are not covered by this section), *and* Florida Statutes Chapter 558.002(1) (2004) (stating that "action" does not include any "proceeding asserting a claim for alleged personal injuries arising out of an alleged construction defect"), *and* Indiana Code Section 32-27-3-1(1) (2003) (stating "action" does not include "any civil action in tort alleging personal injury"), *and* Kentucky Revised Statutes Annotated Section 411.252(1) (2003), *and* Montana Code Annotated Sections 70-19-426(1)(a) (2003), *and* Washington Revised Code Section 64.50.010(1) (2002), *with* Colorado Revised Statutes Sections 13-20-802-5(1) (2003) (defining "action" to include actions for personal injuries), *and* Kansas Statutes Annotated Sections 60-4701(a) (2003) (stating that "action" means any civil action including "a claim for injury"), *and* South Carolina Code Sections 15-3-640(3) (2003), *and* West Virginia Code Section 21-11A-2(8) (2004).

6. H.R. 2761, 187th Gen. Assem., Reg. Sess. (Pa. 2003); *see also* Kansas Statutes Annotated Sections 60-4703 (2003) (stating that the relevant statutes does not apply to claims for personal injury or death).

7. *See, e.g.,* Kentucky Revised Statutes Annotated Section 411.252 (Banks-Baldwin 2003) (defining "construction professional" as a builder).

8. *See* California Civil Code Section 911 (2004) (defining "builder" as "any entity or individual, including, but not limited to a builder, developer, general contractor, contractor, or original seller..."); Florida Statutes Chapter 558.002 (2004); South Carolina Code Annotated Section 40-59-840 (Law. Co-op. 2004) (identifying a "subcontractor" as a potential party to receive notice of a claim).

9. H.R. 2761, 187th Gen. Assem., Reg. Sess. (Pa. 2003). *But see* South Carolina Code Annotated Section 40-59-820 (Law. Co-op. 2004) (defining "claimant" as a "homeowner, including a subsequent purchaser, who asserts a claim against a contractor, subcontractor, supplier, or design professional concerning a defect in the design, construction, condition, or sale of a dwelling or in the remodel of a dwelling").

10. *See* California Civil Code Section 910 (2002) (holding that "prior to an action against a party..., the claimant shall initiate the following prelitigation procedures..."); Florida Statutes Chapter 558.003 (2004) (asserting that "[a] claimant may not file a civil action subject to this chapter" without first complying with the chapter's requirements); Kansas Statutes Annotated Section 60-4702(a) (2003).

11. H.R. 2761, 187th Gen. Assem., Reg. Sess. (Pa. 2003).

12. West Virginia Code Section 21-11A-7(b) (2004); *see also* Nevada Revised Statutes 40.647 (2004) (requiring a court to dismiss without prejudice an action filed before the statutory provisions are followed).

13. *Id.*

14. West Virginia Code Section 21-11A-7(a) (2004).

15. H.R. 2761, 187th Gen. Assem., Reg. Sess. (Pa. 2003).

16. California Civil Code Section 910(a) (2004); *see also* Kansas Statutes Annotated Section 60-4704 (2003); Kentucky Revised Statutes Section 411.258(1) (2003); Montana Code Annotated Section 70-19-427(1) (2003); S. 909, 72nd Leg. Assem., Reg. Sess. (Or. 2003).

17. Florida Statutes Chapter 558.004(1) (2004); *see also* Indiana Code Section 32-27-3-2(a) (2003).

18. Washington Revised Code Section 64.50.020(1) (2004)

19. *See* California Civil Code Section 910(a) (2004) (requiring written notice).

20. H.R. 2761, 187th Gen. Assem., Reg. Sess. (Pa. 2003).

21. *Id.*

22. Indiana Code Section 32-27-3-2 (2003).

23. H.R. 2761, 187th Gen. Assem., Reg. Sess. (Pa. 2003).

24. *Id.*

25. *Id.*

26. *See* Florida Statutes Chapter 558.004(1) (2004); Indiana Code Section 32-27-3-2(a) (2003); Nevada Revised Statutes 40.645 (2004); Washington Revised Code Section 64.50.020(1) (2002).

27. Colorado Revised Statutes Section 13-20-803 (2003).

28. S. 909, 72nd Leg. Assem., Reg. Sess. (Or. 2003).

29. *Id.*

30. Nevada Revised Statutes 40.645 (2004).

31. California Civil Code Section 913 (2004).

32. *Compare* Nevada Revised Statutes 40.6472 (2004) (requiring a response to the notice of a claim within 90 days after receipt), *with* California Civil Code Section 913 (2004) (requiring a response within 14 days after receipt).

33. H.R. 2761, 187th Gen. Assem., Reg. Sess. (Pa. 2003).

34. California Civil Code Section 913 (2004).

35. See California Civil Code Section 915 (2004).

36. *See, e.g.,* H.R. 2761, 187th Gen. Assem., Reg. Sess. (Pa. 2003); Nevada Revised Statutes Section 40.6472 (2004); Montana Code Annotated Section 70-19-427 (2003).

37. H.R. 2761, 187th Gen. Assem., Reg. Sess. (Pa. 2003).

38. *Id.*

39. Indiana Code Section 32-27-3-4 (2003); Florida Statutes Chapter 558.004(2) (2004).

40. S. 909, 72nd Leg. Assem., Reg. Sess. (Or. 2003).

41. *See* Indiana Code Section 32-27-3-4 (2003).

42. California Civil Code Section 916(a) (2004).

43. Florida Statutes Chapter 558.004(2) (2004).

44. *Id.*

45. *Id.*

46. *Melissa C. Tronquet, Comment, There's No Place Like Home … Until You Discover Defects: Do Prelitigation Statutes Relating To Construction Defect Cases Really Protect The Needs Of Homeowners And Developers?,* 44 Santa Clara L. Rev. 1249, 1278 (2004) (citations omitted).

47. H.R. 2761, 187th Gen. Assem., Reg. Sess. (Pa. 2003); California Civil Code Section 916(a) (2004).

48. California Civil Code Section 916(d) (2004).

49. *Id. at* Section 916(e).

50. *Compare* H.R. 2761, 187th Gen. Assem., Reg. Sess. (Pa. 2003) (where the contractor "may serve a written response", *with* Indiana Code Section 32-27-3-4 (where the construction professional "must serve").

51. H.R. 2761, 187th Gen. Assem., Reg. Sess. (Pa. 2003).

52. *Id. See also* Nevada Revised Statutes 40.660 (2004) (stating that an offer of settlement that is not accepted in 45 days if a complex matter or 25 days if not a complex matter is considered rejected).

53. H.R. 2761, 187th Gen. Assem., Reg. Sess. (Pa. 2003).

54. *Id.*

55. *Id.*

56. Indiana Code Section 32-27-3-5 (2003).

57. Kansas Statutes Annotated Section 60-4704(k) (2003).

58. *See, e.g.,* Indiana Code Section 32-27-3-4 (2003).

59. Kentucky Revised Statutes Annotated Section 411.258 (Banks-Baldwin 2003).

60. Nevada Revised Statutes Section 40.650 (2004); *see also* Indiana Code Section 32-27-3-9 (2003).

61. H.R. 2761, 187th Gen. Assem., Reg. Sess. (Pa. 2003).

62. *Id.*

63. *Id.*

64. *Id.*

65. Colorado Revised Statutes Section 13-20-805 (2003); *see also* Indiana Code Section 32-27-3-14 (2003) (holding that if a written notice is served within the time prescribed for the filing of a construction defect action, the statutes of limitations is tolled from the day on which the notice is served until 60 days after the period of time during which the filing on an action is barred).

66. S. 909, 72nd Leg. Assem., Reg. Sess. (Or. 2003).

67. *Id.*

68. *Id.*

69. Kansas Statutes Annotated Section 60-4702 (2003).

70. Florida Statutes Chapter 558.004(10) (2004).

71. California Civil Code Section 927 (2004).

72. *Id.*

73. *Id.*

74. *Id.* at Section 914 (2004) (emphasis added).

75. *Id.* at Section 919 (2004).

76. W. Va. Code Section 21-11A-1 (2004).

77. *Id.*

78. Florida Statutes Chapter 558.001 (2004).

79. *See, e.g.,* Kentucky Revised Statutes Annotated Section 411.260 (Banks-Baldwin 2003).

80. *See, e.g., id.;* Indiana Code Section 32-27-3-12 (2003).

81. Indiana Code Section 32-27-3-12 (2003).

82. *Id.;* see also Kentucky Revised Statutes Annotated Section 411.260 (Banks-Baldwin 2003); Kansas Statutes Annotated Section 60-4706 (2003); S. 909, 72nd Leg. Assem., Reg. Sess. (Or. 2003).

83. H.R. 2761, 187th Gen. Assem., Reg. Sess. (Pa. 2003); Nevada Revised Statutes Section 40.600, *et seq.* (2001); California Civil Code Section 895, *et seq.* (2004).

CHAPTER 10

A Builder's Right-to-Repair: Step-by-Step

To get a better idea of how typical right-to-repair laws affect homeowners and associations, what follows is a step-by-step review of how a case would proceed using California as an example.[1]

1. The Homeowner Notifies the Builder of a Claim

When an association's preliminary investigation turns up construction defects, the association or homeowner must notify the builder of the claim in writing via certified mail, overnight mail, or personal delivery.

The notice must provide the claimant's name, address, and preferred method of contact. It must state that the claimant alleges a violation against the builder, and describe the defect in enough detail to determine its nature and location.[2]

Homeowners aren't precluded from seeking redress according to the terms in a contract, warranty, or other document that the contractor generates; however, this doesn't satisfy the California notice requirements.

2. The Homeowner Requests Documents from the Builder

In response to a written request, a builder must provide copies of all relevant documents that pertain to the residence or appropriate part of a development within 30 days of receipt, if it states that it is made relative to structural, fire safety, or soils provisions of the legislation. The person asking for the documents pays to have them copied.

Builders don't have to supply these documents, if they're lost or destroyed through no fault of the builder. However, the builder must help the homeowner obtain them from their original source.[3]

3. The Builder Acknowledges the Claim

A builder must acknowledge that he or she received the notice of claim in writing within 14 days. If a builder knows that the homeowner or association is represented by an attorney, he or she must copy the attorney on all communication. The builder will know who the homeowner's attorney is because the attorney will likely send the notice of claim or send a letter stating that he or she represents the homeowner. If the builder also has an attorney, only the attorneys will communicate with each other.[4]

If a builder fails to acknowledge receipt of the notice of a claim or to request an inspection within the time specified (or after an alternative non-adversarial proceeding), or elects not to go through the pre-litigation process, the homeowner is released from the requirements of the legislation and may file an action.[5]

4. The Builder Inspects and Tests for Defects

The builder has 14 days to initially inspect and test the defect at a date and time mutually convenient to the homeowner. If the homeowner has an attorney, a representative from the attorney's office should be included in the inspection, if at all possible. The builder is responsible for the costs of the inspection and testing as well as the costs of repairing any resulting damage. The builder must also provide proof that he or she has liability insurance that covers damages or injuries that might occur during inspection and testing. If the homeowner or his or her legal representative wants to observe, record, videotape, or photograph the inspection, the builder must allow it.[6]

If a builder believes a second inspection or test is necessary, he or she must submit a written request to the homeowner specifying the reasons for the additional inspection or test and must complete it within 40 days. All requirements concerning the initial inspection or testing also apply to the second inspection or testing.[7]

If the builder fails to inspect or test the property within the time specified, the homeowner may file an action.[8]

5. Other Responsible Parties are Notified

Sometimes builders hold others responsible to some extent for construction defects. Subcontractors, design professionals, product manufacturers, or material suppliers—including insurance carriers, warranty companies, or service companies—may be involved, and the builder must notify them. Notice must be given sufficiently in advance to allow them to attend the initial or second inspection and to participate in the repair process. Also, the builder must let the claimant or his or her legal representative know prior to the inspection who has been invited to attend. This provision does not apply to the builder's insurance company.

6. The Builder Offers to Repair or Pay

After having a look at the defects, the builder may offer to repair the defect and compensate the homeowner for recoverable damages. This is a written offer that includes a detailed, specific, step-by-step statement that identifies the defect, explains the nature, scope, and location of the repair, and sets a reasonable date for the repair. It includes the names, addresses, telephone numbers, and license numbers of the contractors who will do the work. They must be fully insured—and the homeowner can ask for proof of insurance—and responsible for all damages or injuries they may cause. The homeowner has a right to ask that up to three more contractors be added to the list of candidates to do the repairs, and builder's offer should let them know about this. Also, if the homeowner asks for documentation—in writing and within the prescribed time period—pertaining to the claimed violation, the builder must make it available.[9]

Instead of offering to repair defects, a builder may make a cash offer. In this situation, the homeowner is free to accept the offer, or he or she may reject the offer and file an action.[10]

7. The Homeowner Accepts the Offer or Mediates the Dispute

Based on the builder's offer, the homeowner must authorize the builder to proceed with the repair or provide information about alternative contractors. The builder has 35 days to provide the homeowner with a choice of contractors, and the homeowner has 20 days to authorize the builder or one of the alternative contractors to make the repair.[11]

The builder's offer to repair a defect must also offer to mediate the dispute if the homeowner chooses. If mediation fails, and the builder has made an offer to repair a defect, the homeowner must allow either the builder or a contractor to repair the defect.[12] If the builder or contractor fails to comply in the time or manner specified, the homeowner may proceed to file a legal action.[13]

8. Repairs are Scheduled

Once the builder and homeowner agree on repairs, the builder makes an appointment and all necessary arrangements with the homeowner to get the repair completed. As stated earlier, if the homeowner has an attorney, all communication must be with the attorney—including scheduling repairs. However, because of the time limitations, if the attorney is unavailable, the builder should contact the manager or another legal professional.

Repairs should be scheduled for a date convenient to all parties, but within a limited number of days depending on the last completed step: within 14 days of the homeowner accepting the offer to repair or selecting an alternate contractor, within seven days of mediation, or within five days of the builder obtaining a permit, if needed. The builder should be reasonably diligent about obtaining any such permit.[14]

It's the builder's responsibility to ensure that the repairs are done diligently and quickly—preferably within 120 days.[15]

Many of the rules that applied to inspections also apply to repairs. For example, homeowners may record, videotape, or photograph the repairs; however this documentation can't be used as evidence to support a spoliation defense in later litigation.[16] Also, builders must provide copies of all documents to the homeowners that pertain to the repairs, if they ask.[17]

9. The Homeowner Isn't Satisfied

When repairs are completed, if the homeowner believes the work is inadequate or still doesn't meet standards, he or she can file an action for the work and any damages[18]—but first he or she must request mediation in writing—if the two parties haven't already tried it.[19]

10. When Additional Defects are Discovered

Sometimes, in the middle of a defect claim, another defect is discovered at the same property. Unless the builder and homeowner agree to combine the cases, they are treated as two separate cases. There are exceptions, however. For example, in detached, single-family residences, if defects discovered later are a violation of the same standard as the pending action, the homeowner doesn't need to begin another legal action. The same is true for attached residences—like condominiums—if the subsequent defect in a common area violates the same standard as the pending defect action.[20]

Each of these steps has specific time limits, and, unless both parties agree otherwise, they must be strictly observed. Homeowners can take legal action against builders who fail to act on time unless both parties have agreed in writing to extend the time.[21] Conversely, if the homeowner fails to act on time, the builder can ask the court to disallow any further legal action by the homeowner.[22]

Endnotes

1. California Civil Code Section 938.
2. California Civil Code Section 910(b).
3. California Civil Code Section 912(a).
4. California Civil Code Section 913.
5. California Civil Code Section 915.
6. California Civil Code Section 916(a).
7. California Civil Code Section 916(c).
8. California Civil Code Section 916(d).
9. California Civil Code Section 917.
10. California Civil Code Section 929(a).
11. California Civil Code Section 918.
12. California Civil Code Section 919.
13. California Civil Code Section 921.
14. California Civil Code Section 921(a).
15. California Civil Code Section 921(b).
16. California Civil Code Section 922.
17. California Civil Code Section 923.
18. California Civil Code Section 926.
19. California Civil Code Section 108.
20. California Civil Code Section 932.
21. California Civil Code Section 930(a).
22. California Civil Code Section 930(b).

CHAPTER 11

Other Steps
before Litigation

The initial investigation showed that the association had legitimate construction defect claims, the builder and the association worked together to resolve the problems, but the association isn't satisfied with the outcome and is ready to file a lawsuit. However, before heading to the courthouse, the association must take a few additional steps.

Step 1: Gather Documents

The manager will need to gather an extensive collection of documents from current and past management companies and board members—who may have historical records.

The manager should catalog all records, note the original source, and preserve them in their original files, except for privileged documents that must be segregated.

DEVELOPER'S PERSPECTIVE: Like the association, the developer must gather a substantial amount of information and coordinate the efforts of many people—design professionals, employees, and contractors.

The developer must also assign a project leader to organize and supervise the effort, analyze data, coordinate inspections, and form preliminary conclusions. This developer representative also will work closely with the association manager to coordinate inspections that eliminate duplication of effort for the developer and reduce inconvenience for the residents.

The developer needs to respond and investigate promptly, not only because time limits are mandated in some states, but also because it avoids litigation.

Step 2: Investigate All Responsible Parties

Early in the process, the manager should gather evidence about anyone who might be included in the lawsuit: especially the developer, but also general contractors, architects, engineers, subcontractors, and material suppliers. Once a defect attorney has been hired, he or she can take over this step.

Association Documents Needed in a Lawsuit

Association documents
- Property plans, specifications, maps, and plots
- Governing documents: articles of incorporation, bylaws, CC&Rs, rules and regulations
- Homeowner mailing lists
- Minutes of board meetings, including executive sessions, and annual owners' meetings

Financial documents
- Current and past reserve studies

Insurance documents
- Current and expired insurance policies
- Files from or about the broker concerning applicable coverage

Reports
- Developer's reports as submitted to state and local government, including final subdivision reports
- Engineering reports, including soils, mechanical, and civil
- Reports, photographs, and backup data developed by the association, developer, and consultants relating to defect investigations

Repair documentation
- Temporary repairs
- Repairs and warranty work performed by developer, general contractor, or subcontractors

Correspondence
- Between association and developer regarding defects, warranty claims, and repairs
- Between association and management company regarding defects or warranty claim issues

Developer's marketing materials
- Sales brochures
- Advertising relating to the community or association
- Sales contracts

Managers who are unsure who to investigate or where to find them should check the association's governing documents, reports submitted to state agencies, building department records, project sales brochures, and the initial sales contracts.

If the developer set up a limited liability company (LLC) specifically for your development, find out who formed it, since the LLC itself will seldom have any assets. Online research should quickly provide the status of the corporation; names and addresses of officers, directors, and key personnel; status of contractor licenses; and a history of contractor license disputes. For large builders that are public companies, financial information is also available online, primarily from filings with the Securities and Exchange Commission, as well as judgments, tax liens, defaults, and bankruptcies.

Don't be surprised if the company the association needs to sue is bankrupt or out of business by the time construction defects are discovered. They can still be pursued through their insurance companies. The developer generally undertakes an investigation of available insurance by reviewing its own files on subcontractors.

DEVELOPER'S PERSPECTIVE: Construction defect claims, almost universally, criticize the work of subcontractors. Since developers rely on subcontractors to comply with construction documents, industry standards, and applicable codes, they generally want subcontractors to participate when defect claims are filed against them. They will want to apportion responsibility among subcontractors, suppliers, and design professionals.

Therefore, while a developer investigates a defect or reviews documents, he will put subcontractors on notice and give them the opportunity to respond to allegations of defects in their work. It's in the developer's best interests to involve subcontractors in the process and have them participate financially to resolve defect claims.

Step 3: Try for an Early Settlement

Defect litigation can become extremely expensive; and, invariably, the insurance companies are the ones who pay. Naturally, insurance adjusters want associations and homeowners to engage in negotiations with the developer or builder to resolve disputes as quickly as possible. This approach is particularly appropriate when defects are limited and damages are relatively small. In recent years, even large community associations with significant defects have been able to resolve construction defect claims with developers early in the process without litigation.

Before settlement negotiations begin, the community manager or board should ask the association's attorney to ensure that statutes of limitation do not run during negotiations with the developer.

If an association decides to seek early settlement, it must be well prepared with detailed expert reports, cost-of-repair estimates, and a settlement demand that includes:

- Estimated cost of repair.
- Temporary repair costs.
- Costs of the investigation.
- Claim for attorney's fees, if applicable.

This collection of documents will not only go to the developer, but to the developer's counsel and insurance carrier as well. It should be clearly labeled For Mediation Purposes Only, and the statute regarding privileged settlement communications should be cited prominently on the label. For example:

John Jones, CEO
Mountain Homebuilders, LLC
123 Main Street
Jackson, CA 90887

For Mediation Purposes Only
Evidence California Civil Code, Section 1152

The association should follow up with the developer to arrange for its experts to present photographs, videotape, and other graphic evidence of the defects and for the cost estimator to explain the cost-of-repair estimate in detail.

An early settlement may amount to the developer proposing to repair the association's property—generally using his own crews or selecting the repair contractor. Boards and managers should be cautious if they allow the developer to make the repairs or select the contractor. In this case, the settlement agreement should provide that the association's experts may monitor the reconstruction and comment on its deficiencies. The preferred approach is to require the developer to hire an independent contractor who is acceptable to the association. Regardless of who undertakes the repairs, the settlement agreement should specify in detail the repair work that will be done—this minimizes the possibility of disputes as the work goes forward.

When boards are considering an early settlement offer, the developer and its insurance carrier will ask for a general release. If the association agrees, a general release will bar the association from making any further claims against the developer. This causes two problems: if additional defects are discovered after settlement, the association will have to bear the cost of repairing them, and the board may be held liable for failing to conduct a thorough investigation.

Even when working toward an early settlement, the association should include an experienced defect attorney in the process. This person is familiar with and will keep the association clear of any statute of limitations issues. He or she will ensure that the defect investigation is sufficiently thorough and advise the board whether a developer's response to an offer is reasonable.

Of particular value is the defect attorney's guidance with releases. While the developer will seek a general release barring all future claims, a defects attorney is often able to negotiate an issue release, in which the developer is only released from specific issues. If a new defect is discovered later, the association is not barred from pursuing new and different claims.

Step 4: Try a Neutral Investigation

Another enlightened approach to resolving construction defect claims quickly is to conduct a neutral investigation. In this case, the association and the developer agree that before taking formal pre-litigation steps or filing a lawsuit they will appoint a team of neutral, independent experts to investigate the defects. For best results, the association and the developer should enter into a confidential agreement

—not subject to disclosure, if the case isn't resolved—that details the steps in the neutral investigation and how the parties will attempt to resolve the claims when the neutral investigation is completed.

A typical neutral-investigation agreement between an association and a developer specifies the areas of expertise that are needed on the investigation team and identifies individuals qualified to fill them—for example, an architect, civil engineer, structural engineer, geotechnical engineer, mechanical consultant, roofing consultant, and an electrical consultant. It will also list the specific defects to be investigated, or—absent known defects—the scope of the investigation. Each neutral expert will:

- Identify the scope, nature, and extent of each defect and its cause.
- Determine whether the defect resulted from deficient design, materials, or construction.
- Determine whether the defect resulted from improper original construction, improper subsequent repairs, or improper maintenance.
- Determine whether the alleged defect can be attributed to the actions or neglect of the association, the developer, or some third party.
- Determine the appropriate repairs for each defect.
- Recommend repairs for each defect.

A neutral cost estimator prepares a detailed cost-of-repair analysis based on the expert's reports. The expert team then presents its findings to the association's board, the developer and its insurance carriers, and all attorneys. The presentation covers the nature, scope, and extent of each defect and its cause, the damages caused by each defect, the recommended repairs for each defect and their costs. Considering all the information presented by the neutral experts, the association and the developer attempt to resolve the claims by negotiation.

The association and developer should decide in advance what constitutes a resolution and include it in the written agreement. For example, the parties might agree that claims will be resolved if each accepts the recommendation of the neutral expert team and the cost-of-repair estimate. If one or both parties rejects the expert team's recommendations or cost of repair, this process ends and formal pre-litigation steps begin—or a lawsuit is filed. This is the take-it-or-leave-it approach to neutral investigation.

Another approach is to involve an experienced construction-defects mediator if the parties can't agree with the experts' findings. With this approach, if the mediator can't get the association and the developer to accept the findings of the neutral team, he or she will attempt to reach resolution through traditional mediation techniques.

As part of the written agreement, the association and the developer should also specify who will bear how much of the costs of the neutral expert investigation. Often the developer and its insurance company will agree to pay 100 percent because neutral investigation and early resolution are less expensive for them than litigation.

The entire neutral investigation must be conducted under the mediation privilege so that nothing will be admissible if the case goes to trial. None of the work of the neutral experts can be the subject of discovery. None of the neutral team's reports are admissible at trial. The cost-of-repair analysis prepared by the neutral team cannot be used for any purpose at trial. In short, there will be no reference whatsoever to the neutral process if the case goes to trial.

Step 5: Fulfill State Pre-litigation Requirements

Apart from the builders' right-to-repair laws, some states mandate that certain steps—called pre-litigation steps—be taken before a lawsuit for construction defects can be filed.

The first pre-litigation statutes were enacted in California and are known as the Calderon process after Senator Charles Calderon, the author of the legislation. California's pre-litigation procedures are among the most exhaustive in the country. Therefore, the Calderon process is highlighted as a primary example of sample procedures.

Serve Notice to the Builder

The Calderon process starts by serving a builder with a Notice of Commencement of Legal Proceeding[1], and this starts the statutes of limitations running.

Establish a Dispute Resolution Period

Once notice is served, all parties have a certain number of days—180 in California—to resolve the dispute, and extensions can usually be negotiated.[2]

Convene an Informal Meeting

The builder may meet with the association board at least once, unless they all agree otherwise, and the discussions are privileged communications.[3]

Exchange Documents

The builder provides the association with all plans and specifications, subcontracts, and other construction files regarding the defects. Conversely, the association provides the builder with all files regarding the defects, including reserve studies, maintenance records, survey questionnaires, and test results.[4]

Serve Notice to Other Parties

The builder sends a copy of the notice to all subcontractors, design professionals, their insurers, and others who may be involved and makes arrangements for everyone to participate in selecting a dispute resolution facilitator (DRF).[5]

Provide Statements of Insurance

The subcontractors and design professionals provide the association and the builder with a Statement of Insurance that provides the names of their insurance carriers and their policy numbers.[6]

Designate Peripheral Parties

Subcontractors, design professionals, or insurers may ask to be designated as a peripheral party—that is, someone whose total exposure is below a certain threshold.[7] This excuses them from participating in the pre-litigation process.

Select a Dispute Resolution Facilitator

All parties with responsibility for the defects meet to select a dispute resolution facilitator to preside over the process.[8] The DRF must disclose to all parties whether he or she has any conflicts of interest.[9] If he or she fails to reveal a conflict, and a participant discloses one before the case management meeting, the DRF will be disqualified.[10] If the parties can't agree on a dispute resolution facilitator, then each submits a list of three facilitators they find acceptable, and each strikes one from the others' list. The court makes the final selection.[11]

Convene a Case Management Meeting

All parties participate in a case management meeting in which they draft an agreement, called a case management statement. This statement specifies that certain process and activities—like visual inspections and invasive testing—will take place in a prescribed order, within certain guidelines,[12] and according to established deadlines.[13] The case management statement may also call for a photo exchange between parties; expert presentations and meetings; or anything else that will help resolve the dispute.[14]

Submit a Settlement Offer

After all the work outlined in the case management statement has been completed, the builder may submit a written settlement offer to the association.[15]

At this point, if a settlement isn't forthcoming or the board rejects a settlement offer, the association may initiate legal action.[16]

Endnotes

1. California Civil Code Section 1375(b).
2. California Civil Code Section 1375(c).
3. California Civil Code Section 1375(d).
4. California Civil Code Section 1375(e)(1).
5. California Civil Code Section 1375(e)(1).
6. California Civil Code Section 1375(e)(2).
7. California Civil Code Section 1375(e)(3).
8. California Civil Code Section 1375(f)(1).
9. California Civil Code Section 1375(f)(1).
10. California Civil Code Section 1375(f)(3).
11. California Civil Code Section 1375(f)(4).
12. California Civil Code Section 1375(h).
13. California Civil Code Section 1375(j).
14. California Civil Code Section 1375(i).
15. California Civil Code Section 1375(k)(1)(A)-(B).
16. California Civil Code Section 1375.05.

PART FOUR

The Lawsuit

CHAPTER 12

Who Files Suit—
Association or Owners?

The community association manager and board members have taken all the steps necessary to resolve their construction defects with a builder or developer, but they just aren't getting acceptable results. It's time to file a lawsuit, but who should file—the association, the individual owners, either or both? In legal terminology, who has the standing to sue?

Is It the Community Association's Case?
What Type of Association Is It?
A community association's standing to sue for construction defects depends on what type of association it is.

Many housing developments are referred to, generally, as common-interest developments, and community associations are the nonprofit corporations or unincorporated associations created to manage them.[1] Common-interest developments can include condominiums, community apartments, planned developments, homeowner associations, and stock cooperatives.[2]

In a community apartment development, each unit owner holds an undivided interest in the entire property and the right to occupy an apartment. Here, the owners have standing, rather than the association.[3] In a stock cooperative, by contrast, the association has standing to sue for defects because the stock cooperative owns the entire property.[4] In a planned development, the owners generally hold title to their individual lots and homes, and the association may own or lease the common areas. The owners have standing to sue for defects in their homes and lots; the association has standing for the common areas.[5]

Is It a Common Element or a Separate Interest?
Another way to determine who has standing to sue is to identify whether a common element (sometimes called common areas) or a separate interest (an individual unit) is affected by the construction defect. When construction defects affect a common element, the association has standing to sue because it has maintenance responsibility for the common areas. When individual units are affected, the individual owner has standing to sue.[6]

As straightforward as that seems, experienced managers know that delineating one from the other can be challenging. Fortunately, the association's governing documents (generally the CC&Rs) and state law provide guidance. Additionally, the Uniform Common Interest Ownership Act (UCIOA)[7] provides a definition for common elements:[8]

> i. In the case of (a) a condominium or cooperative, all portions of the common interest community other than the units; and (b) a planned community, any real estate within a planned community which is owned or leased by the association, other than a unit; and

> ii. In all common interest communities, any other interest in real estate for the benefit of unit owners which are subject to the declaration.

The definition of a "unit" in the UCIOA is more specific:[9] Unit means a physical portion of the community designated for separate ownership or occupancy. The challenge arises at the points where common elements and units intersect. The UCIOA defines unit boundaries in four ways:[10]

> 1. If walls, floors or ceilings are designated as boundaries of a unit, all lathe, furring, wallboard, plasterboard, plaster, paneling, tiles, wallpaper, paint, finish flooring, and any other materials constituting any part of the finished surfaces thereof are a part of the unit, and all other portions of the walls, floors, or ceilings are a part of the common elements.

> 2. If any chute, flue, duct, wire, conduit, bearing wall, bearing column, or any other fixture lies partially within and partially outside the designated boundaries of a unit, any portion thereof serving only that unit is a limited common element allocated solely to that unit, and any portion thereof serving more than one unit or any portion of the common elements is part of the common elements.

> 3. Subject to paragraph (2), all spaces, interior partitions, and other fixtures and improvements within the boundaries of a unit are a part of the unit.

> 4. Any shutters, awnings, window boxes, doorsteps, stoops, porches, balconies, patios, and all exterior doors and windows or other fixtures designed to serve a single unit, but located outside the unit's boundaries, are limited common elements allocated exclusively to that unit.

When Both Common Areas and Individual Units are Affected

Who has standing to sue when construction defects are present in the common elements *and* individual units? According to the UCIOA:[11] "…the association may …institute, defend, or intervene in litigation or administrative proceedings in its own name on behalf of itself or two or more unit owners on matters affecting the common-interest community." Therefore, when defects appear in both the common areas and the units, the standing to sue would belong to the association on its own behalf and on behalf of two or more unit owners. Indeed, the preferred practice is to name the association and at least two owners as representatives of all affected owners.

Standing to Sue State by State

A number of states have standing-to-sue statutes that echo the UCIOA:

In California, community associations have the authority to initiate and defend against actions involving damage to or defects in the common areas or separate interests:[12]

An association established to manage a common interest development shall have standing to institute, defend, settle, or intervene in litigation, arbitration, mediation, or administrative proceedings in its own name as the real party in interest without joining with it the individual owners of the common interest development, in matters pertaining to the following:

a. Enforcement of the governing documents.

b. Damage to the common areas.

c. Damage to the separate interests, which the association is obligated to maintain and repair.

d. Damage to the separate interest which arises out of, or is intricately related to, damage to the common areas or separate interests that the association is obligated to maintain or repair.

California allows associations to sue for property damage relating to construction defects, except in individual units,—e.g., carpeting, fixtures, paint and wallpaper.

Utah's standing-to-sue statute is even broader[13]:

Without limiting the rights of any unit owner, actions may be brought by the manager or management committee, in either case in the discretion of the management committee, on behalf of two or more unit owners, as their respective interest may appear, with respect to any cause of action relating to the common areas and facilities for more than one unit.

In Colorado, associations have standing to sue for construction defects unless their governing documents prohibit it:[14]

Except as provided in subsection (2) of this section, and subject to the provisions of the declaration, the association, without specific authorization in the declaration, may…institute…litigation.

By contrast, associations in Oregon have standing to sue only if their CC&Rs specifically allow it[15]:

Subject to the provisions of the condominium's declaration and bylaws, and whether or not the association is unincorporated, the association may…institute, defend, or intervene in litigation…

For summaries of the standing-to-sue statutes for common-interest developments in all 50 states and the District of Columbia, see Appendix 1.

HISTORICAL PERSPECTIVE: Developers, builders, subcontractors, and suppliers used to retaliate against community associations that sued for construction defects by counter suing. They would disavow responsibility for the defects and allege that the association's maintenance was substandard—which led to the defects. That's no longer the case, at least in California, where new laws prohibit counter suing for claims arising from construction defects.

Class Actions

Some construction defects are common to many or all owners. Rather than file numerous individual suits against the same defendant that may get inconsistent results, filing a class action ensures that all damages are recouped at once. Some states favor this approach, and (although it lessens the burden on the state's legal system) some don't.

CASE NOTE: An example of a class action brought by a community association is the California case of *Occidental Land, Inc. v. Superior Court.** Approximately 150 homeowners alleged that the developer deliberately underestimated the property maintenance costs during sales of the homes. The developer countered that each owner should file separately because each paid varying amounts of the maintenance costs. But the California Supreme Court disagreed, ruling that the developer's misrepresentations were the same to all members of the class. The damages amounted to the difference between the promised maintenance costs and the actual costs paid by the homeowners. **18 Cal.3d 355, 134 Cal.Rptr. 388 (1976).*

Class actions are inappropriate for common-area defects in community associations; they're used primarily to recover for defects in large tracts of single family homes. Qualifying (or being "certified") as a class, i.e., authorized to bring a class-action suit, requires an association to meet a number of prerequisites that have been laid out in federal guidelines[16] and are followed by many states. Broadly stated, the group is so large it's impractical for each person to sue individually, and all group members have essentially the same type of claim.

CASE NOTE: The circumstances that make a construction defect case a class action are illustrated by the recent California case of *Hicks v. Kaufman and Broad Homecorp.** In this case, homes purchased from developer Kaufman and Broad were built on conventional concrete foundations. Historically, concrete foundations contained welded wire mesh to strengthen the concrete; however, Kaufman and Broad incorporated a new product called Fibermesh. When the slabs and stem wall foundations cracked, moisture, dirt, and insects invaded the homes and caused humps in the flooring. The homeowners sued alleging that Fibermesh did not resist ground movement as well as traditional welded wire. Again, the developer wanted each homeowner to make the case separately for each home. But, the court ruled that the case was, indeed, a class action. **89 Cal.App.4th 908, 107 Cal.Rptr.2d 761 (2001).*

Class actions are the most economical approach for homeowners, but which construction defect cases qualify as class actions? Generally, it's a class action if all homes are showing the same defect and the lawsuit is restricted only to defects that are common throughout the community. There are six factors to consider:[17]

1. **How many people are affected by the defect?** There are no rigid numerical guidelines for the number of homes that makes class certification appropriate in a construction defect case; however, it's the point at which the people who might be in the class are so numerous that naming all of them as individual plaintiffs becomes impractical. One California court placed the number at more than 40,[18] and others certified class actions in a 65-unit community involving landscape defects,[19] an 88-unit community with defects attributable to negligent grading and filling,[20] and a 192-unit community with damaged common areas.[21] The Nevada Supreme Court has approved certification of a class consisting of 60 condominium owners.[22]

2. **How common are the defect, damages, and proposed theory of recovery?** If all homeowners in a defect case have experienced similar damages from the same defect,[23] e.g., cracked foundations, or they're suing on the same theory of recovery, e.g., breach of contract, class action certification is likely. It doesn't matter that different owners suffered differing amounts[24] of damages.

3. **How typical are the defects among the group?** Are the claims made by the class representatives typical of the claims of the class as a whole? In other words, are the class representatives experiencing construction defect damages similar to those of all class members? Again, it doesn't matter if group members have varying amounts[25] of damage.

4. **Are the group representatives and the attorney adequate?** First, there can be no antagonism or conflict between the class representatives and the members of the class.[26] Second, the attorney for the class must be experienced in handling construction defect cases.

5. **If separate suits were filed, would the outcomes be inconsistent?** To qualify for class status, an association has to show that prosecution of separate actions would create a risk of inconsistent or varying rulings if the case did proceed as a class action.

6. **Is a class-action approach the best way to proceed?** Is the number of class members too numerous to make separate lawsuits practical, and the typical individual claim too small from an economic standpoint for each individual class member to bring a separate lawsuit?

Past, Present, or Future Property Owners?

In single-family home communities, the owner of the real property has standing to sue. But, who has standing when the property changes hands? The original purchaser? The owner when a defect arises? The owner when a defect is discovered? The current owner? Few reported cases have addressed these issues.

CASE NOTE: The first reported case addressing the question of standing among successive owners was *Vaughn v. Dame Construction Company.** In that case, the California Court of Appeal held that the party with standing to sue is the owner at the time of injury to the property. The essential element in this court's view was injury to one's interest in the property, as opposed to ownership of the property. The owner does not lose the right

to sue for damages by selling the property unless he or she transfers that right to a subsequent purchaser. In the Vaughn case, the original purchaser brought an action for construction defects in her condominium; but, after filing the lawsuit, she sold the property. The trial court dismissed the case, ruling that the plaintiff no longer had standing to sue once the property was sold. The court of appeal reversed that ruling, saying that the plaintiff suffered the construction defects, and she retained the right to recover for them unless she transferred those rights to the subsequent purchaser. Thus the owner at the time of injury got to recover from the developer even though the property had been sold. *223 Cal.App.3d 144, 372 Cal.Rptr. 261 (1990).*

An owner may, of course, choose to deliberately transfer a cause of action to a subsequent owner; but he or she must clearly indicate the intention to do so, otherwise a cause of action doesn't automatically transfer to the next owner.

Clearly, the message from the courts is that buyers must thoroughly investigate any property before purchasing. If potential defects are found, the owner should assign the claims to the seller or remedy the defects.

Endnotes

1. California Civil Code Section 1351.
2. California Civil Code Section 1351(a).
3. California Civil Code Section 1351(d).
4. California Civil Code Section 1351(m).
5. California Civil Code Section 1351(k).
6. *See, for example,* California Civil Code Section 1364.
7. The Uniform Common Interest Ownership Act has been adopted by the legislatures in Alaska, Connecticut, Minnesota, Nevada, Vermont, and West Virginia. The Act is being considered by the legislatures of other states, including New Jersey and Utah.
8. Uniform Common Interest Ownership Act Section 1-103(4).
9. Uniform Common Interest Ownership Act Section 1-103(31).
10. Uniform Common Interest Ownership Act Section 2-102.
11. This Act has been adopted in Alaska, Connecticut, Minnesota, Nevada, Vermont, and West Virginia.
12. California Code of Civil Procedure Section 383(a).
13. Utah Code Section 57-8-33.
14. Revised Statutes Section 38-33.3-302.
15. Oregon Revised Statutes Section 100.405.
16. Federal Rule of Civil Procedure 23(a).
17. Deal v. 999 Lakeshore Association, 94 Nev. 301, 579 P.2d 775 (1978).
18. Lockwood Motorists, Inc. v. General Motors Corporation, 162 F.R.D. 569 (D.Minn. 1995).
19. Ravens Cove Townhomes, Inc. v. Knuppe Development Co., 114 Cal.App.3d 783 (1981).
20. Erreca's v. Superior Court, 19 Cal.App.4th 1475 24 Cal.Rptr.2d 156 (1993).
21. Del Mar Beach Club Ass'n v. Imperial Contracting Co., 258 Cal.App.3d 898, 176 Cal.Rptr. 886 (1981).

22. Deal v. 999 Lakeshore Association, 94 Nev. 301, 579 P.2d 775 (1978).

23. Meyer v. District Court, 110 Nev. 1357, 885 P.2d 622 (1994).

24. Johnson v. Travelers Insurance Company, 89 Nev. 467, 515 P.2d 68 (1973).

25. Meyer v. District Court, 110 Nev. 1357, 885 P.2d 622 (1994).

26. Lerwill v. Inflight Motion Pictures, Inc., 582 F.2d 507 (9th Cir. 1978).

CHAPTER 13

Legal Theories of Recovery

Construction defect claims are pursued according to a number of legal theories—negligence, fraud, breach of contract, and others. The approach the attorney selects will vary depending on the state and the facts of a particular case.

Negligence

Negligence has been, and continues to be, one of the most frequently used legal theories applied to construction defect cases. Negligence has been defined in various ways. One early California decision defined negligence as either the omission of a person to do something which an ordinarily prudent person would have done under given circumstances, or the doing of something which an ordinarily prudent person would not have done under such circumstances. It is not an absolute, or to be measured in all cases in accordance with some precise standard, but always relates to some circumstance of time, place, and person.[1] Negligence has also been defined as conduct that falls below the standard established by the law for the protection of others against unreasonable risk of harm. It does not include conduct that recklessly disregards the interests of others.[2]

A typical instruction given to a civil jury deliberating a negligence case is as follows:[3]

Negligence is the doing of something which a reasonably prudent person would not do or the failure to do something which a reasonably prudent person would, under circumstances similar to those shown by the evidence.

It is the failure to use ordinary or reasonable care.

Ordinary or reasonable care is that care which persons of ordinary prudence would use in order to avoid injury to themselves or others under circumstances similar to those shown by the evidence.

In the landmark California Supreme Court case of *Rowland v. Christian,*[4] the court established the general principle that all persons are required to use ordinary care to prevent others from being injured as a result of their conduct. Unless the law says otherwise, there are no exceptions to this principle. The California Supreme Court has established broad criteria for deciding negligence:

A departure from this fundamental principle involves the balancing of a number of considerations; the major ones are the foreseeability of harm to the plaintiff, the degree of certainty that the plaintiff suffered injury, the closeness of the connection between the defendant's conduct and the injury suffered, the moral blame attached to the defendant's conduct, the policy of preventing future harm, the extent of the burden to the defendant and consequences to the community of imposing a duty to exercise care with resulting liability for breach, and the availability, cost and prevalence of insurance for the risk involved.[5]

CASE NOTE: In *Sabella v. Whistler,** the foundation of a house, built by Whistler, cracked after sewer pipes leaked in unstable soil conditions and caused the soil to expand and contract. Whistler argued that the doctrine of *caveat emptor* protected him from negligence suits by the purchaser. The California Supreme Court rejected the argument, stating that *caveat emptor* didn't apply to the construction of a residence, even though all the work that was negligent had been done by subcontractors. The court of appeal also ruled that it was Whistler's duty to discover the nature of the soil upon which the house was constructed. **59 Cal.2d 21, 27 Cal.Rptr. 689 (1963).*

Who Can Be Sued for Negligence?

Virtually anyone involved in the design, sales, and construction of residential housing can be sued under negligence theories. While developers and general contractors may be sued in many jurisdictions under other theories that are easier to prove, every person involved in the construction process can be sued under a negligence theory.

In states where developers can be sued under the legal theory of strict liability, subcontractors generally cannot be sued under that theory. Therefore, in virtually all jurisdictions, claims against subcontractors are grounded in negligence.[6]

Design professionals also cannot be sued under strict liability, so they're most frequently sued under a negligence theory. The basic test of whether a design professional has been negligent is whether he or she has exercised the ordinary skill and competence of members of the profession.[7] Negligence claims against design professionals have been upheld by the appellate courts in many construction contexts, including faulty soil testing,[8] failure to stabilize slopes,[9] inadequate drainage design,[10] improper environmental impact reports,[11] faulty filling, cutting, and compacting of soil,[12] land subsidence and improper soil compaction,[13] improper design of sewage systems,[14] and improper building design.[15]

Aside from design professionals, other service providers can be sued for negligence in construction defect related claims. For instance, construction managers and project managers can be sued for negligence if they fail to properly supervise construction if the failure causes injury to the property owner.[16] Similarly, real estate agents and brokers can be sued for negligence if they fail to investigate or inspect the property with reasonable diligence.[17]

Construction defect investigations often reveal that building codes have been violated, and boards and individual homeowners will ask if the government offices that inspected the buildings can be sued for the construction defects. Many states bar claims against public entities under the doctrine of sovereign immunity.[18] However, other states permit negligence actions against public entities for construction defects.[19]

Government employees are also immune from negligence lawsuits for construction defects in those states that apply sovereign immunity.[20] However, negligence can be extended to state-employed planners, engineers, and other design professionals if the government entity actually designs the construction project in question. The courts distinguish between a government entity reviewing design and construction by others, as opposed to engaging in design or construction itself.[21]

Boards of common-interest associations in many states may find themselves on the receiving end of negligence claims. The directors' duty of care in the negligence context is defined by common law; however, their corporate duty of care is created by statutes in many jurisdictions.[22]

Statutes in some jurisdictions have been enacted in recent years to shield volunteer directors from liability for negligence. For instance, California statutes provide that officers and directors who are volunteers in homeowner associations cannot be liable to individuals who suffer bodily injury, emotional distress, or wrongful death caused by a negligent act or omission of an officer or director if prescribed conditions are met, including the following: 1. the act was performed in good faith; 2. the act or omission was not willful, wanton, or grossly negligent; 3. the association maintained and had in effect, at the time of the incident, general liability insurance with coverage as specified in the statute; 4. the act was performed within the scope of the association duties of the officer or director; and 5. the development is exclusively residential.

A 1997 amendment includes a new criterion that provides that the scope of the officers' or directors' association duties include both of the following decisions: 1. whether to conduct an investigation of the common-interest development for latent or patent deficiencies prior to the expiration of the applicable statute of limitations; and 2. whether to commence a civil action against the builder for defects and design of construction.

Finally, community association managers may find themselves exposed to claims for negligence as agents for common-interest associations. No industrywide standard of care exists for community association managers as it does for design professionals—although it can be established by expert testimony. Community managers can protect themselves by learning about the construction defect claim process and by urging boards to investigate thoroughly and consult with a defect attorney.

Must Property Be Damaged to Recover for Negligence?

Over the past few decades, a legal debate has raged whether construction defects must cause physical property damage before a builder can be held liable in negligence.

Contrast the two following scenarios to understand whether property damage has occurred: 1. A roofing contractor installs roofing materials in violation of building codes. The negligent installation allows water to saturate wallboard in the ceiling, which separates from the framing and crashes to the floor. The roofer's negligence results in property damage. 2. A builder fails to install fire blocking while framing a home, which violates building codes and threatens harm to life, health, and property. But property damage has not occurred, even though the failure to follow the codes has created safety issues.

CASE NOTE: The question of whether property damage is required in a negligence claim against a developer, contractor, or subcontractor was addressed in one of the most frequently cited construction defect cases of all time, *Aas v. Superior Court of San Diego County,* a decision by the California Supreme Court.* In this case, homeowners brought consolidated claims for construction defects in two developments: one comprising single family homes and the other condominiums. The homeowners claimed numerous construction defects, and developer William Lyon Company filed motions to exclude evidence of defects that had not caused property damage. In response to these motions, the homeowners offered proof that many of the defects arose from violation of building codes that had been enacted to prevent harm to life, health, and property. The trial court agreed with the William Lyon Company that evidence of defects where no property damage had occurred would not be allowed at trial. The homeowners sought review by the California Court of Appeal. The court of appeal upheld the trial court's ruling. The homeowners then appealed to the California Supreme Court. Ultimately, a divided Supreme Court affirmed the decisions by the trial court and the court of appeal. **24 Cal.4th 627, 101 Cal.Rptr.2d 718 (2000).*

The Economic-Loss Rule

The economic-loss rule states that a claimant cannot recover in negligence when he or she has only experienced economic losses rather than property damage. Economic damages only injure a claimant's economic interests, not his or her person or property. While economic damages can be recovered under the legal theories of breach of contract and breach of warranty, such damages cannot be recovered under the negligence theory.[23]

The Aas decision has generated much controversy in California and other states across the nation since it was handed down by the California Supreme Court. However, the consequences of the decision are actually quite restricted: they deal only with claims asserted under the negligence theory. The decision does not deal with claims asserted under a strict liability theory, which is the primary theory used by homeowners against developers in California and elsewhere. Additionally, the Aas decision does not prevent homeowners from introducing evidence of economic losses under the legal theories of breach of contract or breach of warranty. Finally, the impact of the Aas decision has been limited by legislation that applies to homes sold in California on or after January 1, 2003.

CASE NOTE: The Nevada Supreme Court has weighed in on the economic-loss rule in construction defect claims in the case of *Calloway v. The City of Reno*—a class action on behalf of the owners of 164 townhouses.* The homeowners alleged that the townhouses were built with defective roofing and siding, which led to extensive water intrusion. The homeowners sued the developer, general contractor, roofing contractor, siding contractor, and the City of Reno. The homeowners alleged that inspectors for the city had approved construction with actual knowledge of defects. The Calloway case came before the Nevada Supreme Court twice. On its second review, the Nevada Supreme Court concluded that the economic-loss doctrine precluded the homeowners' claims in both negligence and strict liability. Because the homeowners had previously dismissed their contract claims in the case, they were left without any remedy. **993 P.2d 1259 (Nev. 2000).*

The Nevada Legislature has enacted certain statutory implied warranties and even enacted a statute that directly conflicts with the Calloway decision. This statute provides that a contractor is liable for his acts or omissions or the acts or omissions of his agents, employees, or subcontractors.[24] By using the phrase "a contractor is liable for his acts," the Nevada Legislature has, in effect, imposed strict liability on contractors because the statute does not reference any degree of fault. Additionally, the term *omission* can imply a tort liability for negligence. The Nevada Legislature went on to confirm that the following economic losses, which were not recoverable under the Calloway decision, could be recovered to the extent they're caused by a construction defect:[25]

a. Any reasonable attorneys' fees;

b. The reasonable cost of any repairs already made that were necessary and of any repairs yet to be made that are necessary to cure any construction defect that the contractor failed to cure and the reasonable expenses of temporary housing necessary during the repair;

c. The reduction in market value of the residence or accessory structure;

d. The loss of use of all or any part of the residence;

e. The reasonable value of any other property damaged by the construction defect;

f. Any additional cost reasonably incurred in investigating the defects; and

g. Interest as provided by statute.

Courts in other jurisdictions also have reached conflicting conclusions on the application of the economic-loss rule to residential construction defects. South Carolina holds builders liable for all deviations from building codes and industry standards that diminish the value of a house.[26] Maryland ordinarily permits homeowners to recover in a negligence action the reasonable cost of correcting construction defects that present a clear danger of death or personal injury, but not conditions that present merely a risk to general health, welfare, or comfort.[27] A North Carolina court has held that plaintiffs stated a cause of action for negligence by alleging they were forced to undergo extensive demolition and repair to correct defective, dangerous, and unsafe conditions caused by the defendant's negligence.[28]

Breach of Implied Warranty

Breach of implied warranties is another legal theory available to construction defect claimants in many states. Some states have created implied warranties through appellate court decisions. Other states have embellished the implied warranty theory by enacting statutes. Many states have adopted the Uniform Commercial Code (UCC), which includes a number of implied warranties that have been made applicable to construction defects by court decisions. The UCC warranties are called the implied warranty of merchantability and the implied warranty of fitness.[29]

CASE NOTE: An example of a construction defect case in which a builder in California was found liable under the implied warranties of merchantability and fitness is *Eichler Homes, Inc. v. Anderson.** In this case, a group of homeowners sued a developer because the steel-tube radiant heating system in their homes failed. Eichler Homes filed cross-complaints against the tubing manufacturer and the subcontractors who installed it. The trial court found that the manufacturer and the installing contractor had implied that the product was merchantable—fit to be sold—for the intended purpose, and the implied warranties had been breached. The court of appeal agreed.** *9 Cal.App.3d 224, 87 Cal.Rptr. 893 (1970).*

The implied warranties of merchantability and fitness for a particular purpose found in the UCC were originally enacted to protect consumers when buying personal property. However, many states, either by statute or by case law, have extended these implied warranties to buying mass produced homes. Colorado was an early leader in this field with the case of *Carpenter v. Donohoe.*[30] In Carpenter, the Colorado appellate court used the terms "implied warranties that the home was built in a workmanlike manner and is suitable for habitation."[31]

The appellate courts in Arizona have ruled that the law imposes on new home builders an implied warranty called "workmanship and habitability."[32] In the *Columbia Western Corp. v. Vela* case, the court reasoned that the implied warranty could be established based on several factors:

1. Home developers operate on a large scale.
2. Developers hold themselves out as skilled in home construction and in the business of building and selling to individual homeowners.
3. Developers contract with builders that actually construct the homes.
4. Building construction by modern methods is complex and intertwined with government codes and regulations.
5. The ordinary home buyer is not in a position to discover defects.
6. The building's components are usually covered up and not available for inspection.[33]

The UCC as enacted in some states specifically excludes real property from its coverage. However, in many states, the implied warranty doctrine has been applied to real property, and the courts have specifically held that these implied warranties are not grounded in the provisions of the UCC.[34]

Plaintiffs in construction defect cases may pursue not only developers under theories of implied warranty, but subcontractors as well.[35]

HISTORICAL PERSPECTIVE: An important consideration in deciding whether to pursue claims for construction defects based on implied warranty theories used to be the legal doctrine known as *privity of contract*—when one party to a contract sues another party to the contract. In construction defect claims, the original home buyer is in privity of contract with the developer. Many states require privity of contract for a claimant to proceed under a breach of implied warranty theory.* More recently, courts in some states have rejected the privity of contract requirement and permitted subsequent purchasers to pursue claims against the original developers.** These courts reason that our society is increasingly mobile, and homes will eventually change ownership. Furthermore, the latent defects will be just as catastrophic for a subsequent owner as for the original owner, and the builder will be just as responsible for improper or substandard work. Because the developer is in a better position than a subsequent owner to prevent defects, the costs of poor workmanship should be the developer's to bear.*** Like caveat emptor, privity of contract has become a disfavored theory. **House v. Thornton, 6 Wash.App. 595, 494 P.2d 1371 (1972). **Richards v. Powercraft Homes, Inc., 139 Ariz. 242 (1984). ***Id. at 245, See also, Moxley v. Laramie Builders, Inc. 600 P.2d 733 (Wyo. 1979); Hermes v. Staiano, 181 N.J. Super. 424 (Law Div. 1981).*

In some states, the implied warranty remedy is restricted to claims for new construction. For instance, the California Supreme Court recognized the implied warranties in the landmark case of *Pollard v. Saxe & Yolles Development Co.,*[36] but limited its application to new construction.

Breach of Express Warranty

Developers, builders, and manufacturers of building components frequently provide express warranties to original home buyers. An express warranty is defined in the UCC as "any affirmation of fact…made by the seller to the buyer which relates to the goods and becomes part of the basis of the bargain."[37] This creates an express warranty that the goods will conform to the affirmation.[38]

In addition to promises or representations in express warranties, promises or representations made in advertisements or manufacturer's brochures may also serve as the basis of express warranties.[39] If a homeowner can prove that a written or express warranty was breached, the party issuing the warranty is liable whether or not it was negligent.[40]

A typical claim based on breach of an express warranty might involve building components like windows or sliding glass doors. Manufacturers of these products frequently provide warranties against defects in materials or workmanship for periods of many years or even for the life of the product. When these product brochures are provided to new homebuyers, claims for breach of express warranty can be made against both the developer and the manufacturer. Since claims for breach of an express warranty arise from contract law rather than tort law, privity of contract is required to assert such claims; that is, only the original purchaser can sue. However, an original purchaser can assign a claim under an express warranty theory to a subsequent purchaser. Such assignments must be made for valuable consideration and in writing.

Strict Liability

The rights of homeowners to sue developers for construction defects have increased in those states where the doctrine of strict liability has been applied to mass produced housing. Until strict liability was applied to construction defect claims, homeowners generally proceeded on the theories of negligence or breach of implied warranty—each with its limitations.

HISTORICAL PERSPECTIVE: The doctrine of strict liability has evolved over time. In 1944* a justice of the California Supreme Court suggested that a manufacturer's liability should be imposed "irrespective of fault."** Approximately 20 years later, the same justice established the doctrine of strict liability. *24 Cal.2d 453, 150 P.2d 436 (1944). **24 Cal.2d at 461.*

The doctrine of strict liability was adopted by courts across the nation, particularly when it was incorporated in the *Restatement (Second) of Torts* in 1995. The *Restatement* sets forth the doctrine as follows:

1. One who sells any product in a defective condition unreasonably dangerous to the user or consumer is subject to liability for physical (personal) harm caused to the ultimate user or consumer, or to his property if

    a. The seller is engaged in the business of selling such a product; and

    b. It is expected to and does reach the user or consumer without substantial change in the condition in which it was sold.

2. The rule stated in subsection (1) applies although

    a. The seller has exercised all possible care in the preparation and sale of his product; and

    b. The user or consumer has not bought the product from, or entered into any contractual relation with, the seller."[41]

Thus, the *Restatement* clearly eliminated the requirement of privity of contract, allowing an injured consumer to seek recovery from the manufacturer even though the product had passed through distributors, retailers, and prior consumers.

Developers

Strict liability was first applied to the sale of mass produced homes in a New Jersey case.[42] A 16-month-old child had been scalded by hot water in the bathroom of a new home because the developer had failed to install a valve to mix cold water with extremely hot water before the water was drawn from the faucet. The developer had provided the homeowners with instructions on how to avoid scalding when the home was purchased; however, the child was clearly below the reading age. Although the claim was brought under the traditional theories of negligence and breach of implied warranty, the New Jersey Supreme Court, on its own, found that housing units were manufactured products, and thus subject to strict liability. Thus, in an unusual move by an appellate court, the New Jersey Supreme Court created a cause of action in strict liability. In so ruling, the court found no meaningful distinction between the mass production of homes and the mass production of automobiles, finding that the policy consideration should be the same.[43]

CASE NOTE: In the landmark case of *Greenman v. Yuba Power Products,** the plaintiff, relying on a manufacturer's brochure, purchased a power tool that turned out to be defective and sustained serious personal injuries. The manufacturer tried to have the resulting suit dismissed because of a delay in providing notice of breach of warranty. The court declared that there was no need to rely on the warranty: "A manufacturer is strictly liable in tort when an article he places on the market, knowing that it is to be used without inspection for defects, proves to have a defect that causes injury to a human being." The Supreme Court went on to explain the decision as follows:

> Although in these cases liability has usually been based on the theory of express or implied warranty running from the manufacturer to the plaintiff, the abandonment of the requirement of a contract between them, the recognition that the liability is not assumed by agreement but imposed by law…, and the refusal to permit the manufacturer to define the scope of its own responsibility for defective products…makes clear that the liability is not one governed by the law of contract warranties but by the law of strict liability in tort….The purpose of such liability is to ensure that the cost of injuries resulting from defective products are borne by the manufacturers that put such products on the market, rather than by the injured persons who are powerless to protect themselves.** **59 Cal.2d 57, 27 Cal.Rptr. 697 (1963). **59 Cal.2d at 63.*

It was only four years later that a California court of appeal, in the landmark case *Kriegler v. Eichler Homes,*[44] expanded strict liability to construction defects that did not result in personal injuries, but rather in monetary damages.

The California Supreme Court in Kriegler focused on the number of homes built by the developer—at least 4,000. Other courts have looked at different factors in imposing strict liability. In *Avner v. Longridge Estates,*[45] the California court of appeal focused not on the number of homes, but rather the complexity of the building process itself. Another California court looked to the homeowner's reliance on the activities of the developer, rather than the size or complexity of the project.[46] A New Jersey court pointed out that a consumer is in no better position to judge the quality of a house than to judge the quality of an automobile.[47]

Courts in other jurisdictions have focused on the character of the business of the developer, rather than number, complexity, or expertise.[48] Developers that build homes only occasionally would probably not be subject to strict liability.

Courts have reasoned that these developers are unable to protect themselves financially by spreading their losses among many homes.[49]

CASE NOTE: In the case of *Kriegler v. Eichler Homes,** Eichler was a well known, large-scale builder in the 1950s. Because of a copper shortage during the Korean War, a sub contractor used steel—rather than copper—tubing in the heating systems in approximately 4,000 Eichler Homes. Eichler sold the home to its first buyer in 1952. Kriegler purchased the home in 1957, and two years later the heating system failed because the steel tubing had corroded. Kriegler had to install a new system at a cost of approximately $5,000. Kriegler sued Eichler under numerous legal theories, including strict liability. The trial court ordered judgment in favor of the homeowner on a strict liability theory. The California court of appeal agreed, noting that Kriegler had relied on Eichler to produce a home with a heating system reasonably fit for its intended purpose. The court said:

> We think, in terms of today's society, there are no meaningful distinctions between Eichler's mass production and sale of homes and the mass production and sale of automobiles and that the pertinent overriding policy considerations are the same. Law, as an instrument of justice, has infinite capacity for growth to meet changing needs and mores. Nowhere is this better illustrated than in the recent developments in the field of products liability. The law should be based on current concepts of what is right and just and the judiciary should be alert to the never-ending need for keeping legal principles abreast of the times. These are distinctions that make no sense in today's society, and that tend to discredit the law and should be readily rejected as they were step by step in Greenman...** *269 Cal.App.2d 224, 74 Cal.Rptr. 749 (1969). **Id. at 227.

Landlords

Landlords as well as developers have been held liable for construction defects. For instance, in *Becker v. IRM Corp.,*[50] a tenant sued a landlord for personal injuries caused by a defective shower door. The court said that a landlord is part of the "stream of commerce" and is, therefore, liable for injuries that result from defects that exist at the time the unit is leased.[51]

Material Suppliers

When manufactured products such as windows, sliding glass doors, fixtures, fireplaces, roofing materials, and siding are damaged, the results can damage the homes where they're installed. Can their manufacturers be held liable for harm resulting from their defective products? Are they liable for the physical damage to other parts of the residence that results? The California Supreme Court answered Yes to both of these questions in the case of *Jimenez v. Superior Court of San Diego County.*[52] There is little law on this issue in other states.

Financial Institutions

Generally speaking, financial institutions that lend money to developers are not subject to strict liability for construction defects. However, the California Legislature recognized that there are exceptions:

> A lender who makes a loan of money, the proceeds of which are used or may be used by the borrower to finance the design, manufacture, construction, repair, modification, or improvement of real or personal property for sale or lease to others, shall not be held liable to third persons for any loss unless such loss or damage is a result of an act of the lender outside the scope of the activities of the lender of money, or unless the lender has been a party to misrepresentations.[53]

Thus, a lender whose only involvement in a development is to provide the necessary funds cannot be held liable for construction defects.[54] On the other hand, a lender may be liable for construction defects if that lender is operating outside the scope of the traditional activities of a lender.[55]

Subcontractors

The courts have held that contractors are not strictly liable to homeowners for construction defects. The leading case is *La Jolla Village Homeowners Assn, Inc. v. Superior Court.*[56] The court in this case did caution, however, that a subcontractor could be held liable if it was also a co-developer of a project, had a financial interest in the project, or controlled the project. The Nevada Supreme Court first held in 1997 that construction defect actions against subcontractors based on strict liability were permitted;[57] however, the Supreme Court reversed course and rejected the application of strict liability to subcontractors in its second decision in the same case.[58]

Design Professionals

The courts have also uniformly held that design professionals, such as architects and engineers, cannot be held liable for construction defects based on the theory of strict liability.[59]

Statutory Causes of Action

In recent years, states have enacted statutory schemes that lay out certain steps that must be taken by a homeowner association or individual homeowners before a lawsuit can be filed against the developer and others for construction defects. Many of these statutory schemes give the developer or builder the right to make repairs prior to the commencement of litigation.

Some of the pre-litigation statutory schemes, in addition to providing the builder with the right to repair, establish local building standards that can give rise to separate causes of action for construction defects. Examples of theories of recovery created by statute follow. In some cases, these statutes give rise to causes of action that did not exist under the common law of the state in question. In other cases, statutes modify the common law by taking away common law causes of action and substituting statutory causes of action in their place.

Colorado is an example of a state that has enacted statutes that take away the rights of homeowners to pursue common law claims and substitutes in their place the right to pursue limited statutory claims:[60]

1. No negligence claims seeking damages for residential construction defects may be

asserted in an action if such claim arises from the failure to construct a residential improvement to real property in substantial compliance with an applicable building code or industry standard; except that such claim may be asserted if such failure results in one or more of the following:

a. Actual or potential damage to real or personal property;

b. Actual or potential loss of the use of real or personal property;

c. Bodily injury or wrongful death; or

d. A risk of bodily injury or death to, or a threat to the life, health, or safety of, the occupants of the residential real property.

2. Nothing in this section shall be construed to prohibit, limit, or impair the following:

a. The assertion of tort claims other than claims for negligence;

b. The assertion of contractible warranty claims; or

c. The assertion of claims that arise from the violation of any statute or ordinance other than claims for violation of a building code.

Additionally, the California Legislature has adopted a detailed set of building standards, the violation of which gives rise to causes of action for construction defects. The statute begins:

In any action seeking recovery of damages arising out of, or related to deficiencies in, the residential construction, design, specifications, surveying, planning, supervision, testing, or observation of construction, the builder, subcontractor, material supplier, individual product manufacturer, or design professional shall be liable for, and the claimant's claims for causes of action shall be limited to, violation of the following standards.[61]

Washington State provides homeowners with warranties that were not available in common law. The implied warranties of quality include:[62]

1. A declarant [developer] and any dealer warrants that a unit will be in at least as good condition at the earlier of the time of the conveyance or delivery of possession as it was at the time of contracting, reasonable wear and tear and damage by casualty or condemnation excepted.

2. A declarant and any dealer impliedly warrants that a unit and the common elements in the condominium are suitable for the ordinary use of real estate of its type and that any improvements made or contracted for by such declarant or dealer will be

a. Free from defective materials; and

b. Constructed in accordance with sound engineering and construction standards, and in a workmanlike manner in compliance with all laws then applicable to such improvements.

3. A declarant and any dealer warrants to a purchaser of a unit that may be used for residential use that an existing use, continuation of which is contemplated by the parties, does not violate applicable law at the earlier of the time of conveyance or delivery of possession.

The Washington Legislature made clear that a contract is not required: "Any conveyance of a unit transfers to the purchaser all of declarant's implied warranties of quality."[63]

Some states have also created statutory express warranties. For instance, the Washington Legislature provided the following definition in its Condominium Act:

1. Express warranties made by any seller to a purchaser of a unit, if relied upon by the purchaser, are created as follows:

a. Any written affirmation of fact or promise which relates to the unit, its use, or rights appurtenant thereto, area improvements to the condominium that would directly benefit the unit, or the right to use or have the benefit of facilities not located in the condominium creates an express warranty that the unit and related rights and uses will conform to the affirmation or promise.

b. Any model or written description of the physical characteristics of the condominium at the time the purchase agreement is executed, including plans and specifications of or for improvements, creates an express warranty that the condominium will conform to the model or description.

c. Any written description of the quantity or extent of the real property comprising the condominium, including plans or surveys, creates an express warranty that the condominium will conform to the description, subject to customary tolerances; and

d. The written provision that a buyer may put a unit only to a specified use is an express warranty that the specified use is lawful.

2. Neither formal words, such as "warranty" or "guaranty" nor specific intention to make a warranty are necessary to create an express warranty quality, but a statement purporting to be merely an opinion or commendation of the real estate or its value.

Breach of Fiduciary Duty

Developers of common-interest communities are frequently sued under the legal theory of breach of fiduciary duty.

Breach of Duty by the Developer

Developers are required by state law to prepare the association's governing documents—articles of incorporation, bylaws, and the declaration of covenants, conditions, and restrictions (CC&Rs). Developers are also generally required to prepare the documents that will be used to sell units—escrow instructions, purchase agreements, association operating budgets, and reserve requirements—and get them approved by the state real estate department. Developers in some states are required to obtain a Final Subdivision Public Report, known in California as a White Report.[64]

In addition to preparing the association's governing documents, the developer appoints the first governing board. As more units are sold, the composition of the board changes—owners gradually replace developer-controlled board members. When the developer's last unit is sold, governance of the association transfers entirely to the owners.

Until transition of the board occurs, the developer has a fiduciary duty to the association. Frequently, statutes spell out the duties of corporate directors. For instance, the California code provides:

A director shall perform the duties of a director, including duties as a member of any committee of the board upon which the director may serve, in good faith, and in a manner such director believes to be in the best interests of the corporation and its shareholders and with such care, including reasonable inquiry, as an ordinarily prudent person in a like position would use under similar circumstances.[65]

During the early years of a common-interest development, developers expose themselves to a charge of breach of fiduciary duty in certain circumstances:

1. Failure to enforce the association's CC&Rs.
2. Failure to establish a proper operating budget.
3. Failure to establish and fund adequate reserve accounts.
4. Conflicts of interest.

Breach of Duty by the Board

Lawsuits can be brought against any community association board—not just those controlled by developers—if it breaches its fiduciary duty to the association. Since community association boards sometimes comprise well meaning but unknowledgeable volunteers, they may make mistakes; however, a legal doctrine known as the business judgment rule shields them from liability if they act in good faith and according to what they believe is in the best interests of the association.[66] This means that directors seek opinions, reports, financial data, and other necessary information from reliable sources, independent experts, or association committees before making decisions.[67]

In addition to the protections offered by the business judgment rule, boards also receive a relative degree of support from the judicial system, i.e., courts are disinclined to second-guess board decisions. The standard of review is typified by the California Supreme Court's decision in *Lamden v. La Jolla Shores Clubdominium*:[68]

> Where a duly constituted community association board, upon reasonable investigation, in good faith and with regard to the best interests of the community association and its members, exercises discretion within the scope of its authority under relevant statutes, covenants, and restrictions to select other means for discharging an obligation to maintain and repair a development's common areas, the court should defer to the board's authority and presumed expertise.[69]

Nuisance

Nuisance is another legal theory frequently pursued in construction defect cases. The term nuisance (French for *harm*) covers two unrelated types of invasion of the property interests of others that involve harm, inconvenience, or annoyance.[70]

Public nuisance covers the invasion of rights common to all members of the public, such as the right to free and safe use of the public highways. Public nuisance is normally a criminal offense, and only people who have suffered a particular harm—different from the public in general—can recover damages.[71]

Private nuisance covers the invasion of the private right of a person to use and enjoy land. Rather than being a criminal act, it is a tort—i.e., a landowner can sue another for private nuisance if his or her interest in the land has been affected.[72] Stated another way, a public nuisance affects an entire community or many people, albeit unequally,[73] and any nuisance that isn't public is a private nuisance.[74] Another distinction is that private nuisances have statutes of limitation—expiration dates—while public nuisances do not.[75]

The burden of proof is lower for nuisance when compared with other possible causes of action;[76] however, a landowner must show substantial harm.[77]

The most obvious nuisance is actually interfering with another's use of his or her land—building the shed two feet over the property line,[78] blocking the

CASE NOTE: Circumstances in which an association brought a claim against a developer on a breach of fiduciary duty theory can be illustrated by the leading California case of *Raven's Cove Townhomes, Inc. v. Knuppe Development Co.** Raven's Cove comprised 65 town homes in Alameda, California. In November 1972, the developer conveyed the common areas and facilities to the association. At the same time, the developer used subcontractors who added and then improperly compacted fill at the site. By October 1973, Raven's Cove was completed and sales began. The association was responsible for maintaining and repairing roofs and siding on the individual units, assessing and collecting dues, and establishing operating and reserve funds. However, the developer had neither established nor turned over to the association reserve or operating funds. By 1974, when the developer transferred all control of the association to the owners, various defects in landscaping and siding had developed.

A landscape architect testified for the association that the soil type was improper for plant growth, and there were problems with soil compaction. To grow plants properly, the topsoil would have to be replaced with a deeper layer of planting material. Drainage and irrigation did not match the plans and specifications for the project. In addition, the siding was decomposing for lack of paint, and an expert testified that the siding was damaged because it had been fastened with ungalvanized nails.

The association sued the developer and the developer's agents in 1976 under legal theories of declaratory relief, strict liability, breach of warranty, and breach of fiduciary duty for conflicts of interest and failing to establish an adequate reserve fund. The judge dismissed the case on the grounds that there was no breach of fiduciary duty by the developer-controlled directors before the transition to owners took place.

The court of appeal reversed the judgment, stating that the developer knew that the bay-front exposure created particular exterior maintenance problems and should have established a reserve fund. Failure to do so constituted a breach of fiduciary duty by the developer.

The first board of a new association has a fiduciary relationship with the owners analogous to a corporate promoter to shareholders. Fiduciary duty takes on greater magnitude considering that membership in the association is mandatory for buyers. In this case, the court found that Raven's Cove's first board (comprising the developer and the developer's employees) failed to manage association operations properly because it failed to assess each unit for an adequate reserve fund. Thus, the individual directors were liable to the association for a breach of basic fiduciary duty because they failed to act in good faith and failed to exercise good management.** *114 Cal.App.3d 783, 171 Cal.Rptr. 334 (1981). **114 Cal.App.3d at 794.

---

neighbor's entrance,[79] piling trash on the neighbor's front lawn,[80] or constructing a berm that collapses into the neighbor's driveway.[81]

The statute of limitations regarding public nuisance is one reason developers and contractors frequently pursue nuisance as a legal remedy. Nuisances are classified either as permanent or continuing. A permanent nuisance is one that presumably will continue indefinitely. A continuing nuisance is one that can be stopped at any time. This is an important distinction when determining when the statute of limitations starts running. Permanent nuisances start the statute of limitations running as soon as they are created. On the other hand, every repetition of a continuing nuisance is a separate wrong that starts the statute of limitations running anew.[82]

HISTORICAL PERSPECTIVE: Through the close of the 19th century, the courts employed the Latin term *caveat emptor*—let the buyer beware—in deciding disputes between sellers and buyers of real property.* While courts were beginning to protect the general public from poorly designed or manufactured consumer products, the same protections were not yet provided to buyers of real property. If a buyer didn't receive the property in the condition bargained for, there was no available remedy. In the 20th century, however, American courts began to move away from the doctrine of caveat emptor as they recognized that houses were just like other mass-produced items like automobiles or toasters.

*Gustafson v. Dunman, Inc., 204 Cal.App.2d 10, 22 Cal.Rptr. 161 (1962).

Fraud and Deceit

Associations or individual owners may bring claims against a developer for fraud or deceit—which falls in several categories. Fraud involves contracts, whereas deceit may arise from any relationship among parties. Fraud may be either constructive or actual. Constructive fraud is a breach of a duty without fraudulent intent that gives the person breaching the duty an advantage by misleading the other to his or her prejudice.[83]

Actual fraud, on the other hand, occurs when a developer or contractor induces a buyer to enter a contract[84] by providing false information—whether he knows it's false or believes it to be true, withholding truthful information, making promises with no intention of keeping them, or doing anything else that's designed to deceive.

Deceit occurs when a person willfully deceives another into changing his position to his own injury or risk.[85] Like actual fraud, deceit[86] occurs when one person provides another with false information—whether he knows it's false or believes it to be true, withholds truthful information, makes promises with no intention of keeping them, or does anything else that's designed to deceive.

Examples of actionable fraud and deceit in construction defect claims include:

- Intentionally misrepresenting information called for in documents filed with state agencies.[87]
- Continued sales of units after notice of construction defects.[88]
- Failing to disclose dangerous soil conditions.[89]
- Failing to disclose that homes cannot safely be occupied.[90]

Endnotes

1. Fouch v. Werner, 99 Cal.App. 557, 279 P.183 (1929).

2. Restatement Second, Torts, Section 282.

3. BAJI Instructions (7th Edition), no. 3.10.

4. 69 Cal.2d 108, 70 Cal.Rptr. 97 (1968).

5. 69 Cal.2d at 112.

6. Massei v. Lettunich, 248 Cal.App.2d 68, 56 Cal.Rptr. 232 (1967).

7. Gagne v. Bertran, 43 Cal.2d 491, 275 P.2d 15 (1954).

8. *Id.*

9. Churpin v. Elmhirst, 148 Cal.App.3d 94, 195 Cal.Rptr. 737 (1983).

10. Mozzetti v. City of Brisbane, 67 Cal.App.3d 565, 136 Cal.Rptr. 751 (1977).

11. Coac, Inc. v. Kennedy Eng'rs, 67 Cal.App.3d 916, 136 Cal.Rptr. 890 (1977).

12. Oakes v. McCarthy Co., 267 Cal.App.2d 231, 73 Cal.Rptr. 127 (1968).

13. Bonadiman-McCain, Inc. v. Snow, 183 Cal.App.2d 59, 6 Cal.Rptr. 52 (1960).

14. Alisal Sanitary Dist. v. Kennedy, 190 Cal.App.2d 69, 4 Cal.Rptr. 379 (1960).

15. Bayuk v. Edson, 236 Cal.App.2d 309, 46 Cal.Rptr. 49 (1965).

16. Allied Properties v. John P. Blume and Assocs., Eng'rs., 25 Cal.App.3d 848, 102 Cal.Rptr. 259 (1972).

17. Easton v. Strassburger, 152 Cal.App.3d 90, 199 Cal.Rptr. 393 (1984).

18. See, for example, Trianon Park Condominium Ass'n v. City of Hialeah, 468 So.2d 911 (Fla. 1985); Cancun Homeowners Ass'n v. City of San Juan Capistrano, 215 Cal.App.3d 1352, 264 Cal.Rptr. 288 (1989).

19. J & B Development Co. v. King County, 100 Wash.2d 299, 669 P.2d 468 (1983).

20. Mozzetti v. City of Brisbane, 67 Cal.App.3d 565, 136 Cal.Rptr. 751 (1977).

21. *Id.*

22. Smith v. Superior Court, 217 Cal.App.3d 950, 266 Cal.Rptr. 253 (1990).

23. Seely v. White Motor Co., 63 Cal.2d 9, 45 Cal.Rptr. 17 (1965).

24. Nevada Revised Statutes Section 40.640.

25. Nevada Revised Statutes Section 40.655.

26. Kennedy v. Columbia Lumber & Mfg. Co., 299 S.C. 335, 384 S.E.2d 730 (1989).

27. Council of Co-Owners v. Whiting-Turner, 308 Md. 18, 517 A.2d 336 (1986).

28. Oates v. Jag, Inc., 314 N.C. 276, 333 S.E.2d 222 (1985).

29. UCC Section 2314.

30. 154 Colo. 78, 388 P.2d 399 (1964).

31. *Id.* at 83-84.

32. Columbia Western Corp. v. Vela, 122 Ariz. 28, 592 P.2d 1294 (1979).

33. *Id.* at 32.

34. Richards v. Powercraft Homes, Inc., 139 Ariz. 242 (1984).

35. Continental Townhomes East Unit One Association v. Brockbank, 152 Ariz. 537, 733 P.2d 1120 (1986).

36. 12 Cal.3d 374 (1974).

37. UCC Section 2313(2).

38. UCC Section 2313(1)(a).

39. Greenman v. Yuba Power Products, 59 Cal.2d 57, 27 Cal.Rptr. 697 (1963).

40. Basin Oil Co. v. Baash-Ross Tool Co., 125 Cal.App.2d 578, 271 P.2d 122 (1954).

41. *Restatement (Second) of Torts*, Section 402(A), 1995.

42. Schipper v. Levitt & Sons, 44 N.J. 70, 207 A.2d 314 (1965).

43. 44 N.J. at 78.

44. 269 Cal.App.2d 224, 74 Cal.Rptr. 749 (1969).

45. 272 Cal.App.2d 607, 77 Cal.Rptr. 633 (1969).

46. Del Mar Beach Club Owners Assn. v. Imperial Contracting, 123 Cal.App.3d 898, 176 Cal.Rptr. 886 (1981).

47. Schipper v. Levin & Sons, 44 J.J. 70, 207 A.2d 314 (1965).

48. Patitucci v. Drelich, 153 N.J. 177, 379 A.2d 297 (1977).

49. Oliver v. Superior Court, 211 Cal.App.3d 86, 259 Cal.Rptr. 160 (1989).

50. 38 Cal.3d 454, 213 Cal.Rptr. 213 (1985).

51. *Id.* at 464.

52. 29 Cal.4th 473, 127 Cal.Rptr.2d 614 (2002).

53. California Civil Code Section 3434.

54. U.S. Financial v. Sullivan, 37 Cal.App.3d 5, 112 Cal.Rptr. 18, (1974).

55. Connor v. Great Western Savings & Loan Ass'n., 69 Cal.2d 850, 73 Cal.Rptr 369 (1968).

56. 212 Cal.App.3d 1131, 261 Cal.Rptr. 146 (1989).

57. Calloway v. City of Reno, 971 P.2d 1250 (1997).

58. Calloway v. City of Reno, 993 P.2d 1259 (2000).

59. Del Mar Beach Club Owners Ass'n v. Imperial Contracting Company, 123 Cal.App.3d 898, 176 Cal.Rptr. 886 (1981).

60. Colorado Revised Statute 13-20-804.

61. California Civil Code Section 896.

62. Revised Code of Washington Section 64.34.445.

63. *Id.* at subparagraph 6.

64. California Business and Professions Code Sections 11018 through 11024.

65. California Corporations Code Section 309(a).

66. California Corporations Code Section 309(a).

67. California Corporations Code Section 309(b).

68. 21 Cal.4th 249, 87 Cal.Rptr.2d 237 (1999).

69. 21 Cal.4th at 270.

70. *Restatement (Second) of Torts*, Section 821A.

71. *Restatement (Second) of Torts*, Section 821B, 821C.

72. *Restatement (Second) of Torts*, Section 821D, 821E.

73. California Civil Code Section 3480.

74. California Civil Code Section 3481.

75. California Civil Code Section 3490.

76. Curtis v. Kastner, 220 Cal. 185, 30 P.2d 26 (1934).

77. Shields v. Wondries, 154 Cal.App.2d 249, 316 P.2d 9 (1957).

78. Lussier v. San Lorenzo Valley Water Dist., 206 Cal.App.3d 92, 253 Cal.Rptr. 470 (1988).

79. Marshall v. Standard Oil Co., 17 Cal.App.2d 19, 61 P.2d 520 (1936).

80. Turlock v. Bristow, 103 Cal.App. 750, 284 P. 962 (1930).

81. Spaulding v. Cameron 38 Cal.2d 265, 239 P.2d 625 (1952).

82. Phillips v. Pasadena, 27 Cal.2d 104, 162 P.2d 625 (1945).

83. California Civil Code Section 1573.

84. California Civil Code Section 1572.

85. California Civil Code Section 1709.

86. California Civil Code Section 1710.

87. Barnhouse v. City of Pinole, 133 Cal.App.3d 171, 183 Cal.Rptr. 881 (1982).

88 Oakes v. McCarthy Co., 267 Cal.App.2d 231, 73 Cal.Rptr. 127 (1968).

89. Karoutas v. HomeFed Bank, 232 Cal.App.3d 767, 283 Cal.Rptr. 809 (1981).

90. Prichard v. Rietz, 178 Cal.App.3d 465, 223 Cal.Rptr. 734 (1986).

CHAPTER 14

Construction Defect Litigation Step by Step

In recent years, many state legislatures have attempted to stem the increasing number of construction defect lawsuits by requiring that homeowners attempt to resolve problems before pursuing litigation. These pre-litigation steps, including builders' right-to-repair provisions, are based on good legislative intentions. However, as a practical matter, most construction defect claims are not resolved in pre-litigation—a lawsuit is usually required. What are the steps in a lawsuit? This chapter will trace the formal litigation process from beginning to end.

In those lawsuits brought on behalf of common-interest developments, the community manager and the association's board will be heavily involved in the process. The community manager, in particular, must make certain that effective and secure communication is open among the association's members, board, attorneys, and investigative team throughout the process.

Homeowners will be called on to make their homes available for inspection and testing. Later, as defect cases approach trial, community managers, board members, and other owners become even more involved with the litigation. While the association's attorney will do everything possible to spare volunteers from discovery, board members and other members will probably have to be deposed while the attorney positions the case for settlement. If the construction-defect case goes to trial, community managers, board members, and other owners become important witnesses for the association.

The Association Files a Complaint

The first step in a construction-defects lawsuit is for the association's attorney to file a complaint. In a homeowners association, the complaint may either be brought as a class action (depending on the claims and jurisdiction) or as an action in which all homeowners are named as plaintiffs.

Complaints alleging construction defects typically contain multiple causes of action, including breach of implied warranty, breach of express warranty, negligence, nuisance, breach of fiduciary duty, strict liability, and other legal theories. The causes of action will depend on the facts of the case, the legal theories that are best suited to those facts, and state law.

Construction defect lawsuits are generally filed in the county where the community is located.

Defendants Answer the Complaint and File Cross Complaints

Developers—together with corporations, partnerships, and individuals—often form limited liability corporations, or LLCs. When associations sue developers for construction defects, the association's attorney will frequently name these related entities and individuals in the lawsuit in addition to naming the LLC. Once the lawsuit is filed, the court requires those named in the suit to respond (called a responsive pleading) generally within 30 to 60 days.

During this time, developers will invariably file cross actions—sometimes called cross complaints or cross claims. A cross complaint is quite similar to the original complaint, except the developer files it to bring general contractors, sub-contractors, design professionals, and material suppliers into the lawsuit.

In the cross action, the developer typically proceeds under the legal theories of express indemnity, implied indemnity, and contribution, among others.

Express indemnity means that a subcontractor agrees to cover the developer's losses if a defect results from the subcontractor's work.[1]

Implied indemnity, on the other hand, gives developers and general contractors a remedy when their subcontractor's fail to perform and a claim against the developer results.[2]

Contribution is a legal theory that applies when more than one party is responsible for the same damage.[3] For instance, the roof-tile manufacturer has to pay for roof leaks since the tiles are deteriorating long before they should. The roof-leak damage is $500,000. However, the roof installers could have prevented the leaks if they had placed the underlayment correctly, but they didn't. Instead, they left open areas on the plywood. Thus, both parties are responsible to the association for $500,000 in damages.

The tile-manufacturing company wants out of the case early, so it pays the entire $500,000. This discharges all the tile manufacturer's obligations to the judgment.[4] However, since the roof installers are also responsible, the tile manufacturer then seeks contribution from them for part of the $500,000. The tile manufacturer files an action against the roof installer who eventually contributes $200,000 to the tile manufacturer.

Filing a cross action follows the same procedure as filing the original complaint: the parties named in the cross-action have a prescribed amount of time to respond.

Traditional Litigation or Case Management Order?

Construction-defect litigation can proceed via one of two routes—the traditional lawsuit or case management order (CMO).

Traditional Litigation

Traditional construction-defect lawsuits filed on behalf of community associations are fraught with shortfalls, delays, and unnecessary expense, and they involve dozens of parties. Initially, there are two parties to the case: the association and the developer. However, the developer invariably files cross actions against all subcontractors, material suppliers, and design professionals, which immediately increases the parties to the lawsuit. Then the subcontractors, material suppliers, and design professionals may file counterclaims against each other. When the dust settles, the typical construction defect lawsuit has blossomed into dozens of parties, and there may be dozens of complaints, cross-complaints, and third-party complaints on file. And, at this point in a traditional case, that file could be several *feet* thick.

But this is only the beginning of the blizzard of paper. Next comes the discovery phase: interrogatories, requests for documents, requests for admissions, inspections, testing, and depositions—by every party in the lawsuit! And, in traditional litigation, there is no limit on the discovery that can be conducted by any party—unless another party files to limit it.

Case Management Orders

A case management order is a set of procedures that is customized for construction defects claims. It's based on an agreement between the opposing parties and approved by the court. Standardized CMOs achieve consistency, reduce negotiation time, and reduce everyone's expenses. The CMO provides ground rules and schedules for conducting the case; in fact, the CMO schedule is the backbone of the chronology of a construction defect case.

HISTORICAL PERSPECTIVE: As construction defect lawsuits increased, attorneys and courts alike soon concluded that traditional rules of discovery made the cost of resolving construction defect claims unacceptably high.

Thus the CMO was introduced. CMOs were first used for construction defect cases in Southern California as early as the 1980s. By 2003, CMOs had been refined into final case management orders.* The legal community agreed that final CMOs would be used in all construction defect cases, and no deviations would be permitted except by court order. Final CMOs varied somewhat depending on the type of construction defect case involved. For example, one final CMO was for homeowner associations; a second form was for individual homeowners in single-family home developments; and another was designed for use in cases involving commercial buildings. *Letter from Judges May and Enright, San Diego County Superior Court, to all construction litigation counsel, dated February 13, 2003, with three forms of final case management orders enclosed.*

CMOs typically begin by stating their purpose, such as the following contained in the San Diego County final case management order for use in association cases:

The court deems this matter to be complex litigation....As such, this is a case that requires specialized management to avoid placing unnecessary burdens on the court or the litigants. The primary areas that require specialized management are discovery and settlement discussions.[5]

A Discovery Referee and Mediator Are Appointed

CMOs typically designate both a discovery referee and a mediator, which—in small cases—may be the same person. The discovery referee hears only discovery disputes and motions. Substantive motions are heard by the judge, and a mediator is appointed to facilitate settlement.

The CMO not only names the discovery referee and mediator, but also specifies their hourly rates. It contains a means to object to the appointment of the discovery referee and mediator, to appeal their rulings, and to divide their costs and fees among the participants.[6]

Limits on Discovery

A key element of CMOs used in construction defect cases is that they specify the discovery that is permitted among the parties to the dispute—generally documents, special interrogatories, statements of work, and inspections and testing. An exception is that the CMO does not specify or limit the discovery that is permitted from others in the construction process who are not parties to the lawsuit[7]—local building departments, state departments of real estate, contractors performing temporary repairs, and testing services.

A Document Depository is Established

In traditional litigation, each document generated by each party to the construction defect case must be served on all other parties to the case. CMOs eliminate all this paperwork by creating a document depository[8] where every party must place the originals of all their documents. Each time a document is added, all the other parties are notified. Everyone in the suit has access to the depository, and anyone can order copies of documents as needed.

Litigation support firms are common document depositories. If their court reporting services are contracted and they take all the depositions in the case, they often provide and maintain the document depository at no charge.

Typical CMOs specify what documents must be placed in the depository. Plaintiffs (association or individual homeowners), defendants (developer and/or general contractor), and cross-defendants (subcontractor, design professional, or material supplier) will be required to deposit different types of documents.

Association Documents

Associations and homeowners typically deposit:[9]

1. Documents regarding the defects.

2. Plans, specifications, contracts, and other documents relating to the design and construction of the community.

3. Documents relating to landscaping, grading, flatwork, and post-purchase improvements undertaken by the association or homeowners.

4. Documents that identify current and past members of an association's board, architectural committee, landscaping committee, and other association committees.

5. Documents identifying property management firms and maintenance companies employed by the association or homeowners.

6. Governing documents of the associations, including CC&Rs, articles of incorporation, bylaws, rules, and regulations.

7. Records relating to the repair and maintenance of the community or homes

8. Records relating to the claimed construction defects, including meeting minutes, notes, correspondence, memoranda, photographs, and reports.

9. Reports, notes, correspondence, and memoranda relating to complaints by homeowners, tenants, and other individuals concerning construction deficiencies.

10. Documents in the possession of the association or homeowners relating to:
   a. Original design and construction
   b. Maintenance
   c. Proposed or actual repairs of any defects
   d. Reserve accounts and reserve reports
   e. Operating budgets
   f. Sales and marketing literature
   g. Appraisals
   h. Property management agreements and records

11. Documents showing the ownership interests of the plaintiffs in the association.

Developer's Documents

Developers, general contractors, subcontractors, design professionals, and material suppliers deposit:[10]

1. Written agreements and contracts pertaining to the original construction.

2. Plans, specifications, diagrams, shop drawings, as-built plans, calculations, journals, invoices, purchase orders, change orders, job diaries, project files, daily job logs, field orders, superintendent reports, time cards, governmental inspection records, and all other documents relating to the original construction, repair, or maintenance of the community.

3. Insurance policies, certificates of insurance, and additional insured endorsements that potentially provide insurance coverage for the claims asserted in the lawsuit, regardless of whether coverage has been reserved or denied by the insurance companies in question.

4. All documents relating to repairs, alterations, modifications, or improvements.

5. Sales files, customer service files, advertising files, marketing documents, warranty claims, and warranty documents.

6. Documents generated or possessed by experts for the party in question.

7. All documents subpoenaed from third parties.

Special Interrogatories Are Answered

Interrogatories are simply written questions posed by one party to another during the course of litigation that must be answered under oath. Special interrogatories are custom designed for a particular type of litigation like construction defects.

In traditional discovery procedures, a party can object to an interrogatory that isn't relevant or that isn't seeking admissible evidence. A special interrogatory, by contrast, fits the circumstances of a particular case and has been pre-approved by the court; therefore, the question must be answered without objection.

Special interrogatories in construction defect CMOs take different forms depending on who is answering them—plaintiff or defendant.

The Association Answers

If an association or owner (the plaintiff) is answering, special interrogatories may cover:[11]

1. The type of entity, such as a corporation or unincorporated association, together with the status of a corporation or association.

2. A description of the association's or owner's ownership interest in the real property and improvements, such as residential buildings, clubhouses, pools, and perimeter walls.

3. A description of claims made by the association or owner under insurance and warranty policies.

4. A description of attempts to repair any of the defects identified in the lawsuit.

5. Descriptions of professionals, such as contractors, architects, or engineers that the association or owner has retained to inspect the defects or damages, other than those hired by the attorney.

The Developer Answers

If a developer, general contractor, subcontractor, design professional, or material supplier (the defendant) is answering, special interrogatories may cover:[12]

1. Identity of the defendant as a corporation, partnership, joint venture, unincorporated association, or sole proprietorship.

2. Whether the defendant possesses a license, such as a general contractor's license.

3. A description of the work performed, the person or company contracted to perform it, or whether the work was subcontracted to another person or company.

4. A description of materials supplied.

5. The person or company from whom the defendant purchased the materials.

6. The last known addresses and telephone numbers of the person most knowledgeable about the services performed or the materials supplied to the project.

7. The insurance agent or broker who provided coverage to the defendant.

8. Regarding insurance:

   a. The name of each insurance carrier who provided coverage from the time the work began until the interrogatory.

   b. A description of each policy, including number, type, limits, dates of coverage, and the estimated amount of remaining aggregate coverage.

   c. A disclosure of whether each carrier is defending the lawsuit in question with or without a reservation of rights.

   d. An explanation for any insurance coverage that has been denied.

   e. Confirmation that policies have not been revoked, rescinded, or purchased back by the carrier.

   f. Dates when coverage was denied, revoked, rescinded, or bought back.

   g. The names of insurance brokers and agents involved in the placement of all coverages.

   h. The names of all insurance representatives with full authority to settle claims.

   i. A description of additional insured endorsements to each policy.

   j. The names of the present custodians of all insurance policies.

k. The name of the person responsible for obtaining insurance policies during the construction project.

l. Names, addresses, and phone numbers of each insured named on all policies.

Those answering special interrogatories must respond within a limited time, such as 30 days.[13]

The Association Files a Preliminary Defect List

Following special interrogatories, the association files a preliminary defect list[14] that gives the other parties to the lawsuit an idea of the scope of the issues. The defect list is preliminary at this stage because inspections and testing have not yet taken place.

Visual Inspections are Made

Based on the preliminary defect list, the property will be visually inspected.[15] For homeowner associations, the inspection frequently encompasses common areas and sometimes includes interiors of units. Interiors are inspected either because defects in the common areas have damaged interiors, or defects can only be inspected from inside units—faulty plumbing, HVAC, or electrical components. In a defect case involving multiple defects and many parties, several rounds of visual inspections may be necessary.

How to Select Units for Inspection

Selecting the individual units for inspection—and later testing—is an important process that can be approached in several ways.

First, units may be selected that demonstrate the damage on the preliminary defect list. These will be identified by reviewing responses to homeowner surveys and temporary repair records.

Second, units may be selected as representatives of the whole. For instance, a condominium may comprise several buildings, and a designated number of units per building are selected for inspection. Or, a community may contain homes with varying types of plans, and a certain number from each plan type will be selected.

Third, units may be selected at random, and there are varying degrees of sophistication to this method. The least sophisticated method is to contact owners until an inspection schedule is filled. At the other end of the spectrum, the most sophisticated type of random sample—indeed, the only kind certain to be admissible at trial—is generated by a statistician applying scientifically-accepted techniques.

Selecting units for visual inspections and subsequent testing requires the association to balance competing factors: expense, practicality, and credibility. Using a statistician will be expensive, but the results will have maximum credibility in mediations and at trial. If the association chooses this approach, it's essential that it follow the random sample selected by the statistician. There is also the practical question whether the owners of the units selected by the statistician will make their units available for inspection or testing. Nothing is accomplished if they won't. They may be willing to open their homes for visual inspection, but they're much less likely to allow invasive testing.

During visual inspections, defendants and their experts may inspect, photograph, videotape, and measure exteriors and interiors, but they cannot sample, test, or mark anything.[16]

Invasive Tests are Conducted

After visual inspections, invasive testing (sometimes called destructive testing) begins.[17] Tests can be undertaken either sequentially—the plaintiff first followed by the defendant later in the case—or jointly with all parties testing at the same time.

When the association (the plaintiff) tests first, its experts provide the association attorney with information about the components and units to be tested, and the attorney publishes a testing schedule that meets the CMO schedule.

When all parties test jointly, each submits a request to the association attorney specifying the scope, location, and type of testing to be conducted, whether special equipment is necessary, and whether they are prepared to share the cost of testing.[18]

Invasive testing should be governed by rules established in advance in the CMO that include:[19]

1. Test areas must be protected from inclement weather.

2. Test areas must be repaired and restored to pre-testing condition quickly.

3. If personal property is damaged during testing, the responsible party must pay for it immediately.

4. During testing, those conducting the tests are prohibited from communicating with residents or association personnel except as needed to conduct the tests and make repairs.

5. All construction and engineering companies performing tests or making repairs must be licensed contractors and carry adequate liability and workers compensation insurance.

The Association Makes Temporary Repairs

During the course of a construction defect case, it's inevitable that temporary repairs will be needed. When this happens, the association's attorney must provide advance notice to the defendants so that they can observe and document the defect and how it's repaired.[20]

The Association Presents its Claims

After testing, the association's experts typically present the association's claims to the mediator, all defendants and cross-defendants, and all defense experts. The board and community manager should attend the presentation as well.

This presentation is frequently referred to as a show-and-tell in which each association expert makes a slide presentation illustrating the defects within his or her expertise and answers questions from the audience.

The association's attorney should videotape the entire presentation for the benefit of subcontractors or others who join the litigation later.

Latecomers Conduct Cleanup Testing

In a complex construction defect case, the CMO schedule will provide for cleanup testing after all other testing is complete. This allows those who joined the suit late to conduct their tests and provides for any additional tests that might be necessary to resolve conflicts in expert opinions or narrow issues in mediation. Like other procedures in the process, cleanup testing requires detailed requests that specify the scope of the testing, and it is subject to a deadline.

The Association Compiles a Final Defect List and Estimates Costs

Invasive testing provides sufficient information for the association to compile a final defect list and to estimate the cost of repairs.

The cost-of-repair report (referred to simply as the cost-of-repair), lists each defect, how it will be repaired, the nature and location of the repair, and how much labor and material are needed to make it. In some instances, one repair may cover several defects. From this information, the association's professional cost estimator projects how much the repair will cost.[21]

The Association Serves a Global Settlement Demand

After the association has completed its final defect list and cost-of-repair and placed them in the depository, the association attorney serves the defendant— contractor, developer, or other—with a global settlement demand. The global demand encompasses all categories of defects discovered to date and all components of the association's demand, which vary from state to state. The settlement demand could contain the following components, depending on the jurisdiction:

1. The association's total cost of repair.
2. Temporary repair costs incurred to date.
3. Investigation costs to date.
4. Attorney's fees.

The association's global settlement demand is the opening shot across the bow in settlement negotiations. It should be served as soon as possible after the final defect list and cost-of-repair are completed and as far in advance of the first mediation as possible.

The Developer Allocates Costs

The developer's experts will allocate the costs listed in the global settlement demand among the subcontractors, design professionals, and material suppliers that have been brought into the case as soon as possible, but typically no later than 14 days before the first mediation session.[22]

Expert Witnesses are Named

As the mediation phase of a construction defect lawsuit approaches, each party must specify the name and contact information for each of its expert witnesses, a general description of the subject of each expert's testimony, each expert's hourly rates for deposition and trial testimony, and a copy of each expert's resume.[23]

In many instances, CMOs provide for both an initial and supplemental designation of expert witnesses. Typically, the first designation is served by all parties as the first mediation approaches, and the supplemental declaration follows some months later, before expert depositions commence.[24]

Mediation Begins

The mediation process begins shortly after allocation of the settlement demand. Depending on the facts of the case and the agreed order of mediations, the first round of mediation may include the association and the developer alone, or it may include all parties.

Unless excused by the mediator, each party must appear at mediation sessions with representatives who have the authority to settle the disputes. In the case of a homeowner association, members of the board should participate in mediation sessions. Attorneys and insurance representatives will participate for the developer.[25]

The sequence of mediations will depend on the size and complexity of the case, the number of parties involved, and the insurance picture. The first mediation generally involves the association and the developer and developer's insurance representatives. The next round or two is typically conducted between the developer and the subcontractors, design professionals, and material suppliers. Finally, mediations involving all parties would be conducted until the case was resolved or until it was decided that mediation would not achieve a settlement.

The Experts Meet

During initial mediations, sometimes everyone agrees that some defects exist and they agree on the scope of the repair. With respect to other defects, the parties and their experts may be far apart. When this happens, it's useful for the experts on all sides to meet among themselves—without attorneys or others—to resolve their disagreements. These expert meetings, facilitated by the mediator, can narrow the gaps between opinions about the existence, nature, and extent of the defects and the appropriate scope and cost of repair.

Depositions are Taken

If the case hasn't been resolved after several rounds of mediation, it's time to prepare for trial—beginning with taking depositions. Again, the CMO provides a timeline and protocol for this most time consuming and expensive of trial preparations.

Witnesses that may be deposed in a typical construction defect case—that hasn't settled within 18 to 24 months—include:

- Present and former community managers.
- Present and former members of the board.
- Owners other than board members.
- Persons most knowledgeable (PMKs) about the original construction, repair history, and present defects—usually the developer, general contractor, subcontractors, design professionals, and material suppliers.

Third parties are frequently deposed as well, including PMKs from companies that did the temporary repairs, companies that tested and investigated before the attorneys became involved, and the experts who contributed to the process.

The typical order of depositions is as follows:

1. Present and past community managers.
2. Present and past association board members.
3. Owners other than board members.

4. Third parties.
5. Developer PMKs.
6. Subcontractor, design professional, and material supplier PMKs.
7. Experts.

Expert depositions in particular should be spelled out clearly in the CMO. For example, the data, reports, and documents of each expert should be placed in the depository seven business days before the deposition. Experts are usually deposed according to areas of expertise—e.g., roofing. First the association's roofing experts are deposed, then the developer's roofing experts are deposed, and finally the subcontractor's roofing experts are deposed.[26]

All Parties Meet for Final Mediation and Mandatory Settlement Conference

It's not unusual for mediations to continue while the depositions take place, a process that frequently consumes several months. However, at some point as the trial date approaches, the mediator will announce a final mediation that will involve all parties and their insurance representatives. This is the mediator's final push to settle the case before going to trial.

After the final mediation, the parties may request, or the court may require, a mandatory settlement conference. An experienced settlement judge—other than the trial judge—will conduct the conference at the courthouse with all parties and the association's insurance claims adjusters present.

Mandatory settlement conferences can be extremely effective. Confronted with the formality of the courtroom and stern lectures from the judge about the expense and risks of proceeding with a trial, the chances of resolution increase greatly. The mediator works hand in hand with the settlement judge at the mandatory settlement conference. He or she is not only experienced in settling cases, but is familiar with the background and dynamics of the case. It isn't unusual for mandatory settlement conferences to continue past normal business hours or even into the next day.

The Court Convenes Pretrial Conferences

As the trial date approaches, if no settlement has been achieved, courts generally convene pretrial conferences in complex cases such as those involving construction defects. Generally speaking, the pretrial conference is designed to narrow the issues in the case and prepare for an organized approach to the trial, which is achieved by requiring the parties to identify all the witnesses that will be called, all documents that will be introduced, and all uncontested facts that do not need to be proved.

Construction defect cases invariably involve thousands of documents, dozens of witnesses, and myriad factual and legal issues. Pretrial conferences may run on for several days before the trial judge is satisfied that everything is in order.

The Trial is Held

As mentioned earlier, it's widely believed in the construction industry that only about five percent of construction-defect lawsuits make it to trial. And for good

A Sample CMO Schedule and Timeline

1. Complaint is filed and non-privileged documents are deposited in a document depository. (July, year 1.)

2. Responses to agreed upon interrogatories are due (related to insurance and subcontractor scope-of-work issues).

3. Plaintiff's preliminary defect list is due. (October, year 1.)

4. Deadline to name and serve new parties.

5. Plaintiff and developer meet and confer regarding unit selection for inspections and testing.

6. Defendants provide plaintiff with list of units requested for visual inspections.

7. Plaintiff publishes visual inspection schedule.

8. Visual inspections take place. (January, year 2.)

9. Plaintiff identifies units for invasive testing and describes the scope of invasive testing.

10. Plaintiff publishes invasive testing schedule.

11. Plaintiff's invasive testing takes place. (March, year 2.)

12. Plaintiff's presentation of claims to all parties and mediator takes place.

13. Plaintiff's final defect list is submitted. (May, year 2.)

14. Parties exchange expert witness designations.

15. Plaintiff's cost of repair is submitted. (July, year 2.)

16. Plaintiff serves a global settlement demand on the developer.

17. Initial mediation between plaintiff and developer takes place. (August, year 2.)

18. Defendants designate units for invasive testing and the scope of invasive testing.

19. Defendants publish defense invasive testing schedule.

20. Defense invasive testing takes place. (October, year 2.)

21. Developer submits allocated settlement demands on all subcontractors, material suppliers, and design professionals.

22. Second round of mediation takes place. (November, year 2.)

23. Parties meet and confer concerning deposition schedules if necessary of persons most knowledgeable, management representatives, board members, homeowners, and experts.

24. Developer serves deposition schedule on all parties.

25. Third round of mediations among all parties takes place.

26. Depositions take place.

27. Final mediation takes place. (February, year 3.)

28. Discovery ends.

29. Pretrial conference takes place.

30. Trial begins. (March, year 3.)

reason—the process is drawn out and extremely expensive. A trial involving even a few defects can easily take several weeks. Normal trial steps include:

- Arguing pretrial motions.
- Selecting the jury.
- Presenting evidence—first the association (plaintiff), followed by the developer (defendant), and finally the subcontractors, design professionals, and material suppliers.
- Presenting rebuttal evidence from the association.
- Presenting final arguments.
- Instructing the jury.
- Deliberating and deciding by the jury.
- Issuing a judgment.

During the course of a construction defect trial, thousands of documents may be admitted into evidence, including the original project plans and specifications, reams of photographs, temporary repair records, cost-of-repair reports and their supporting materials, and expert reports—in short, everything from the document depository. Trial witnesses will include the same people who were deposed during discovery.

After all evidence has been presented, attorneys for all sides will propose jury instructions to the trial judge, and it may take several days of arguing for the final instructions to be agreed on. Final arguments aren't delivered until all parties agree on the instructions to the jury. Then, the jury deliberates until it reaches a decision.

Frequently, juries must answer detailed questions regarding how to divide fault among various defendants for each defect and how much monetary damage to allocate to each. This is called the special-verdict procedure. After the jury presents its verdict, the trial judge will enter a judgment based on that verdict.

After the Trial

After the trial, attorneys on both sides may file post-trial motions, including motions for new trials. Appeals may follow from the jury's verdict and judgment.

Following a trial in which judgment is rendered in favor of the association, the case is ultimately resolved by a settlement, or judgment, or both. The judgment may be satisfied by tapping the defendants' assets or by proceeding against their insurance companies. The post-trial process can drag on for years.

Endnotes

1. MacDonald & Kruse v. San Jose Steel Co., 29 Cal.App.3d 413, 105 Cal.Rptr. 725 (1972).
2. White v. Huntington Beach, 21 Cal.3d 497, 146 Cal.Rptr. 614 (1978).
3. Id.
4. Atkinson Co. v. Consani, 223 Cal.App.2d 342, 35 Cal.Rptr. 750 (1963).
5. San Diego Standard CMO, Paragraph 1(A).
6. Id.
7. San Diego Standard CMO, Paragraph 2(A).
8. San Diego Standard CMO, Paragraph 2(B).

9. San Diego Standard CMO, Exhibit "E (A).

10. San Diego Standard CMO, Exhibit "E (B)"

11. San Diego Special CMO, Exhibit "A."

12. San Diego Special CMO, Exhibit "B."

13. San Diego Standard CMO, Paragraph 2(C)(2).

14. San Diego Standard CMO, Paragraph 2(E)(1).

15. San Diego Standard CMO, Paragraph 2(D)(1).

16. *Id.*

17. San Diego Standard CMO, Paragraph 2(D)(2).

18. San Diego Special CMO, Exhibit "F."

19. San Diego Special CMO, Paragraph 2 (D)(3).

20. San Diego Special CMO, Paragraph 2 (D)(4).

21. San Diego Special CMO, Paragraph 2 (E)(3).

22. San Diego Special CMO, Exhibit "G" Subparagraph (C)(2).

23. San Diego Special CMO, Paragraph 2 (F)(1).

24. *Id.*

25. San Diego Special CMO, Paragraph 2 (3)(A).

26. San Diego Special CMO, Paragraph 2 (F)(1).P

PART FIVE

Alternative Dispute Resolution

CHAPTER 15

Mediation

Over the past few decades, homeowners, attorneys, and judges have turned to alternative dispute resolution, or ADR, because formal litigation simply does not work to resolve defect claims. Indeed, all construction defect claims, at least in states where many such claims are filed, are now resolved using ADR.

Traditional litigation is ineffective in construction defect cases for several reasons. First, it's adversarial—one side wins, one loses. Second, cases sometimes don't go to trial for many years. Third, traditional litigation includes extensive pretrial discovery and exorbitant costs. Fourth, when a case finally goes to trial, it's dumped in the laps of judges and juries who have no experience or knowledge of complex and technical construction issues. Finally, associations and developers in a traditional trial have very little opportunity to participate meaningfully in the process. On the contrary, their rights and obligations are based on narrow legal issues rather than real world factors.

Alternative dispute resolution, on the other hand, resolves defect claims quickly and inexpensively. In contrast to traditional litigation, ADR narrows the issues and encourages both sides to achieve an amicable resolution. ADR recognizes that lawsuits often result from lack of communication; therefore, it encourages all parties to participate in and control the dispute resolution process. This approach achieves a mutually-acceptable solution earlier and at much lower cost.

Alternative dispute resolution can be either binding or non-binding. Mediation is the most widely used non-binding ADR—particularly in construction defect cases. Since it's non-binding, the ruling can be rejected by either party.

General Principles of Mediation

Traditionally, mediation has been a non-binding, voluntary process. However, recently in some states, mediation has become one of the required steps before a construction defect lawsuit can be filed. The mediation isn't binding; but both sides are compelled to participate. Additionally, states that use case management orders now invariably incorporate mediation in the CMO.

Mediation is guided negotiation. A mediator is a neutral person who guides and facilitates a negotiated settlement between and among disputing parties.

CONSTRUCTION DEFECT LITIGATION

The result of a successful mediation is an agreement, not an imposed decision as in an arbitration or litigation. Parties remain in control, not having to agree to a settlement unless each feels that it is in its best interests.

The success of mediation depends on how persuasive the mediator is, how determined the parties are to resolve their disputes, and how creative the attorneys are in proposing solutions. While mediation can be useful at any stage, it produces best results if used early in a dispute—before participants become fixed in their positions and while they're all still communicating with each other.

Mediation has no strict rules or procedures; indeed, the rules are suggested by the mediator and agreed to by the parties. Each mediation session proceeds in its own way depending on the nature of the dispute, the goals of the participants, and the techniques employed by the mediator.

Mediation is especially effective in multi-party, multi-issue disputes. A skilled mediator can help to organize negotiations by categorizing claims and identifying potentially responsible parties in each category. Mediators also facilitate the scheduling of negotiating sessions. Effective mediators can also be helpful in negotiating with insurance adjusters for the general contractor and subcontractors.

The first step in the process is getting everyone to agree to mediation. Unfortunately, the greater the number of potential parties, the harder it is to gain agreement to mediate as well as to agree on a mediator and to apportion costs. There are some parties who believe that they are peripheral to the main issues and therefore are unwilling to pay significant amounts for mediation. They likewise feel that it is a waste of time and money to have their legal counsel sit through hours of negotiation or worse, to wait around while negotiations take place that do not involve their particular issues.

Mediation of a large defect case can take many months. The mediator must make initial contact with all parties and the parties' representatives. This will include adjusters for any of the parties' insurers. At the same time, position papers of the various parties will be assembled. In the case of the association, the claims and potentially responsible parties will be listed. The developer will also put its position in writing and will implicate any material supplier, contractor or subcontractor and the portion of the work for which that party may be responsible. At this stage, it is common for subcontractors or suppliers to have only a general idea of the extent and nature of their involvement in the case and will request additional information prior to taking a position. The early stages of the mediation can—and must—serve as an educational process for both the mediator and the parties, especially those that consider themselves small or marginal parties.

Subsequent to an initial general meeting, much of the mediation is conducted without all parties present at the same time. Mediators conduct meetings with individual parties or groups of parties as the circumstances may require. For example, the mediator may have a meeting with the general contractor, material suppliers, and all subcontractors who were involved in the construction of roofs. This enables the mediator to give close examination to a single significant defect and to begin a discussion with those possessing potential liability regarding the apportionment of responsibility.

Individual meetings may also be required, for example, when a particular defendant has insurance coverage issues. Since insurance coverage is directly relevant to the parties' ability to meaningfully participate in a settlement, the mediator will try to resolve disputes between the insurer and the contractor or between insurers as to their respective responsibilities. Creating settlements very often depends on the mediator's success in packaging offers from various insurers.

Meetings between the association and smaller groups of suppliers, contractors, and subcontractors will also occur to allow the matter to be resolved issue by issue. The developer and general contractor are involved in virtually all of the issues; some of the subcontractors will be involved in multiple discussions. The design professionals can also be involved in many of the negotiations as their responsibilities usually span the entire project.

In addition to face-to-face meetings, mediators employ conference calls, individual telephone calls, emails, and all other types of communications. The main purposes of the mediation are to encourage the parties to discuss correction of the defects present at the project and to secure work, materials, money, or a combination thereof, in order to achieve such corrective work. Any communication method that moves the discussion towards those results is acceptable.

It sometimes bothers the parties to mediation that a mediator may be spending more time with one party than another. A good mediator will anticipate this and explain to the parties that there is no significance to the amount of time spent with a given party or parties. Even though the association is a claimant, the mediator may spend more time with a developer and/or general contractor, simply because the developer is attempting to piece together a proposal involving all of the subordinate parties.

There is no universal script for a mediation process. The mediator must evaluate the claims and the parties and convince the various participants of the value of settlement. One of the techniques used by the mediator is to advise each of the parties, including the association, of the weaknesses in their positions. In the case of the association, this means that the mediator will point out claims for which the proof of fault is less persuasive than others. He or she will emphasize weaknesses in evidence of causation, fault, or damages. The difficulties involved in collecting judgments are also discussed. The mediator will in turn focus the defendants on their exposure; that is, the possibility of damage claims far in excess of the amount that might settle the case.

When mediation takes place outside of a case management order, the parties should agree in writing to the scope of the process and the responsibilities of the players. This is particularly important when activities like inspections and testing will take place between mediation sessions. A typical written mediation agreement would address the following:

1. Description of the participants—the developer on the one hand and the homeowners association on the other.

2. Description of the disputes that will be the subject of mediation.

3. Agreement by the homeowners association not to begin or continue with a law suit until the mediation is concluded.

4. Agreement by the developer to suspend all applicable statutes of limitation

and repose until the mediation is concluded.

5. Agreement by the developer to notify the general liability insurance carriers about the claims.

6. A method for selecting the mediator.

7. Agreement on allocation of costs and the mediator's fees.

8. Outline of the duties of the mediator.

9. Outline of the powers of the mediator—to schedule, conduct, coordinate inspections and invasive testing, and regulate all other means of discovery.

10. Agreement on a timeline and the steps in the process, including inspections, invasive testing, exchange of expert information, and mediation sessions.

11. Agreement on the division of costs and expert fees if joint investigations are conducted by neutral experts.

12. Confidentiality.

DEVELOPER'S PERSPECTIVE: Right-to-repair legislation evolved because, from the developer's perspective, defect litigation appeared to have become a profitable industry for many lawyers. Rather than allow developers to repair defects, it seemed that attorneys instead encouraged associations to sue. Mediation is considered a key component of the remediation process, and as such is an integral part of right-to-repair laws

Many developers now agree that alternative dispute resolution (ADR), principally mediation, should be used to avoid litigation and resolve real problems. Not just the association's problems, but also the developer's; namely, mediation allows developers to place the burden of correcting deficiencies on those who actually created them. For example, if a soils engineer designed a foundation system incorrectly, the developer will insist that the engineer contribute to the settlement. Likewise, the subcontractor who failed to properly flash around windows will be held responsible for that failure. Therefore, through mediation the developer can convince the suppliers, designers, and subcontractors to bear some of the financial responsibility for the association's claims.

Confidentiality

The mediation process must be confidential to be effective. Oral and written communications made during mediation aren't admissible if mediation fails and the case is submitted to binding arbitration or goes to trial.

While virtually all states have recognized the confidentiality of mediation proceedings, some states have gone one step further and enacted statutes dealing specifically with the confidentiality of mediation. For example, California's legislature, an early leader in embracing the mediation process as an alternative to trial, enacted California Evidence Code Section 1119 addressing confidentiality. Its main points include:

■ Nothing said in mediation is admissible in evidence or subject to discovery— unless it is otherwise admissible outside of mediation. In that case, introducing it during mediation doesn't insulate it.

- No documents used in mediation are admissible in evidence or subject to discovery.
- All communications, negotiations, or settlement discussions among the participants are confidential.
- Communications and documents are confidential unless all participants agree otherwise.

What to Look for in a Mediator

An experienced, qualified mediator is critical to the success of the process. Private firms that provide mediation services and specialize in construction defects have sprouted up across the country, particularly in large metropolitan areas in the west.

To be successful in construction defect disputes, a mediator must have construction defect expertise, i.e., a thorough understanding of residential construction and of the interrelationships among developers, general contractors, subcontractors, design professionals, and material suppliers. Most important, a mediator must have the ability to recognize and resolve insurance coverage issues relating to construction defect claims.

Mediators must also possess the ability to educate participants about the mediation process, to inspire confidence, to convey an awareness of the dynamics of the parties in the process, to listen, and to be creative. They must also have integrity, a sense of timing, objectivity, sensitivity to everyone's circumstances, honesty, and, when necessary, a sense of humor.

Prospective mediators should have no actual or potential conflicts of interest, and they should be required to disclose potential conflicts that arise during the course of the mediation—not unlikely when mediation lasts for several months.

Pre-litigation Mediation

State legislatures across the nation have included either mandatory or voluntary mediation provisions in their statutes for construction defect claims, including builder's right-to-repair statutes. For example, the builder's right-to-repair legislation in Nevada embraces mandatory mediation:. According to Section 40.680 of the Nevada Revised Statutes:

- Before anyone can file a claim for construction defects against a contractor, subcontractor, supplier, or design professional, the matter must be submitted to mediation.
- All parties select a mediator by agreement.
- The mediator may discover only those documents or records that are necessary to the mediation.
- The mediator has a time limit for beginning and ending the mediation.
  Even in states that don't make mediation mandatory prior to filing a construction defect lawsuit, a person may still be able to force uncooperative parties to mediation by filing a motion seeking court-ordered mediation. Although such rules compel the parties to engage in some form of ADR, it remains non-binding.

Mediation in Case Management Orders

Mandatory mediation procedures are embodied in virtually every case management order for construction defect cases. For example, the typical case management order will include:

1. Appointing a mediator. The CMO will contain the name of the mediator, his or her contact information, hourly rates, and the maximum number of hours of his or her time the parties expect to use.

2. Mediation protocol. Each party must appear at mediations according to the schedule in the CMO along with their insurance representatives and others who have full settlement authority.

3. Settlement demands. Part of the CMO timeline specifies when the association must serve all defendants (developers and general contractors) with a written settlement demand—normally at least 28 days before the first mediation session. The CMO will further specify when defendants must serve all cross-defendants (subcontractors, design professionals, and material suppliers) with allocated settlement demands.

4. Allocating mediation fees. The CMO outlines the allocation of the mediator's fees among the parties.

Most CMO timelines specify numerous mediation dates. In the first mediation session the mediator may meet with only the association and the developer, i.e., without the subcontractors, design professionals, and material suppliers. Or the mediator may elect to include all parties in the first session, in which the association's experts present its claims. In either case, the first session focuses on the history of the project, the defects, the association's demand, and the insurance issues. Rarely is any settlement offer forthcoming at a first mediation session.

Subsequent mediations proceed depending on the facts of the case and the challenges presented by the status of the parties. For example, a developer's status may be bankrupt, or an association's status may be that homes are uninhabitable. The mediator must focus on these and other hurdles to resolve the case quickly —are key players out of business, or, more significantly, do they have inadequate insurance?

A number of insurance companies that historically insured developers and subcontractors have become insolvent. If developers or contractors have no insurance, or limited insurance, the settlement burden is increased for the remaining defendants, and the obstacles to settlement are greater.

The mediator can vary the sequence of mediation events specified in the CMO depending on the results of the first mediation. For example, if insurance disputes are the major impediments to settlement, the mediator may conduct special mediation sessions that focus exclusively on insurance. On the other hand, if the nature and extent of the defects or the cost of repair is the major impediment to settlement, the mediator may conduct special mediation sessions (called facilitated expert meetings) with only the experts—no attorneys—to narrow the gaps in their opinions.

The mediator also frequently conducts follow-up mediation sessions with the developer and subcontractors—without the association. These sessions are used to obtain contributions to a global settlement offer from subcontractors, design professionals, and material suppliers and to resolve disputes about the scope of work performed by particular subcontractors.

After these specialized mediation sessions, the mediator will reconvene all parties to attempt a final resolution of the disputes. If no settlement results, the typical CMO will specify that depositions begin promptly. The threat of expense and time consumed by depositions offers the mediator the best pressure he or she can apply.

Mediation sessions need to take place where numerous separate conference or breakout rooms are available. Each mediation session typically begins with a joint session where all parties establish an agenda, set objectives, and openly state their positions. The mediator meets separately with the different parties; each explains and supports their position confidentially while the mediator attempts to move them toward the common ground necessary for settlement. The mediator must inspire respect for his or her ability to properly evaluate their positions and to accept the strengths and weaknesses in their positions. Eventually, the parties become more receptive to compromise. The mediator's goal is to lay the foundation for a resolution that will be acceptable to everyone.

Documenting Mediated Settlements

In most cases, mediation eventually leads to settlement of construction defect claims; and, when it does, it must be documented in writing and in detail.

Final settlements usually come at the end of long sessions—late in the day when everyone is exhausted. Nevertheless, the mediator must take care and time to document the terms of the settlement, at least in a memo, before all parties leave. Otherwise, subsequent disputes over the terms will result. A deadline can then be set for completing a more detailed settlement agreement.

The mediator should be authorized to resolve disputes over the settlement agreement language based on his or her experience with the parties and knowledge of the case.

The typical construction defect settlement agreement should cover the following subjects:

1. Parties to the settlement.
2. Settlement amount, including a breakdown of the amounts payable by each contributing party.
3. Payment terms.
4. Scope of the releases to be granted to the various contributing parties.
5. Mechanics of dismissal of claims following settlement payments.
6. Provision that each party bears its own costs, attorneys fees, and expert fees incurred in the litigation.
7. Statement that no party admits liability in the settlement.
8. Confidentiality of settlement, if applicable.
9. Mechanisms for enforcement, including statutory citations and designation of the court having continuing jurisdiction.
10. Governing law.
11. Dispute resolution, including designation of mediator or arbitrator to resolve disputes
12. Statement of authority of each signatory to bind the party to the agreement.

If the developer must make repairs as part of the settlement, the agreement should include a detailed scope of repair and provision for monitoring compliance with it.

Mediation takes commitment and patience, but the results can leave all parties in a better position than will litigation that results in a trial and judgment.

CHAPTER 16

Arbitration, Judicial Reference, & Private Judges

Besides mediation, other forms of alternative dispute resolution are available, but they are binding. That is, there's no right of appeal; the ruling is final. Arbitration is the most commonly used binding ADR. Judicial reference and using private judges are also options. Other forms of ADR may be either binding or non-binding, depending on what the participants agree to.

Although arbitration is generally binding, with construction defect cases, it's unclear whether the courts will enforce boilerplate arbitration clauses in real estate sales agreements and CC&Rs.

Arbitration Clauses in Contracts

Many contracts include clauses specifying that any dispute arising from the contract will be submitted to arbitration in lieu of litigation. Groups like the American Arbitration Association (AAA) have offered arbitration services for many decades and have detailed rules for all aspects of the arbitration process, from selecting the arbitrator to conducting the arbitration.

Agreements containing mandatory arbitration provisions are frequently used in contracts between general contractors and subcontractors, insurers and insureds, doctors and patients, lawyers and clients, and architects and homeowners. These are generally supported by state statutes.[1] In fact, if one party refuses to participate in arbitration, the other can petition the court to compel participation. The court will order the arbitration unless the right has been waived, or grounds exist to revoke the agreement, or if one of the signatories is involved in a related court action.[2]

Sometimes the agreement specifies a method for appointing an arbitrator, but if it doesn't the signatories may agree on one. If they can't agree, or can't follow the method, the court will appoint the arbitrator.[3] When the court appoints the arbitrator, the selection depends on the state arbitration statutes. In California, for example, the following procedure is used:[4]

> When a petition is made to the court to appoint a neutral arbitrator, the court shall nominate five persons from lists of persons supplied jointly by the parties to the arbitration or obtained from a governmental agency concerned with arbitration or a private disinterested association concerned with arbitration. The parties to the agreement who seek arbitration and against whom arbitration is sought may within five days of

receipt of notice of the nominees from the court jointly select the arbitrator whether or not the arbitrator is among the nominees. If the parties fail to select an arbitrator within the five-day period, the court shall appoint the arbitrator from the nominees.

When groups like AAA conduct the arbitration, their rules for conducting arbitration are used. Otherwise, the state arbitration statutes are used. In California, for instance, the Code of Civil Procedure provides a detailed road map for conducting an arbitration, including the time and place for the hearing,[5] the right to representation by counsel,[6] the power to subpoena witnesses for the hearing,[7] taking depositions and conducting discovery,[8] and fees to be paid for witness testimony.[9]

The arbitrator's decision is submitted in writing[10] and it's final—there is no right to appeal. The court's role in arbitration is to enforce the judgment.[11]

Boilerplate Arbitration Clauses

Developers of mass-produced houses attempt to force arbitration on homebuyers by burying lengthy arbitration provisions in the fine print of real estate purchase contracts or hiding them at the end of the association's CC&Rs. Such arbitration provisions have been attacked in the legislatures and in the courts.

Some states have established strict guidelines for the form and content of mandatory arbitration provisions in real estate contracts. For instance, California has specified type size and wording for mandatory arbitration clauses, and it requires both parties to initial the arbitration provisions separately in addition to signing the overall contract.[12] The California Legislature went one step further by enacting a statute that precludes arbitration altogether in claims where certain statutes of limitations apply, including the 10-year statute of repose for construction defect claims.[13]

Courts don't like mandatory arbitration provisions much more than legislatures. California courts have a history of consistently rejecting mandatory arbitration clauses in purchase agreements and CC&Rs.[14] Builders have argued in recent years that the California statutes are preempted by the Federal Arbitration Act.[15] But, at least one court has ruled that when housing construction involves interstate commerce, arbitration provisions will be enforced under the Federal Arbitration Act—which preempts state law.[16]

The central issue in cases that attack boilerplate clauses is whether the provision was a negotiated or a take-it-or-leave-it provision. Generally, the courts find them to be in the latter category.[17] Some courts apply a four-part test to decide whether to enforce arbitration clauses in real estate contracts.[18] First, there must be a valid contract between the parties. Second, the validity of the arbitration provision is for the courts to decide. Third, the underlying merits of the dispute should not be considered when determining whether the arbitration provision is enforceable. Finally, the courts have historically favored arbitration. The latter principle is frequently the overriding theme on appeal when no state statute precludes enforcing arbitration provisions.[19]

Judicial Reference

Another alternate dispute resolution technique sometimes employed in construction defect cases is called a judicial reference. Judicial reference is used in two circumstances. First, the parties to a lawsuit can ask a court to appoint a referee to hear their dispute if all parties agree, regardless of whether this was provided for in the contract. Second, one party to a contract can ask a court to appoint a referee if the contract provides for disputes to be heard by a referee.[20]

The referee hears and determines all the issues—factual and legal—and submits his or her decision to the court.[21] Or, a referee can offer factual findings only, and the court rules on the legal issues and makes the final judgment based on the facts reported by the referee.[22]

Judicial reference differs from arbitration in its procedural rules. In arbitration, the procedural rules are set by the parties or by a private arbitration service. In judicial reference, if the parties have not agreed on procedural rules, they will follow the rules of the court where their case is filed.

If the disputing parties can't agree on a referee, court rules provide a procedure for appointing one. For instance, in California, each side submits three names to the court, and the court appoints one or more referees.[23] Either side can object to the appointments for any number of reasons:[24] they're not qualified, they're related to someone involved in the case, they have a relationship to one of the parties such as guardian or employer, they're a family member of a party, they're in business with a party, they're security on an obligation of a party, they were a juror or witness in a trial between the same parties, they have an interest in the outcome, they've expressed an opinion about the merits of the case, or they're biased toward one party.

Referees report their decisions in writing to the court within a specified number of days after the hearing.[25] If both parties consented to the judicial reference, the referee's decision stands as the decision of the court,[26] and judgment may be entered as if the case had actually been tried.[27] If the parties didn't agree to use a referee, but the court used one to decide a particular fact, the referee's decision is advisory.[28]

Developers now use judicial reference in lengthy real estate contracts and CC&Rs. For example, the following procedure would be prescribed:

> All claims relating to the purchase agreement, including construction defect claims, would be determined by a general reference conducted by a single referee, such as a retired superior court judge. The referee would try all issues relating to the defect claims, including all issues of fact and law. The referee would render a decision, and would have the power to grant all legal and equitable remedies. The parties waive their rights to trial by jury and their rights to recover punitive damages. The parties would be entitled to the same discovery rights available in court actions. The referee would apply legal rules, including the rules of evidence.

Homeowners have attacked the enforceability of judicial reference provisions in purchase agreements and CC&Rs on several grounds. First, homeowners argue that judicial reference provisions are contracts of adhesion; that is, a standardized contract imposed and drafted by a party with superior bargaining strength whereas the homeowner only has the opportunity to adhere to the contract provision or reject the contract altogether. Second, homeowners argue that provisions that require submission to judicial reference are unconscionable. Third, homeowners argue that provisions that require them to waive their rights to a jury trial and to recover punitive damages are contrary to public policy.

Appellate courts have been divided in their rulings on the enforceability of judicial references in construction defect cases, just as they have been on the enforceability of binding arbitration provisions.[29]

Private Judges

Another form of ADR is using a private judge—generally a retired judge. This procedure, including selecting the private judge, like most ADR procedures, requires the consent of all parties.

With this method of ADR, claims are tried just as they would be in court. The advantages of using a private judge is that the parties can select a judge with experience in construction defects and the ability to expedite claims resolution. The decision of a private judge is binding if the parties agree.

Endnotes

1. California Code of Civil Procedure Section 1281.
2. California Code of Civil Procedure Section 1281.2.
3. California Code of Civil Procedure Section 1281.6.
4. *Id.*
5. California Code of Civil Procedure Section 1282.2.
6. California Code of Civil Procedure Section 1282.4.
7. California Code of Civil Procedure Section 1282.6.
8. California Code of Civil Procedure Section 1283.5.
9. California Code of Civil Procedure Section 1283.2.
10. California Code of Civil Procedure Section 1283.4.
11. California Code of Civil Procedure Section 1281.4.
12. California Code of Civil Procedure Section 1298(b)-(c).
13. California Code of Civil Procedure Sections 1298.7, 337.1, and 337.15.
14. Villa Milano Homeowners Association v. Il Davorge, 84 Cal.App.4th 819, 102 Cal.Rptr.2d 1 (2000).
15. 9 United States Code Section 2 et seq.
16. Basura v. U.S. Home Corp., 98 Cal.App.4th 1205, 120 Cal.Rptr.2d 389 (2002).
17. Marina Cove Condominium Owners Association v. Isabella Estate, 109 Wash. 8 pp. 230, 34 P.3d 870 (2001).
18. Stein v. Geonerco, Inc., 105 Wash. Ct. App. 41, 17 P.3d 1266 (2001).
19. *Id.*
20. California Code of Civil Procedure Section 638.
21. California Code of Civil Procedure Section 638(a).
22. California Code of Civil Procedure Section 638(b).
23. California Code of Civil Procedure Section 640(b).
24. California Code of Civil Procedure Section 641.
25. California Code of Civil Procedure Section 643.
26. California Code of Civil Procedure Section 644(a).
27. *Id.*

28. California Code of Civil Procedure Section 644(b).

29. Compare Pardee Construction Co. v. Superior Court of San Diego County, 100 Cal.App.4th 228, 123 Cal.Rptr.2d 288 (2002) [judicial reference provision unenforceable] with Woodside Homes of California, Inc. v. Folger, 107 Cal.App.4th 723, 132 Cal.Rptr.2d 35 (2003) [judicial reference provision enforceable].

PART SIX

Finances

CHAPTER 17

The Finances of Litigation

The association that is a party to a construction defect case should understand that litigation is extremely expensive. Resolving claims may last two or more years from start to finish, and the investigation costs may run into the hundreds of thousands of dollars. Managing, monitoring, and controlling expenses require dedication from the board and manager. At the conclusion of the process, securing and allocating recovered damages is an equally demanding task. Throughout the entire process, good financial management of the case's expenses and compensation will be a key component in the association's success.

Expenses

Resolving construction defect cases often involves multiple rounds of testing and investigation. These must be completed before claims can be filed. The experts—and there will be many—undertaking the investigation are specialists who charge substantial fees, and they must be paid long before the association receives a settlement. In addition, temporary repairs must be made during the process—usually at substantial expense.

Document Expenses Thoroughly

The attorney or manager is usually responsible for tracking the investigation and temporary repair costs. It is this author's opinion that the expenses should be tracked by the attorney and provided to the manager on a monthly basis. Regardless of who assumes this responsibility, carefully documenting all expenses will ensure that they are fully recovered in a settlement or judgment.

Obviously, in addition to documenting the expenses, the association must also pay them. If the association prefers to pay the costs up front, various options are available.

Reserves

In some states—California, for example—statutes allow common-interest associations to use reserve funds to finance litigation. The board may use the reserve funds to pursue claims related to the repair, replacement, restoration, or maintenance of major components for which the reserve fund was initially established.

In some states, reserve funds may be transferred to the association's general operating fund to meet short-term cash flow requirements relating to litigation. However, the transferred funds must be restored to the reserve fund within specified time periods; and, the board may levy a special assessment to recover the full amount.

If an association's general fund and reserve funds are not adequate to pay for construction defect investigations or expensive temporary repairs, the community manager and the board will have to consider other ways to cover these expenses. Failing to pay the association's bills would be a breach of the board's fiduciary duty.

Special Assessments

Associations often levy special assessments to finance construction defect investigations. Different states allow different approaches—a percentage increase in the regular assessment or a specific amount.

Bank Loans

Some banks will loan money to community associations to finance construction defect investigations and temporary repairs. It may take a little searching to find lenders who offer this service, and the association can expect the bank to peg cash flow from assessments as collateral. Also, lenders won't approve a loan unless the association has a satisfactory history of assessment collection.

Lenders aren't the only ones who have to approve the loan: Governing documents may require the approval of a certain percentage of the owners as well. The association's attorney can ensure that the loan process complies with the association's governing documents. Many documents require a member vote before the association can borrow funds for any reason, and institutions that routinely finance association operations will ask for a resolution showing that the members gave the necessary approval. The association attorney should assist the board with the procedure needed to obtain this approval when a vote is mandated by the governing documents.

Attorney Financing

The current trend is for the construction defect attorney to advance the costs of testing and repair since associations simply are not budgeted to incur these types of expenses. The attorney is repaid from the eventual recovery.

When the association is deciding which construction defect attorney to hire, it should consider whether the candidate, or his or her firm, might finance the investigation. In areas where defect cases are filed in great numbers, this practice is particularly prevalent.

Understandably, these arrangements are subject to rules of professional conduct. The association's general attorney can advise the board on what's permissible and what approvals and disclosures must be made.

Attorneys who finance investigation costs typically don't take collateral, but often charge interest. Furthermore, they generally require repayment from the first sums the association receives from settlement or judgment. Associations should negotiate the interest percentage, if any, and include it in the attorney's fee agreement.

Managing Settlement Proceeds

Whether the board and developer settle the case or the association is awarded a judgment, at some point large sums of compensation may come to the association. Collecting and allocating these proceeds appropriately are important responsibilities.

Collecting Settlement Proceeds

The association's or the individual homeowners' attorneys will be responsible for collecting the settlement proceeds, which they will deposit in a trust account for their clients. Since it may take at least 60 days to collect the funds from all responsible parties, the association should set up a separate trust account for each different construction defect case. Separate trust accounts make it easier for lawyers, clients, and tax professionals alike to track deposits and disbursements. Additionally, separate trust accounts earn interest for the association or individual homeowners; whereas, if the attorney sets up a general trust account, the interest must go to a general fund.

Until all funds are paid, the attorneys should report to the board frequently on the status of payments. Settlement agreements should provide a means for the association attorney to obtain court orders (called "orders to show cause") to force delinquent parties to pay in a timely fashion.

Allocating Settlement Proceeds

In a typical construction defect settlement, the gross settlement proceeds will be allocated in several categories, including the following:

1. Attorneys' fees—calculated according to the written fee agreement.

2. Loan repayments. Any sums that the association borrowed—whether from its own reserve accounts, its attorneys, a bank, or any other source—must be repaid from the gross settlement proceeds. Interest on these loans must also be paid. On the other side of the equation, the association may be due interest that has accrued on the trust account for the time period before settlement proceeds are disbursed.

3. Expense reimbursements. Law firms typically cover the administrative costs of a lawsuit—court reporting fees, filing fees, copying, and travel expenses. These costs must also be reimbursed from the gross settlement proceeds.

4. Temporary repair costs. Contractors who make temporary repairs may agree to wait until the suit is settled before invoicing the association for some or all of their services. These expenses must be paid from the settlement proceeds.

5. Disbursements to the association or individual homeowners. The bottom line of any settlement accounting is the monies available for reconstruction after deducting the expenses listed above.

At the same time the association attorney is collecting settlement checks, he or she also prepares an expense accounting for the review and approval of the community manager and board (or homeowners, if the case involves individual owners). Documentation such as invoices from experts, temporary repair invoices, and backup for all other costs should be included.

The manager and board should review the accounting carefully, resolve questions with the attorney, sign it, and return it to the attorney so that he or she has the needed authority to disburse the settlement proceeds.

Based on the time it takes to collect settlement funds in a large construction defect case, the community manager may recommend to the board that the association's attorneys make periodic payments from the attorneys' trust account to an investment account established by the association. Trust accounts generally accrue interest at very low rates, whereas the association can earn a higher rate in its own settlement investment account.

Securing Settlement Proceeds

The reconstruction process can take anywhere from a few months to a number of years. During that time, the association will pay the reconstruction contractor periodically as work progresses and withhold the final payment until a final punch list has been completed.

Because the association may be disbursing substantial sums of money over potentially long periods, the board should select a financial institution and establish an investment account for the net proceeds. Based on recommendations from the community manager or others within the management company or the community, the board should consider several institutions and compare interest rates, fees, and the institution's strengths before making a selection.

The Role of Insurance

In most instances, construction defect claims are resolved by insurance companies making payments to the association on behalf of clients. It isn't unusual for dozens of parties to contribute to a settlement, and many of the contributing parties may in turn receive contributions from several different insurance carriers.

Construction defect settlements or verdicts are funded not only by general contractor/developers but also by myriad subcontractors. Clients often ask how the settlements or verdicts will be funded, and the reality is that the insurance industry ends up serving as what one West Coast superior court judge refers to as "the mother's milk" of the construction defect industry.

The various defendants and cross defendants will rely heavily on their commercial general liability policies to fund eventual resolution of these cases. It thus becomes imperative for the attorney to ascertain the existence and status of such policies early in the litigation. Furthermore, in this day and age, the association attorney needs to be well versed in insurance coverage law. A detailed analysis of coverage law is beyond the scope of this text.

Triggers of Coverage

The trigger of coverage of liability policies in a construction defect context has been litigated in jurisdictions throughout the United States. Differing policy language and factual scenarios have been treated differently by courts of various states, as well as by courts within the same state. At times, actual splits in authority have arisen, making the precise trigger difficult to predict. However, in every case, it's most prudent to start the trigger of coverage analysis by reviewing the specific policy language in the insurance contract. While Insurance Services Office, Inc. (ISO) forms are used widely, and key provisions from them are often the subject of reported cases, factual nuances and manuscripted policy provisions and endorsements often dictate application of triggers which may not, at first glance, seem to comport with precedent.

With occurrence-based liability policies such as the standard ISO form commercial general liability policy, consideration of the specific policy's language concerning trigger of coverage leads to the inquiry of when the injury or damage "occurred." Courts have found that the question of when injury or damage occurs can be answered in one of two ways; either 1. when it is discovered, or 2. while it is in progress, prior to discovery. However, under either approach, there should be some actual injury or damages resulting during the policy period. As such, generally five trigger-of-coverage approaches have been adopted by courts: 1. exposure, 2. manifestation, 3. continuous, or "triple-trigger," 4. injury-in-fact, and 5. wrongful act.

Types of Triggers

Exposure. The exposure theory provides that the policies in force at the time the injured person or property was exposed to the harm are the ones that provide coverage. While some courts have held that only the initial exposure to the injury triggers coverage, others have held that if the injury-producing event occurs during several successive policy periods, then all of those policies are triggered.

Manifestation. Courts seeking to apply a "bright-line" rule often adopt this trigger theory which, while not necessarily based on actual policy language, provides that the policy triggered is the one in force at the time a harm is first discovered.

Continuous/Triple. The "triple-trigger theory," as it has been called in some jurisdictions, has evolved into the more commonly referred to "continuous trigger" theory, although some differences should be noted. The triple-trigger provides, hypothetically, that at least three policies are triggered: 1. the policy in force during the time of initial exposure, 2. the policy in force during the time of continued exposure, and 3. the policy in force at the time of manifestation. Theoretically could leave gaps resulting in non-triggered policies between each of the three triggers. However, under the continuous trigger theory, all policies in force from the time of initial exposure to the date of the filing of the lawsuit seeking recovery, and possibly thereafter, are triggered.

Injury-in-Fact. This theory provides that all policies in force at the time the claimant suffered the actual injury are triggered.

Wrongful Act. Under this theory, coverage is triggered on the date the wrongful act is committed, regardless of whether actual harm has actually taken place.

For a state-by-state survey of insurance triggers of coverage, see Appendix 3.

CHAPTER 18

Recoverable Damages

The terms *damage* and *damages* are easily confused, but each has its own legal meaning. Damage is physical harm caused to property such as a building or mechanical equipment. Actual damage is required to trigger insurance coverage. On the other hand, *damages* are those sums of money that a court can award a successful plaintiff at the end of a trial to compensate for loss or injury, thus, they're also called *compensatory damages*.

Damages in construction defect cases may—depending on the jurisdiction—include the costs to repair the defective conditions as well as any physical damage that resulted, the reduction in property value caused by defective conditions, litigation costs, investigation costs, attorneys' fees, relocation costs while repairs are being made, and loss of use of the property.

How much money can be collected depends on where the property is. Many states have laws dealing specifically with damages in construction defect cases. Others determine damages according to the legal theory the suit is based on: is it being pursued for breach of warranty, negligence, strict liability? And finally, the damages that can be recovered in a construction defect case will depend on precedent—how much has been awarded by the courts previously?

What the Law Allows

The same legislation that mandates the steps to be taken before filing a lawsuit also define and limit the types of damages that can be recovered. For example, in California[1] homeowners can recover damages for:

- The value of repairing any violation of the standards and the cost of resulting damage.
- The cost of repairing damage caused by the repair efforts.
- The cost of removing and replacing improper repairs.
- Reasonable relocation and storage expenses.
- Lost business income—if the home was a place of business.
- The cost for investigating each defect.
- Other costs or fees recoverable by contract or statute.

What's missing from the statute in California after 2003 is damages for loss of property value, stigma damages, and attorneys' fees. On the other hand, the cost of repairing defects that have *not* caused damage to the structure (such as violations of building standards) can be recovered.

In Nevada,[2] a claimant in a construction defect action can recover only the following damages:

- Attorneys' fees.
- The cost of repairs already made and yet to be made.
- Temporary housing needed while repairs are made.
- The reduction in market value of the residence, resulting from structural failure.
- The loss of the use of a residence.
- The value of other property damaged by the construction defect.
- Experts' fees.
- Interest.

Elements of Compensatory Damage
Cost of Repair versus Diminution of Value

The first expense to be considered for compensation is the cost to repair the defect. A local expert with general contracting experience usually testifies about the repair costs. This expert should testify that making structural repairs to a finished, occupied home is far more expensive than the original construction because furnishings, fixtures, and personal property must be protected while repairs are underway. In fact, it's often less costly to relocate residents and their possessions during this time. Also, unlike original construction that can be done in volume, repairs must be done individually.

Diminution of property value is the difference between the value of the property with the defective conditions and the value without the defects. A local property appraiser can provide evidence of the diminution of property value.

HISTORICAL PERSPECTIVE: Damages in construction defect cases once depended on whether the association or homeowner claimed a tort theory, such as negligence or nuisance, or a contract theory, such as breach of express or implied warranties. In a tort, damages are generally the amount that will compensate the injured person for all the harm that's been caused, whether or not anyone could have anticipated it. By contrast, in a contract action, damages are generally the amount that will compensate the aggrieved person for all the harm caused by the breach.*

In recent years, the distinction between tort and contract damages in construction defect cases has been blurred by courts who calculate all damages according to either the cost to repair the defect or the diminution in the value of the property.** *California Civil Code Sections 3333 and 3300. **Raven's Cove Townhomes, Inc. v. Knuppe Development Co., 114 Cal.App.3d 783, 171 Cal.Rptr. 334 (1981).*

The Lesser-of Rule

Many courts have required that claimants be awarded the lesser of the cost to repair the defective condition or the diminution in value. Even in states that have embraced the lesser-of rule, courts frequently depart from it and award the cost of repair, regardless of whether it is the lesser amount.[3]

Courts also depart from the lesser-of rule when damage is temporary. In such cases, courts have routinely applied the cost-of-repair rule. They reasoned that, if a building component is destroyed but replaceable, damages should be the amount needed to restore it to its original condition.[4] Some states limit temporary repair damages by not allowing the cost of repair to exceed the diminution in value.[5]

Damages that can be recovered in construction defect cases are also limited by the so-called economic loss rule. Economic losses are the cost to repair or replace defective building components that have not caused damage to other property. Typical examples of economic losses are the lack of fire stops, improper shear wall fastening, improper electrical wiring, and defective HVAC systems.

Litigation Costs

Litigation costs are the expenses incurred in the process of resolving a legal case. These costs may include filing fees, court reporter fees, jury fees and expenses, witness fees, interpreter fees, service-of-process fees, expert fees, costs of bonds or undertakings, photocopies, long distance phone charges, postage, travel and lodging, and legal research.

The judge, at his or her discretion, can award reasonable and necessary costs to the prevailing party in a lawsuit—that is, the loser pays the winner's expenses. The prevailing party has to document the costs and show that they were necessary to the lawsuit.[6]

If the opposing sides reach a settlement before the case goes to trial and judgment, neither prevails and costs cannot be awarded. In many jurisdictions, final judgment can be entered even though the parties have not resolved litigation cost issues.

Attorneys' Fees

Most states follow what is called the *American rule*, which specifies that each party pays its own attorneys' fees—unless a contract or a statute says that fees will be awarded to the prevailing party. Some states follow the *English rule*, which says that the prevailing party is entitled to an award of attorneys' fees whether or not the fees are authorized by contract or statute.[7] Examples of such contracts include the sale agreement between a developer and a homebuyer or, in a case involving a community association, the CC&Rs. For instance, in the case of *Raven's Cove Townhomes, Inc. v. Knuppe Development Co.*,[8] the association's CC&Rs provided that if the association had to take legal action to enforce its rights, attorneys' fees were to be a charge against the land and a personal obligation of the owner. The court used this clause to support an award of attorneys' fees on behalf of the association.

Some states, like Nevada, have enacted specific statutes allowing attorneys' fees as an element of damages in construction defect cases.[9]

Like litigation costs, attorneys' fees must be documented and the association must show that they were necessary and reasonable. Some judges consider the value of the paralegals' and law clerks' time and apply the same standard of necessity and reasonableness that they apply to the lawyer's time. Generally, if an attorney is handling a case on contingency, the percentage of the contingency places a ceiling on the attorneys' fees that can be awarded, although the trial judge can award less.

Expert Fees

Because modern residential construction and government regulations are very complex, associations, homeowners, and even builders and developers must rely on experts in the fields of architecture, civil and soils engineering, structural engineering, electrical engineering, mechanical engineering, metallurgy, industrial hygiene, general contracting, and property appraisal for opinions and guidance.

These experts conduct inspections and tests, make recommendations about how to repair defects, present their findings during settlement discussions and mediation, and provide depositions and trial testimony.

As a general rule, experts are paid by the people who hire them; but, like all rules, there are exceptions. Some states allow a property owner to recover the fees for the expert to make recommendations on how to repair defects. Some courts say that expert's fees are recoverable simply as a portion of the cost-of-repair.[10] Others rationalize that they are recoverable as a cost incidental to the repair.[11] Moreover, an expert may be hired by one party—for example, the association—and also asked by the opposing party—perhaps the developer—to give deposition testimony. In this case, the developer would pay the expert for his or her time spent in deposition.

For the most part, it's up to the judge whether some or all of the experts' fees will be awarded, and the prevailing party must prove the fees were necessary and reasonable.

Relocation and Alternate Living Accommodations

As noted previously, it's often less expensive to repair certain defects if the furniture and residents are moved out while repairs are underway. The cost of moving personal property to and from storage, the storage cost itself, and the cost of alternate accommodations for residents are normally included in compensatory damages. These costs may be allowed by statute or by judges who consider them part of the damages necessary to fully compensate the claimant.[12]

Loss of Use

Some jurisdictions allow damages for the loss of use of property if it cannot be occupied because it's too dangerous or defective construction needs to be repaired. Loss of use is measured by the rental value of similar property in the community.

Punitive Damages

In addition to recovering the actual costs resulting from a construction defect, sometimes an association or homeowner may seek *punitive* damages—additional amounts intended to punish the offending party.

Punitive damages are only appropriate in certain circumstances. The most common is fraud. For example, if a developer is aware of a defect in the way the soil was prepared for construction and instructs the sales staff to keep it quiet, that's tantamount to fraud.[13] Occasionally punitive damages are awarded for negligence, if the defendant consciously disregarded the safety of others;[14] and, occasionally they're awarded for strict liability, if a person (rather than property) is injured.[15]

Punitive damages alone can't be awarded—there must first be actual damages.[16] Also, there is no rule specifying how much should be awarded in punitive damages, but the amount should be in reasonable proportion to the actual damages.[17]

Emotional Distress

In construction defect claims, *emotional distress* includes anxiety, worry, shock, humiliation, grief, and indignity resulting from negligent or intentional misconduct by the defendant. Awards for emotional distress are usually, but not always, for personal injury claims. In recent years, some have been for products liability, but even these involve personal injury, rather than property damage.[18] Damages for emotional distress have also been awarded for nuisance cases involving mudslides,[19] obstructed drains,[20] and aircraft noise.[21]

States differ about just how severe misconduct must be to cause emotional distress. Some states say the misconduct must rise to the level of fraud, malice, or other willful conduct[22]—others don't.[23]

Offset and Comparative Fault

Sometimes owners do things, or fail to do things, that aggravate a construction defect. For example, a minor leak may become a major mold problem if a homeowner refuses to let a contractor in to fix it. Similarly, a component like an HVAC system may fail if an association doesn't follow the manufacturer's recommended maintenance.[24] When this happens, logic suggests that the developer, builder, or manufacturer isn't entirely responsible for the problem. Consequently, the amount of damages paid to the owner or association are offset to some degree or possibly eliminated altogether.

In most jurisdictions, a judge, arbitrator, or jury can offset the compensatory damages by the amount of harm caused by the owner. And, in a few jurisdictions, they can completely bar an award of compensatory damages if they find evidence that the owner contributed to the damages. Also, if the harm caused by the owner is greater than—or even equal to—the harm caused by the builder or developer, it's possible that no compensatory damages will be awarded at all.

Homeowners aren't the only ones to contribute to defects. Sometimes subcontractors also bear some of the responsibility. Comparative fault is a legal doctrine that describes the percentage of responsibility assigned to each party who contributed to the damage—developer, owners, and subcontractors.

Endnotes

1. California Civil Code Section 944.

2. Nevada Revised Statutes Section 40.655.

3. Heninger v. Dunn, 101 Cal.App.3d 858, 162 Cal.Rptr. 104 (1980); Orndorff v. Christiana Community Builders, 217 Cal.App.3d 683, 266 Cal.Rptr. 193 (1990).

4. Stewart v. Cox, 55 Cal.2d 857, 13 Cal.Rptr. 521 (1961).

5. State v. Brockell, 187 Ariz. 226, 928 P.2d 650 (1996).

6. *See, for example,* Arizona Revised Statutes Section 12-332, California Code of Civil Procedure Section 1032.

7. Carroll v. Hanover Ins. Co., 266 Cal.App.2d 47, 71 Cal.Rptr. 868 (1968).

8. 114 Cal.App.3d 783, 171 Cal.Rptr. 334 (1981).

9. *See, for example,* Arizona Revised Statutes Section 12-341.01.

10. Stearman v. Centex Homes, 78 Cal.App.4th 611, 92 Cal.Rptr.2d 761 (2000); Regan Roofing Co. v. Superior Court, 21 Cal.App.4th 1685, 27 Cal.Rptr.2d 62 (1994).

11. Simon v. Coppola, 876 P.2d 10 (Colo.) 1993.

12. California Civil Code Section 3333.

13. Oakes v. McCarthy Co., 267 Cal.App.2d 231, 73 Cal.Rptr. 127 (1968).

14. Silberg v. California Life Ins. Co., 11 Cal.3d 452, 113 Cal.Rptr. 711 (1974); Penner v. Falk, 153 Cal.App.3d 858, 200 Cal.Rptr. 661 (1984).

15. See, for example, Hasson v. Ford Motor Co., 32 Cal.3d 388, 185 Cal.Rptr. 654 (1982).

16. Esparza v. Specht, 55 Cal.App.3d 1, 127 Cal.Rptr. 493 (1976).

17. Oakes v. McCarthy Co., 267 Cal.App.2d 231, 73 Cal.Rptr. 127 (1968).

18. Kately v. Wilkinson, 148 Cal.App.3d 576, 195 Cal.Rptr. 902 (1983); Shepard v. Superior Court, 76 Cal.App.3d 16, 142 Cal.Rptr. 612 (1977).

19. Spaulding v. Cameron, 127 Cal.App.2d 698, 274 P.2d 177 (1994).

20. Sturges v. Charles L. Harney, Inc., 165 Cal.App.2d 306, 331 P.2d 1072 (1958).

21. Greater Westchester Homeowners Ass'n v. City of Los Angeles, 26 Cal.3d 86, 160 Cal.Rptr. 733 (1979).

22. Slovek v. Board of County Commissioners, 697 P.2d 781 (Colo. 1986).

23. Nord v. Shoreline Savings Assoc., 116 Wash.2d 477, 805 P.2d 800 (1991).

24. California Civil Code Section 945.5.

PART SEVEN

The Morning After

CHAPTER 19

Reconstruction

W hether a construction defect case is resolved by settlement or a judgment rendered at trial, eventually funds will be available to the association or individual homeowners for reconstruction. Within 60 days of settlement or judgment, the community manager and members of the board will be very busy working on important tasks on parallel tracks. This chapter outlines these and other steps in the reconstruction process, from the time funds are received through reconstruction.

Setting Reconstruction Priorities

Reconstruction may proceed in stages, with the most important repairs accomplished first. This requires the association or homeowners to categorize the repairs and prioritize the categories. The association will seek reconstruction and repair bids based on these categories.

The association may turn to its experts to help prioritize repairs within their particular disciplines. For instance, the architect will assign the highest priority to repairs that involve life-safety issues—faulty electrical wiring, lack of sprinklers required by fire codes, and deck handrails that are too low.

The category of repairs with the next greatest priority generally involves water intrusion because leaks cause property damage. Other high-priority repairs may include blocked sewage systems, insufficient drainage, and soil deficiencies that damage slabs, foundations, and other structural components.

Landscaping and other cosmetic issues, like paint, are generally the lowest priorities.

Besides getting help from their own experts, associations or homeowners can also get help setting repair priorities from reconstruction consultants. Large communities, especially, hire specialized reconstruction consultants to manage the reconstruction process and administer reconstruction contracts.

Selecting a Reconstruction Contractor
Identifying and Interviewing Candidates

The association should identify candidates for the reconstruction work as soon after settlement as possible and appoint a committee to oversee the reconstruction process. The reconstruction committee will typically include the community manager, board members, and member representatives with construction experience such as architects, engineers, contractors, and attorneys.

The community manager should propose qualified reconstruction contractors to the association board or reconstruction committee based on his or her industry contacts, including the association's attorney, and personal experience in community associations.

Reconstruction contractors frequently are the same groups who make temporary repairs during a lawsuit. Therefore, the association may also want to include on its list of candidates some or all of the contractors who did its temporary repairs—assuming their skills, charges, and integrity were acceptable to the association. However, only rarely should an association simply select the contractor who performed temporary repairs to do the reconstruction work without a formal interviewing and bidding process.

The board, a subcommittee of the board, or the reconstruction committee should conduct the preliminary round of interviews—arranged by and including the community manager. Before the interviews begin, however, the association should ask each candidate to provide background material:

1. Company resumes, including the company's experience with community association reconstruction projects.

2. Client references, including contact information for boards of associations that the contractor has worked for.

3. Construction industry references, including architects, engineers, and reconstruction consultants.

4. A sample proposed contract form.

5. A schedule of labor rates and other standardized charges.

The association should call each candidate's references, eliminate any contractor who receives a negative rating, and interview all remaining candidates. If all interviews can be conducted on the same day, the board or committee can make a side-by-side evaluation while all candidates are fresh in their minds. Saturday is the best day to conduct interviews with candidate contractors, and any contractor not willing to attend a Saturday meeting probably isn't worth serious consideration. After the initial round of interviews, the reconstruction committee should narrow the candidates to two or three finalists.

Preparing the Scope-of-Repair

Each final candidate should be given a scope-of-repair that the manager or committee has prepared based on the cost-of-repair report and information provided by experts at the beginning of mediation. A reconstruction consultant can also provide information or help develop this document. Similar to a request for proposal, this document ensures that the association or homeowners receive "apples-to-apples" bids.

Repairs are prioritized on a list called the priority cost-of-repair, and it's separated into categories with life-safety issues at the top. It shows the association how many repairs it can afford and therefore how many to include on the scope-of-repair. For instance, if an association has $3 million dollars available for reconstruction and the cost of repairs totals $4 million, the association or committee needs to prioritize the repairs and include approximately 75 percent in the scope-of-repair for bidding purposes.

The bid package should be as detailed as possible, but also allow candidates to suggest alternate repair methods and products. For example, the repair recommendations may include replacing all wood siding throughout the community. The scope-of-repair should specify the type of siding to be used. However, contractors should be invited to suggest alternate siding products in the same price range.

The scope-of-repair is part of a bid package that also includes a deadline for submitting bids. Whether contractors submit their bids on time will be an indication of their future performance.

The Final Contractor Selection

The association or committee should review all bids carefully and invite some or all finalists to present their bids and alternate repair methods and products in person. Following these meetings, the committee may wish to conduct additional due diligence on each candidate. For example, additional reference checks may be desired. If feasible, association representatives should visit a jobsite where each finalist is working to observe how it's managed (is it organized, tidy, fenced for safety?) and talk to site superintendents, board members, community managers, and homeowners to learn about the quality of the contractor's work (is it timely, safe, and on budget?).

At this point, the field can generally be narrowed to a single candidate or negotiated between two finalists whose bids are close in terms of dollars.

In either event, the association shouldn't make its final decision strictly on the basis of the low-dollar bidder. The association may select a contractor who was not the lowest bidder, particularly if the two lowest bids were quite close in dollars and scope of work.

The Reconstruction Contract

The agreement the association signs with its chosen contractor is undoubtedly one of the most significant contracts a community association or group of homeowners will ever negotiate. They must take great care and rely on professionals like the association attorney, the project architect, and the reconstruction consultant for guidance before signing.

Sophisticated reconstruction contractors use any one of a number of standard form agreements, such as those prepared by the American Institute of Architects. Which form is appropriate will depend on the size of the project and the basis for payment—a stipulated sum, a time and materials sum, or some combination of the two. In almost all instances, reconstruction contracts are performed on a stipulated-sum or fixed-price basis. For a detailed explanation of the terms used in a stipulated-sum reconstruction contract, see Appendix 4.

Selecting the Reconstruction Architect

The Architect's Role in Reconstruction

Another key player in the reconstruction process is the architect.

First, the architect prepares all plans, drawings, and specifications necessary to obtain building permits for the reconstruction, and to guide the reconstruction contractor through the details of the work.

Second, the architect is the primary liaison between the association or home-owners and the reconstruction contractor: He or she helps finalize the scope-of-repair, assists in negotiating the terms of the reconstruction contract, participates in weekly jobsite meetings during the reconstruction, and ensures that the con-tractor is performing according to schedule and the scope-of-repair. In this regard, the architect is the project manager.

Third, the architect certifies that the contractor has completed work at vari ous stages according to the contract so that payments—including the final pay-ment—can be made on time.

The Final Architect Selection

During reconstruction, the association may want to use the same architect it worked with during litigation. This may not be appropriate if the architect who served on the expert team during defect investigations specializes in forensic work. Architects who have the most experience working with community associ-ations during reconstruction generally are not forensic specialists; therefore, this person will usually not be the same architect who served on the expert team.

When selecting an architect, the association or homeowners should consider any work history between the architect and the reconstruction contractor. Have they worked together—presently or in the past? Was the partnership successful— did they perform well and on budget?

The architect should be selected before the reconstruction contractor so that he or she can help prepare the scope-of-repair and negotiate the final terms of the reconstruction contract. Otherwise, the search for both positions should be conducted on parallel tracks.

The Architect's Contract

Architect candidates should present the association with a proposed architectural agreement—frequently a standard form of agreement for their professional services prepared by the American Institute of Architects (AIA). This isn't a take-it-or-leave-it proposition. All contracts, including the AIA contracts, should be closely scrutinized and modified by the association's attorney to meet the needs of the association.

The architect's fees and professional errors and omissions insurance coverage are the key contract provisions for negotiation. Architects' fees can be hourly, fixed, or a combination of the two. When fees are hourly, the contract should include a not-to-exceed provision. When fees are fixed, the contract should specifically define the architect's scope of work to prevent disputes about the architect's responsibilities or time. When fees are combined, the contract should include both. In a combined fee arrangement, the architect may charge a fixed fee for certain tasks like preparing the scope-of-work and an hourly fee for man-aging the reconstruction work.

The association should take a close look at the professional errors and omis-sions insurance provisions in the architect's contract. Many contracts provide that the architect's liability is limited to an amount not to exceed the architect's fee unless the association or individual homeowners elect to pay an additional charge for errors and omissions coverage for the architect. Generally, these types of contracts have several levels of coverage available in addition to the architect's fee.

Selecting a Reconstruction Consultant

In large reconstruction projects, particularly those for associations with more than 100 homes, the association may want to hire a reconstruction consultant, in addition to the architect. Reconstruction consultants may be licensed general contractors who have special expertise in reconstruction, or they may be firms that work in multiple disciplines, including architecture, engineering, and reconstruction.

The reconstruction consultant can assist with many of the same tasks listed above for the architect—preparing the priority scope-of-repair, selecting candidates for reconstruction contractor, and negotiating the reconstruction contract. In addition, the reconstruction consultant can serve as one of the board's representatives during reconstruction, participate in weekly jobsite meetings, and make presentations to the board and homeowners on the progress of the reconstruction.

Reconstruction consultants work on an hourly rate or a fixed fee, often equal to a percentage of the overall cost of the reconstruction. Like the agreement with the architect, an hourly-rate agreement with a reconstruction consultant should contain not-to-exceed provisions, and fixed-fee agreements should contain a detailed scope-of-work to reduce disputes during reconstruction.

Meetings before Reconstruction Begins

Reconstruction at a common interest development or in a large tract of single family homes can be very chaotic. Heavy traffic, construction noise, safety concerns, and tension are all side effects of the process. Community managers and board members can minimize the negative impacts of what should be, in the end, a positive process by maintaining clear, consistent lines of communication among everyone.

Organizational Meetings

After the reconstruction agreement has been signed, but before the reconstruction begins, the key players should convene a meeting to get organized. The key players for the association include the community manager, board representatives or the association's reconstruction committee, the contractor's representatives, the architect, the association's attorney, and the reconstruction consultant or project manager, if the association has hired one in addition to the architect.

Key players from the contractor's firm who will be involved in the actual reconstruction should be at the meeting so that the association's representatives can meet and get to know them by name. This will be an entirely different group than those who negotiated the reconstruction contract. (Owners and administrators negotiate contracts, while operations and estimating staff work on reconstruction.) The association representatives should get contact information for each of these contractor staff members so that they can reach them day or night as needed.

The meeting should begin with an overview from the homeowners' viewpoint made by the person who negotiated the reconstruction contract for the association or homeowners, perhaps the attorney. This person should begin the meeting by reviewing the reconstruction process, and he or she should set the tone by emphasizing that the objective is to complete the reconstruction safely, quickly, and on budget.

The association's representative should describe the scope-of-work, how the contractor was selected, and the highlights of the reconstruction agreement negotiations. The funds available for reconstruction should be reviewed in some detail to emphasize the importance of keeping the project on budget.

The reconstruction contractor should also make a presentation describing the project's schedule, safety procedures, the project office location, material staging areas, and the reconstruction sequence. Clear lines of communication should be established at the meeting between and among:

1. The contractor and architect.
2. The contractor and the board.
3. The contractor and the reconstruction consultant or project manager (if different from the architect).
4. The contractor and homeowners.

All meeting participants should agree on who will communicate with homeowners in what circumstances:

1. Scheduling interior work.
2. Informing homeowners of project progress.
3. Fielding homeowners' complaints and answering questions.
4. Answering homeowners' questions about the scope of work.
5. Answering homeowners' questions about the schedule.

All meeting attendees should review the procedures for administering the construction contract. It's important for the contractor to submit applications for progress payments and certificates for payments on time; and, it's equally important for the association to pay the contractor promptly. This first meeting is the time also for everyone to review and understand change order procedures.

Before adjourning the initial organizational meeting, the key players should agree to conduct weekly meetings during reconstruction. Not all key players need to attend these jobsite meetings. Generally attendance is limited to one association representative, the contractor, the architect, and the construction consultant or project manager.

Less frequent meetings involving the full association board or the reconstruction committee should also be scheduled in advance. At these meetings, attendees will review construction progress, actual costs versus contract amount, and new developments requiring significant changes in the agreement or significant change orders.

Meeting with the Members

In addition to the meeting of key players involved in the reconstruction process, the board should convene a meeting with all members before reconstruction begins. The homeowners will have many questions about the reconstruction

The Community Association's Reconstruction Team Roles and Responsibilities

The community association's reconstruction team comprises several important people and groups—each with an important role to play and responsibilities to all other players.

Association Board or Reconstruction Committee
- Define procedures to avoid problems and issues for homeowners in contractor operations.
- Establish a system to resolve construction-related problems quickly.
- Communicate regularly to keep homeowners and contractor's employees fully informed.
- Meet regularly with contractor staff and project managers (architects and reconstruction consultants) to track progress, plan future activities, and address issues and problems.
- Inspect worksites and material storage areas to assure safety, compliance with the reconstruction agreement, and satisfactory visual appearance.
- Pay the contractor promptly as work is completed satisfactorily.
- Establish methods (whether fining or withholding amenities or privileges) to encourage homeowners to comply with construction-related board decisions and to not interfere with contractor operations.

Homeowners
- Inform the board promptly of concerns and complaints through established procedures.
- Comply with procedures, instructions, and signs posted by the association and the contractor to assure safety and avoid disrupting the contractor's work.
- Cooperate with the board and contractor personnel to expedite work and reduce costs.
- Park vehicles only in allocated spaces consistent with reconstruction worksites.
- Offer suggestions and ideas to the board to avoid disruptions, problems, or complaints on any issues affecting the reconstruction process.
- Make units available to contractors as needed to expedite repairs.
- Ensure that guests comply with homeowner responsibilities.

Contractor
- Safety!
- Provide information periodically to all homeowners, and provide notice of construction involving their units well in advance.
- Ensure that material storage areas are neat, orderly, and locked up after work hours.
- Keep job trailers and other staging areas neat and orderly.

continued on page 164

continued from page 163

- Clean up all work areas promptly.
- Identify all employees and vehicles with badges and signs.
- Safeguard homeowner property and regulate noise.
- Define how the association and homeowners can support the contractor to save time and expense.
- Define a procedure to prevent homeowner intrusion into daily contractor operations.
- Define a procedure to address homeowner concerns and complaints.
- Appoint a responsible person who will act as the contractor's agent on site and who has the authority to address issues of concern promptly.
- Bring issues of concern to the attention of the board promptly.

Architect and Other Project Managers
- Meet weekly and as needed with contractor on site to assure reconstruction is proceeding according to the scope-of-work and schedule.
- Meet with contractor as required on site to define scope-of-work and cost for change orders.
- Keep the board and community manager informed of progress and any issues that require board decisions.
- Review applications for payment and promptly issue certificates for payment.
- Promptly resolve any objections to applications for payment.
- Ensure that certificates for payment are processed and checks delivered to contractor on time.
- Prepare plans and specifications as required to obtain permits.
- Monitor progress payments versus overall contract sum to keep the project on budget.
- Maintain records of change orders.
- Meet at least monthly with the board to review overall progress and contract sum versus actual cost.
- Report monthly to the board in writing the total cost of change orders and their impact on the budget.

Community Manager
- Assist the board, contractor, architect, and other project managers in facilitating communications with owners about the reconstruction.
- Assist the contractor in scheduling access to homeowner's units for repairs.
- Ensure that progress payments are processed in a timely manner.
- Provide monthly accounting to board on actual project cost versus contract sum.
- Conduct weekly site visits and recommend ways to improve communications with homeowners, site appearance, and safety.

process and how their individual units will be impacted, and these questions and concerns can best be addressed in a general membership meeting. At this meeting, the key people involved in the reconstruction process should be introduced and their roles and responsibilities explained.

Reconstruction

If the association plans properly when it selects the reconstruction contractor, architect, and other consultants, and if it negotiates the reconstruction contract carefully, the actual reconstruction process should run smoothly. The key to bringing the project to a successful conclusion will be for all the players to carry out the responsibilities described above. Additionally, community managers, board members, and construction committee members must constantly monitor certain broad areas:

1. Keep the homeowners informed of reconstruction progress and the requirements for entry into individual units.

2. Keep the project on schedule.

3. Keep the project on budget.

4. Ensure that the contractor is completing all items in the scope of work using skilled labor and the appropriate materials.

5. Ensure that workplace safety is maintained throughout the project.

6. Keep the lines of communications among all players open at all times.

Substantial Completion, Final Completion, and Final Payment

Substantial completion is that stage in the reconstruction work when homeowners can occupy or use their property for its intended use. When the architect determines that the work is substantially complete, he or she will issue a certificate of substantial completion that establishes the date and responsibilities of the owner and contractor for security, maintenance, heat, utilities, damage to the work, and insurance. The certificate of substantial completion will also specify the time when the contractor must finish all items on an accompanying punch list. The punch list includes all items that the contractor has yet to finish and any remaining responsibilities of the owner.

When the contractor has completed all items on the punch list, the contractor will notify the owner and architect that the work is ready for final inspection and acceptance. The architect, other project manager, and representatives of the association should walk the entire project with contractor representatives and verify that all punch list repairs have been satisfactorily completed.

Completing the punch list satisfactorily may require several site visits and considerable time to complete. When it's finished and the contract has been fully performed, the architect will issue a final certificate for payment stating that the work has been completed in accordance with the contract and the entire balance is due to the contractor. Although the contractor is entitled to final payment, it isn't actually due until the contractor completely releases all liens or provides a bond that indemnifies the association against any outstanding liens. If the association is compelled to discharge unsatisfied liens after making final payment, the contractor must refund all money to the association including legal costs and reasonable attorneys' fees.

When the association makes its final payment, it waives any further claims it might make, except for unsettled liens, as described above, failure of the work to comply with the contract, or claims that might arise from special warranties on components like siding, windows, and doors.

DEVELOPER'S PERSPECTIVE: A number of developers are now proactively eliminating defects from their construction by instituting quality-control programs. For example, several developers in the Northeast now use engineering firms to inspect construction while it's still underway or as soon as it's completed. With these inspections, developers are attempting to find and correct deficiencies as early as possible and to prevent claims once the association comes under owner control.

Identifying problems early has many advantages. Early detection allows developers to correct deficiencies easily—subcontractors are usually still working on site, so the developer has substantial leverage in getting defects repaired. Identifying problems early also allows developers to eliminate—rather than repeat—design problems, improper materials, or inferior methods as the project moves forward. Also very important: early detection saves money. Repair costs are significantly lower during construction—subcontractors, equipment, and materials are still available on site, and much less demolition is needed to make repairs. And, of course, the potential for later expenses to resolve claims is greatly reduced. Finally, early detection minimizes or eliminates disruption for residents.

Disclosure Requirements

Each state requires that certain information be disclosed when a construction defect case is settled. For instance, in California, homeowners associations are required to prepare and distribute to all members a pro forma operating budget that includes:[1]

1. The estimated revenue and expenses on an accrual basis.

2. A summary of the association's reserves; the amount of funds received either from a compensatory damage award or settlement for injuries to real or personal property; the expenditure or disposition of funds, including the amounts expended for the direct and indirect cost of repair of construction or design defects.

Additionally, California now defines reserve accounts as:[2]

1. Monies that the association's board has identified to defray the future repair or replacement of, or additions to, those major components that the association is obligated to maintain.

2. The funds received, and not yet spent, from either a compensatory damage award or settlement of a construction or design defect case.

In some instances, an association may elect to place some portion of its net proceeds from a construction defect settlement in its reserve accounts, rather than expend all sums in reconstruction. This may occur if a board decides to make some repairs, observe the structures, and subsequently decide if additional repairs are required.

Endnotes

1. California Civil Code Section 1365.
2. California Civil Code Section 1365.5(f).

PART EIGHT

Special Considerations

CHAPTER 20

High-Rise Building Claims

Community managers, board members, and attorneys now face a new challenge: construction defect claims involving high-rise buildings. Florida, Hawaii, Illinois, and New York have long been home to luxury high-rise condominium developments offering amenities such as valet service, health spas, fine dining, and personal services. These buildings are literally their own community with each including a homeowners association, common areas, separate areas, and the attendant maintenance and repair obligations.

The success of high-rise communities is due to the buildings' close proximity to work, shopping, and restaurants. Today, Manhattan alone has 391 high-rise condominium projects and Chicago has 350 high-rise condo buildings. Due to lack of available land, developers in other cities have decided it is time to build toward the sky.

With home prices skyrocketing, cities running out of land, and traffic congestion nearing gridlock, cities such as Los Angeles, San Diego, Las Vegas, and Phoenix are undergoing a transformation from horizontal to vertical growth. Many cities have passed ordinances to allow high-density, mixed use development in city centers. Even small towns eager to retain central cores are opting for vertical development by developing residences above shops or offices, reminiscent of European designs from past centuries.

Security and privacy are of ultimate concern to today's homebuyers. Residents of high-rise buildings buy into the lifestyle, in large part, to enjoy the peace of mind of a controlled access lobby, as well as services such as a concierge to receive packages and a doorman to screen guests.

With staff in the lobby 24 hours a day, high-rise living creates a sense of security and respite from the worry of modern life. Restricted access entry into the building, gated underground parking structures, and high speed elevators are commonplace. Extensive video surveillance, built-in security, and electronic access all add to the sense of security.

Luxury high-rise developments impress owners with gourmet kitchens, open living areas for entertaining, lots of glass, great views, fireplaces, room size terraces, wine storage, huge luxurious bathrooms, separate quarters for the maid, and private elevators. For instance, Regatta Seaside, a 224-unit condominium developed by Crescent Heights in Marina Del Rey, California, offers ocean, city, and mountain views through floor to ceiling windows. Unfortunately, the project now finds itself in construction defect litigation over claims for water intrusion, cracking marble, and myriad other defective conditions. Likewise, Turnberry One in Las Vegas, the first of four towers, is already in construction defect litigation. Additionally, Hawaiki Tower, a recently built luxury high rise in Honolulu, is in litigation.

In recent years, San Diego, Los Angeles, and Las Vegas have experienced a surge in building permits for condominiums, many of which are high-rise developments. This has not always been the case. Most of these developments are downtown, bringing people closer to their jobs, relieving traffic, improving air quality, and enhancing the basic quality of life.

Los Angeles, the nation's second largest city, currently has only 20 high-rise residential projects. But permits have been issued and construction has commenced on more than 50 new high-rise developments. In San Diego, Vancouver, Canada based BOSA Development Corporation is bringing its high-rise expertise to several projects both built and underway including The Grande at Santa Fe Place, which comprises twin 39-story, 222-unit luxury condominium towers downtown. Additionally, the Horizons project comprises two 25-unit towers in the heart of the Gas Lamp District. The bottom line is that cities like San Diego are running out of land. Thus, developers are changing their business plans, looking back into the city's core for development opportunities.

In Arizona, luxury is also on the rise, literally. Arizona's real estate market is changing in highly populated areas like greater Phoenix, with the valley seeing a virtual explosion of luxury townhome and condominium tower projects. Examples are Esplanade Place in Phoenix and Benton-Robb's proposed 426-unit Edgewater condo tower on Tempe Town Lake. Additionally, a new 12-story tower has been proposed for Anchor Centre.

In Las Vegas, hiked prices are leading builders to squeeze in more units per acre and are driving the skyline sky-high for some new residential developments in the region. Las Vegas is quickly growing up…and up, with some 25 high-rise developments under construction following the model of Turnberry Towers. The new term being used is "Vertical Vegas." As the city is running out of elbow room, the only direction builders can go is up.

Construction Issues Impacting High Rises

Will construction defect litigation, once commonplace in San Diego in the 1980's and Orange County in the 1990's, find its way to these developments and, if so, how will the cases differ from traditional wood framed (Type V) building defect litigation? There have always been construction defects, ever since the Parthenon was built. As these new developments are organized as common interest developments or homeowner associations, maintenance and repair of the common areas fall on the homeowner associations as does standing to sue for construction defect claims.

Issues that affect high rises, while similar to Type V construction, generally involve: water intrusion from roofs and windows; plumbing deficiencies; water migrating from floor to floor; sound attenuation; and electrical defects. Ensuring against water infiltration and providing for acoustical integrity is much more than a matter of good design. These are the two primary areas of potential liability for developers and design professionals in high-rise condominium design and development. Design against water infiltration in a high rise is a complex science that requires a team of specialists including a knowledgeable architect with substantial high-rise experience, a seasoned waterproofing consultant, and a curtain-wall specialist.

What do defects in these high-rise projects have in common? Primarily, waterproofing issues. In a low-rise project, a leak usually only involves one or two units. By contrast, leaks in high rises can occur at the top of a building or at a bathtub location and flow down floor to floor. Mechanical, electrical, and even elevator problems often follow water intrusion through high-rise buildings.

Then there is the M word. Mold is ugly, damaging, and hard to clean. High rises are not immune to mold claims, as the legal showdown over Hilton's Kalia Tower shows. Hilton Hotels Corporation has unleashed a litany of construction defect claims against some 18 construction firms and design professionals who helped design and build the $95 million hotel tower completed in May 2001.

Can these high-rise developments be built without being followed by construction defect litigation? Development of a high-rise residential tower is not without substantial risk, especially when a community association is involved. As new high rises are being completed, lawsuits such as the Hilton's Kalia Tower, Regatta Seaside, and Turnberry One, just to name a few, have followed.

Standing to Sue

So you are the manager of a new tower with 224 units. Who is the proper plaintiff if construction defect claims must be pursued in a high rise? All unit owners or the community association? As these new developments are being built as common interest developments or as traditional homeowner associations, it is the association that will have standing to sue for the following:

1. Common area defects;
2. Separate area damages caused by common area defects; and
3. Separate area damages that are integrally related with common area defects.

By contrast, where an issue arises as to separate areas but the defect is commonplace, such as defective floor tile, depending on the jurisdiction, the plaintiffs will either be individual homeowners or a class of homeowners. More and more individual issues are becoming part of either a class action or settlement with attendant release of the particular issue so that the developer does not have to be concerned with future litigation from homeowners.

A gray area frequently exists on standing to sue for water damage from plumbing, either within the common area walls or around bathtubs. Where separate area bathtubs leak due to tile integration issues, the leaks migrate from floor to floor. While one can make an argument that the bathtub tile is separate area for which individual homeowners would have standing, the damages occur to the common areas and continue from floor to floor, giving rise to standing to sue by the association.

It is imperative to determine at the outset what claims the association should pursue in a high-rise construction defect case. Where there are common issues occurring in individual units, a determination must be made whether the association has standing, either by statute or the association's governing documents. If not, counsel must seek class certification or join all of the unit owners as co-plaintiffs.

Inspections and Testing

When it comes time to inspect and test, the high rise can pose unique challenges. Observing and testing windows high in the sky is an example of the high-rise challenge. Hopefully there is a swing stage allowing easy access. However, in some cases, the swing stage may be one of the defects. In such a case, counsel and experts may have no choice but to have the window washers photograph the exterior surface from window to window.

High rises should be visually inspected from top to bottom. The roofing substrate and sheet metal copings must be examined. The stairwells also must be inspected for proper pressurization and fire protection. Likewise, the mechanical rooms and utility rooms must be examined along with the underground parking and waterproofing.

As for invasive testing, the common areas should be tested at random locations with test pits for waterproofing. Random samples of the exterior should be analyzed by a lab, along with deck surfaces, transitions, and windows. The key here is to know just how you plan on testing exterior surfaces 50 floors up. It can be done with the proper swing stage, but the procedure must be established prior to the testing to assure a random sampling.

Case Management

There is very little difference in managing a high-rise construction defect case and a traditional case except that case management orders (CMOs) should be utilized at an earlier stage. In states where there is either a builder's right to repair statute or a pre-filing mediation requirement, the association must serve the required notice on the developer. Next, it is the developer's responsibility to put the involved subcontractors, design professionals, and material suppliers on notice of the claims. During any prelitigation process, a CMO should be entered into even though there is no formal litigation yet. In this way, a mediator can be appointed and a schedule established for inspection, testing, and mediation, designed to expedite the process and avoid duplication.

Should the matter not settle during the prelitigation process, then the complaint is filed by the association, a cross-complaint is filed by the developer against allegedly responsible subcontractors, design professionals, and material suppliers, and the formal litigation process continues. Hopefully, all the data developed in the pre-litigation stage can be used during litigation. The following 10-step protocol should be utilized:

1. Plaintiff's visual inspections.
2. Plaintiff's invasive testing.
3. Plaintiff's expert presentation to mediator and all parties.
4. Plaintiff produces defect list and methodology for repair.

5. Plaintiff produces cost of repair.
6. Defense visual inspections.
7. Defense invasive inspections.
8. Expert meditations regarding existence of defects and repair methodology.
9. Insurance coverage meditations.
10. Final all-party meditations.

It is imperative that the mediator keeps this process flowing by following up with each of the parties to see what, if any, impediments there are to moving forward to settlement. High-rise cases should be handled in essentially the same manner as traditional construction defect cases, but with an emphasis on clearly understanding what is and is not within the scope of the association's standing.

Unique Aspects of High Rise Cases

Apart from the challenges of conducting inspections and testing in high-rise buildings, there are other unique features involved in litigating high-rise construction defect claims. Some of these features add to the complexity of high-rise cases as compared to traditional low-rise projects, while others simplify the claims resolution process.

While many of the same defects are found in high-rise projects, the nature of the project development and the relationships between the construction entities are different. In a typical low-rise condominium or single family development, construction occurs in phases. Frequently, different subcontractors are used not only in different phases but sometimes even in the same phase. During mediations, this type of development structure permits the mediator to focus on individual subcontractors with limited scopes of work, with the objective of carving out individual settlements. By contrast, in high-rise construction, subcontractors generally do not change. Because of the integrated fashion in which high rises are constructed, it can be very difficult to isolate one trade from another for the purpose of allocating settlement demands among individual subcontractors.

Compared to a low-rise project, high-rise cases involve mountains of paperwork. A common complaint in traditional residential construction defect cases is the lack of a complete paper trail. By contrast, in a high-rise case, the volume of available paper can be overwhelming. It is extremely important that the documentation in a high-rise case be thoroughly catalogued and that a CMO be utilized beginning in the prelitigation stage.

Construction documents in a high-rise case are generally much more sophisticated than in a traditional low-rise construction defect case. The project's plans and specifications are more complex. The contracts between and among developers, general contractors, design professionals, subcontractors, and material suppliers are also generally more sophisticated, particularly with respect to insurance coverage requirements and indemnity provisions. Because of the nature of the contractual relationships placing heavy responsibility on subcontractors and material suppliers, mediators typically find developer and general contractor entities are far less willing to accept a significant percentage of the liability in high rise cases. Instead, these entities look to the subcontractors, design professionals, and material suppliers to shoulder the lion's share of any settlement contributions. This places a tremendous strain on these parties and creates a high degree of tension between those carriers on the one hand and the carriers for the developer and general contractor on the other hand. While this dynamic exists in the traditional low-rise case, it is not as far reaching because the contract documents in a typical low-rise case are not of the same level of sophistication.

Another unique aspect of high-rise construction defect claims is in the insurance arena. In recent years, a new type of policy, known either as "owner selected insurance policies" or "contractor selected insurance policies" is being utilized. These policies provide all aspects of coverage required for a project under the umbrella of one policy. In a traditional low-rise project, the developer, general contractor, and subcontractors typically have separate policies for general liability coverage, workers' compensation coverage, and vehicular coverage. Under the owner selected insurance policies or contractor selected insurance policies, all coverages are contained in one policy. While there are a number of legal problems surrounding these new policies that have yet to be resolved through litigation, they are growing in popularity. One of the significant benefits of this type of policy is that one defense counsel will be handling the matter for a party being defended under one of these new policy types, rather than several defense counsel being involved for a single party. The single counsel handling a construction defect matter for a developer, for instance, streamlines the mediation process, particularly from the standpoint of the mediator.

As indicated above, high-rise buildings are not immune from toxic mold problems. As is the case in low-rise projects, mold typically originates from water intrusion or poor ventilation. All units in a high-rise project can be susceptible to mold because water from roof and window leaks can travel from floor to floor and unit to unit through common walls, ventilation systems, and plumbing. On the positive side, mold can be easier to remediate in a high-rise building because walls, ceilings, and floors are generally constructed of concrete and steel, rather than wood. Concrete and steel are not susceptible to the same degree of degradation as wood from water intrusion and mold.

PART NINE

Appendices

Appendix 1: State Standing-to-Sue Statutes

Alabama

A nonprofit association, in its name, may institute, defend, intervene, or participate in a judicial, administrative, or other governmental proceeding or in an arbitration, mediation, or any other form of alternative dispute resolution.

A nonprofit association may assert a claim in its name on behalf of its members if one or more members of the nonprofit association have standing to assert a claim in their own right, the interests the nonprofit association seeks to protect are germane to its purposes, and neither the claim asserted nor the relief requested requires the participation of a member. See Ala. Code Section 10-3B-8 (2004).

The association under the Alabama Uniform Condominium Act may institute, defend, or intervene in litigation or administrative proceedings in its own name on behalf of itself or two or more unit owners on matters affecting the condominium; and make contracts and incur liabilities. See Ala. Code Section 35-8A-302 (2004).

Alaska

The association for a common interest community may institute, defend, or intervene in litigation or administrative proceedings or seek injunctive relief for violations of its declaration, bylaws, or rules in its own name on behalf of itself or two or more unit owners on matters affecting the common interest community; and make contracts and incur liabilities. See Alaska Stat. Section 34.08.320 (2004).

Arizona

The association of a condominium may: Institute, defend or intervene in litigation or administrative proceedings in its own name on behalf of itself or two or more unit owners on matters affecting the condominium; and make contracts and incur liabilities. See Ariz. Rev. Stat. Section 33-1242 (2004).

Arkansas

A nonprofit association, in its name, may institute, defend, intervene, or participate in a judicial, administrative, or other governmental proceeding or in an arbitration, mediation, or any other form of alternative dispute resolution.

A nonprofit association may assert a claim in its name on behalf of its members if one or more members of the nonprofit association have standing to assert a claim in their own right, the interests the nonprofit association seeks to protect are germane to its purposes, and neither the claim asserted nor the relief requested requires the participation of a member. See Ark. Code Ann. Section 4-28-507 (2004).

California

An association established to manage a common interest development has standing to institute, defend, settle, or intervene in litigation, arbitration, mediation, or administrative proceedings in its own name as the real party in interest and without joining with it the individual owners of the common interest development, in matters pertaining to the following: enforcement of the governing documents; damage to the common area; damage to a separate interest that the association is obligated to maintain or repair; damage to a separate interest that arises out of, or is integrally related to, damage to the common area or a separate interest that the association is obligated to maintain or repair. See Cal. Civ. Code Section 383(a) (2004).

Colorado

A nonprofit association, in its name, may institute, defend, intervene, or participate in a judicial, administrative, or other governmental proceeding or in an arbitration, mediation, or any other form of alternative dispute resolution.

A nonprofit association may assert a claim in its name on behalf of its members if one or more members of the nonprofit association have standing to assert a claim in their own right, the interests the nonprofit association seeks to protect are germane to its purposes, and neither the claim asserted nor the relief requested requires the participation of a member. See Colo. Rev. Stat. Section 7-30-107 (2004).

Under the Colorado Common Interest Ownership Act, the association, without specific authorization in the declaration, may institute, defend, or intervene in litigation or administrative proceedings in its own name on behalf of itself or two or more unit owners on matters affecting the common interest community and make contracts and incur liabilities. See Colo. Rev. Stat. Section 38-33.3-302 (2004).

Connecticut

Under the Condominium Act, the unit owners' association, whether incorporated or unincorporated, shall have the power to sue and be sued in any court; appear on behalf of all unit owners before any officer, agency, board, commission or department of the state or any political subdivision thereof and appeal from any judgments, orders, decisions or decrees rendered by the same. See Conn. Gen. Stat. Section 47-80a (2003).

Under the Common Interest Ownership Act, the association, even if unincorporated, may institute, defend or intervene in litigation or administrative proceedings in its own name on behalf of itself or two or more unit owners on matters affecting the common interest community, and make contracts and incur liabilities. See Conn. Gen. Stat. Section 47-244 (2003).

Delaware

A nonprofit association, in its name, may institute, defend, intervene or participate in a judicial, administrative or other governmental proceeding or in an arbitration, mediation or any other form of alternative dispute resolution.

A nonprofit association may assert a claim in its name on behalf of its members if 1 or more members of the nonprofit association have standing to assert a claim in their own right, the interests the nonprofit association seeks to protect are germane to its purposes and neither the claim asserted nor the relief requested requires the participation of a member. See Del. Code Ann. tit. 6 Section 1907 (2004).

District of Columbia

A nonprofit association, in its name, may institute, defend, intervene, or participate in a judicial, administrative, or other governmental proceeding or in an arbitration, mediation, or any other form of alternative dispute resolution.

A nonprofit association may assert a claim in its name on behalf of its members if one or more members of the nonprofit association have standing to assert a claim in their own right, the interests the nonprofit association seeks to pro-

tect are germane to its purposes, and neither the claim asserted nor the relief requested requires the participation of a member. See D.C. Code Ann. Section 29-971.07 (2004).

Under the chapter on Control and Governance of Condominiums, the unit owners' association shall have the: Power to institute, defend, or intervene in litigation or administrative proceedings in the name of the unit owners' association on behalf of the unit owners' association or 2 or more unit owners on any matter that affects the condominium, and Power to make a contract or incur liability. See D.C. Code Ann. Section 42-1903.08 (2004).

Florida

The condominium association may contract, sue, or be sued with respect to the exercise or non-exercise of its powers. For these purposes, the powers of the association include, but are not limited to, the maintenance, management, and operation of the condominium property. After control of the association is obtained by unit owners other than the developer, the association may institute, maintain, settle, or appeal actions or hearings in its name on behalf of all unit owners concerning matters of common interest to most or all unit owners, including, but not limited to, the common elements; the roof and structural components of a building or other improvements; mechanical, electrical, and plumbing elements serving an improvement or a building; representations of the developer pertaining to any existing or proposed commonly used facilities; and protesting ad valorem taxes on commonly used facilities and on units; and may defend actions in eminent domain or bring inverse condemnation actions. If the association has the authority to maintain a class action, the association may be joined in an action as representative of that class with reference to litigation and disputes involving the matters for which the association could bring a class action. Nothing herein limits any statutory or common-law right of any individual unit owner or class of unit owners to bring any action without participation by the association which may otherwise be available. See Fla. Stat. Ann. Section 718.111 (2004).

After control of the homeowners' association is obtained by members other than the developer, the association may institute, maintain, settle, or appeal actions or hearings in its name on behalf of all members concerning matters of common interest to the members, including, but not limited to, the common areas; roof or structural components of a building, or other improvements for which the association is responsible; mechanical, electrical, or plumbing elements serving an improvement or building for which the association is responsible; representations of the developer pertaining to any existing or proposed commonly used facility; and protesting ad valorem taxes on commonly used facilities. See Fla. Stat. Ann. Section 720.303 (2004).

Georgia

An action may be maintained by and in the name of any unincorporated organization or association. See Ga. Code Ann. Section 9-2-24 (2004).

The condominium association shall have the capacity, power, and standing to institute, intervene in, prosecute, represent in, or defend, in its own name, litigation, administrative or other proceedings of any kind concerning claims or other matters relating to any portions of the units or common elements which the association has the responsibility to administer, repair, or maintain. See Ga. Code Ann. Section 44-3-106 (2004).

A tort action alleging or founded upon negligence or willful misconduct by any agent or employee of the [property owners'] association or in connection with the conditions of any portion of the instrument which the association has the responsibility to maintain shall be brought against the association. No lot owner shall be precluded from bringing such an action by virtue of his membership in the association. A judgment against the association arising from a tort action shall be a lien against the assets of the association.

The [property owners'] association shall have the capacity, power, and standing to institute, intervene, prosecute, represent, or defend in its own name litigation or administrative or other proceedings of any kind concerning claims or other matters relating to any portion of the lots or common area which the association has the responsibility to administer, repair, or maintain. See Ga. Code Ann. Section 44-3-231 (2004).

Hawaii

A nonprofit association, in its name, may institute, defend, intervene, or participate in a judicial, administrative, or other governmental proceeding or in an arbitration, mediation, or any other form of alternative dispute resolution.

A nonprofit association may assert a claim in its name on behalf of its members if one or more members of the nonprofit association have standing to assert a claim in their own right, the interests the nonprofit association seeks to protect are germane to its purposes, and neither the claim asserted nor the relief requested requires the participation of a member. See Haw. Rev. Stat. Section 429-7 (2004).

Without limiting the rights of any apartment owner, actions may be brought by the manager or board of directors [of condominiums], in either case in the discretion of the board of directors on behalf of two or more of the apartment owners, as their respective interests may appear, with respect to any cause of action relating to the common elements or more than one apartment. Service of process on two or more apartment owners in any action relating to the common elements or more than one apartment may be made on the person designated in the declaration to receive service of process. See Haw. Rev. Stat. Section 514a-93 (2004).

Idaho

A nonprofit association, in its name, may institute, defend, intervene or participate in a judicial, administrative or other governmental proceeding or in an arbitration, mediation or any other form of alternative dispute resolution.

A nonprofit association may assert a claim in its name on behalf of its members if one (1) or more members of the nonprofit association have standing to assert a claim in their own right, the interests the nonprofit association seeks to protect are germane to its purposes and neither the claim asserted nor the relief requested requires the participation of a member. See Idaho Code Section 53-707 (2004).

Without limiting the rights of any condominium owner, actions may be brought by the management body on behalf of two (2) or more of the condominium owners with respect to any cause of action relating to the common areas or more than one (1) unit. See Idaho Code Section 55-1513 (2004).

Illinois

A voluntary unincorporated association may sue and be sued in its own name, and may complain and defend in all actions. For the purposes of this Code, "voluntary unincorporated association" means any organization of 2 or more individuals formed for a common purpose, excluding a partnership or corporation. See 735 Ill. Comp. Stat. 5/2-209.1 (2004).

The unit owners' association is responsible for the overall administration of the property through its duly elected board of managers. Each unit owner shall be a member of the association. The association, whether or not it is incorporated, shall have those powers and responsibilities specified in the General Not For Profit Corporation Act of 1986 [805 ILCS 105/101.01 et seq.] that are not inconsistent with this Act or the condominium instruments, including but not limited to the power to acquire and hold title to land. Such land is not part of the common elements unless and until it has been added by an amendment of the condominium instruments, properly executed and placed of record as required by this Act. The association shall have and exercise all powers necessary or convenient to effect any or all of the purposes for which the association is organized, and to do every other act not inconsistent with law which may be appropriate to promote and attain the purposes set forth in this Act or in the condominium instruments. 765 Ill. Comp. Stat. 605/18.3 (2004).

Indiana

The board of directors, or the manager with the approval of the board of directors, may bring an action on behalf of two (2) or more of the condominium unit owners, as their respective interests appear, with respect to any cause of action relating to: (1) the common areas and facilities; or (2) more than one (1) condominium unit. See Ind. Code Ann. Section 32-25-9-2 (Michie 2004).

Iowa

Under the Multiple Housing Chapter, upon filing such articles the persons signing and acknowledging the same and their associates and successors shall become a body corporate with the name therein stated and shall have power to sue and be sued in its corporate name. See Iowa Code Section 499A.2 (2003).

Kansas

An association may bring an action to recover damages resulting from construction defects in any of the units, common elements or limited common elements of the common-interest community only:(1) Upon a vote of the units' owners to which at least a majority of the votes of

the members of the association are allocated; and (2) upon a vote of the executive board of the association.

An association may commence an action only upon a vote or written agreement of the owners of the units to which at least a majority of the votes of the members of the association are allocated. In such a case, the association shall provide written notice to the owner of each unit of the meeting at which the commencement of an action is to be considered or action is to be taken within 21 calendar days before the meeting. Kan. Stat. Ann. Section 60-4709 (2003).

Kentucky

Under the chapter on Business Corporations, each officer shall have the authority and shall perform the duties set forth in the bylaws or, to the extent consistent with the bylaws, the duties prescribed by the board of directors or by direction of an officer authorized by the board of directors to prescribe the duties of other officers. See Ky. Rev. Stat. Ann. Section 271B.8-410 (2004).

Louisiana

Subject to the provisions of the declaration, the association, even if unincorporated, may institute, defend, or intervene in litigation or administrative proceedings in its own name on behalf of itself or two or more unit owners on matters affecting the condominium, and make contracts and incur liabilities. See La. Rev. Stat. Ann. Section 9:1123.102 (West 2004).

Maine

Under the Maine Condominium Act, and subject to the provisions of the declaration, the association may institute, defend or intervene in litigation or administrative proceedings in its own name on behalf of itself or 2 or more unit owners on matters affecting the condominium; and make contracts and incur liabilities. See Me. Rev. Stat. Ann. tit. 1603-102 (2004).

Maryland

Council-Incorporation and powers. The council of unit owners [of condominiums] may be either incorporated as a nonstock corporation or unincorporated and it is subject to those provisions of Title 5, Subtitle 2 of the Corporations and Associations Article which are not inconsistent with this title. The council of unit owners has, subject to any provision of this title, and except as provided in paragraph (22) of this subsection, the declaration, and bylaws, the following powers: To sue and be sued, complain and defend, or intervene in litigation or administrative proceedings in its own name on behalf of itself or two or more unit owners on matters affecting the condominium; To transact its business, carry on its operations and exercise the powers provided in this subsection in any state, territory, district, or possession of the United States and in any foreign country; To make contracts and guarantees, incur liabilities and borrow money, sell, mortgage, lease, pledge, exchange, convey, transfer, and otherwise dispose of any part of its property and assets. See Md. Real Prop. Code Ann. Section 11-109 (2004).

Massachusetts

Such corporation, trust or association [of the condominiums] shall have, among its other powers, the following rights and powers: to conduct litigation and to be subject to suit as to any course of action involving the common areas and facilities or arising out of the enforcement of the by-laws, administrative rules or restrictions in the master deed. See Mass. Gen. Laws ch. 183A, Section 10 (2005).

Michigan

Under the Condominium Act, actions on behalf of and against the co-owners shall be brought in the name of the association of co-owners. The association of co-owners may assert, defend, or settle claims on behalf of all co-owners in connection with the common elements of the condominium project. See Mich. Comp. Laws Section 559.160 (2004).

All real estate owned or purchased by any association, created under and by virtue of this act, shall be held and owned and conveyance thereof shall be made in the association name; said association shall sue and be sued in their association name; and when suit is brought against any such association, service of process and other papers in such suit prior to appearance therein by defendant, shall be made upon the chairman, secretary or treasurer thereof: Provided, If no such officer reside in the county where the principal office or place or [of] business or [of] such association is located, or no such officer be found in such county within five [5] days after the commencement of such suit, service of such process and papers may be made upon such association by service thereof upon

any clerk, agent or attorney thereof in its office or place of business named in its articles of incorporation, which service shall be as complete and effective as if made upon each and every member of such association. See Mich. Comp. Laws Section 449.310 (2004).

Minnesota

Under the Uniform Condominium Act, unless limited by the provisions of the declaration, the [condominium] association may institute, defend, or intervene in litigation or administrative proceedings in its own name on behalf of itself or two or more unit owners on matters affecting the condominium. See Minn. Stat. Section 515A.3-102 (2004).

Under Minnesota Common Interest Ownership Act, except as provided in subsection (b), and subject to the provisions of the declaration or bylaws, the [owners'] association shall have the power to institute, defend, or intervene in litigation or administrative proceedings (i) in its own name on behalf of itself or two or more unit owners on matters affecting the common elements or other matters affecting the common interest community or, (ii) with the consent of the owners of the affected units on matters affecting only those units; and make contracts and incur liabilities. See Minn. Stat. Section 515B.3-102 (2004).

Mississippi

Each [nonprofit] corporation shall have and exercise all powers necessary or convenient to effect any or all of the purposes for which the corporation is organized including, without limitation, power: to sue and be sued, complain and defend, in its corporate name. See Miss. Code Ann. Section 79-11-151 (2004).

Missouri

Subject to the provisions of the declaration, the [condominium] association, even if unincorporated, may institute, defend, or intervene in litigation or administrative proceedings in its own name on behalf of itself or two or more unit owners on matters affecting the condominium and make contracts and incur liabilities. See Mo. Rev. Stat. Section 448.3-102 (2004).

Montana

Actions may be brought on behalf of two or more of the [condominium] unit owners, as their respective interests may appear, by the manager with respect to any cause of action relating to the common elements or more than one unit. See Mont. Code Ann. Section 70-23-901 (2004).

Nebraska

Under the Nebraska Condominium Act, except as provided in subsection (b) of this section and subject to the provisions of the declaration, the association, even if unincorporated, may institute, defend, or intervene in litigation or administrative proceedings in its own name on behalf of itself or two or more unit owners on matters affecting the condominium and make contracts and incur liabilities. See Neb. Rev. Stat. Section 76-860 (2004).

Under the Nebraska Nonprofit Corporation Act, unless its articles of incorporation provide otherwise, every corporation has perpetual duration and succession in its corporate name and has the same powers as an individual to do all things necessary or convenient to carry out its affairs including, without limitation, the power to sue and be sued, complain, and defend in its corporate name. See Neb. Rev. Stat. Section 21-1928 (2004)

Nevada

Except as otherwise provided in subsection 2, and subject to the provisions of the declaration, the association [of a common-interest community] may: institute, defend or intervene in litigation or administrative proceedings in its own name on behalf of itself or two or more units' owners on matters affecting the common-interest community; Make contracts and incur liabilities. See Nev. Rev. Stat. Section 116.3102 (2004).

New Hampshire

The declarant, every unit owner, and all those entitled to occupy a unit shall comply with all lawful provisions of this chapter and all provisions of the condominium instruments. Any lack of such compliance shall be grounds for an action or suit to recover sums due, for damages or injunctive relief, or for any other remedy available at law or in equity, maintainable by the unit owners' association, or by its board of directors or any managing agent on behalf of such association, or, in any proper case, by one or more aggrieved unit owners on their own behalf or as a class action. See N.H. Rev. Stat. Ann. Section 356-B:15 (2004).

New Jersey

Any unincorporated organization or association, consisting of seven or more persons and having a recognized name, may sue or be sued in any court of this state by such name in any civil action affecting its common property, rights and liabilities, with the same force and effect as regards such common property, rights and liabilities as if the action were prosecuted by or against all the members thereof. Such an action shall not abate by reason of the death, resignation, removal or legal incapacity of any officer of the organization or association or by reason of any change in its membership. See N.J. Stat. Ann. Section 2A:64-1 (2004).

The association provided for by the master deed shall be responsible for the administration and management of the condominium and condominium property, including but not limited to the conduct of all activities of common interest to the unit owners. The association may be any entity recognized by the laws of New Jersey, including but not limited to a business corporation or a nonprofit corporation. See N.J. Stat. Ann. Section 46:8B-12 (2004).

Subject to the provisions of the master deed, the bylaws, rules and regulations and the provisions of this act or other applicable law, the association shall have the following powers: Whether or not incorporated, the association shall be an entity which shall act through its officers and may enter into contracts, bring suit and be sued. If the association is not incorporated, it may be deemed to be an entity existing pursuant to this act and a majority of the members of the governing board or of the association, as the case may be, shall constitute a quorum for the transaction of business. Process may be served upon the association by serving any officer of the association or by serving the agent designated for service of process. Service of process upon the association shall not constitute service of process upon any individual unit owner. See N.J. Stat. Ann. Section 46:8B-15 (2004).

New Mexico

Except as provided in Subsection B of this section, and subject to the provisions of the declaration, the [condominium] association may institute, defend or intervene in litigation or administrative proceedings in its own name on behalf of itself or two or more unit owners on matters affecting the condominium; make contracts and incur liabilities. See N.M. Stat. Ann. Section 47-7C-2 (2004).

Such club or association may sue or be sued in its name without the individual members thereof being made parties to such suit, and may sue any member as a defendant in any matter arising out of his membership in said club or association or the termination thereof, and may recover judgment if necessary, for any dues or obligations due and owing by such member to the club or association, whether such member has ceased to become [be] such or not. See N.M. Stat. Ann. Section 53-10-5 (2004).

New York

Under the Condominium Act, actions may be brought or proceedings instituted by the board of managers in its discretion, on behalf of two or more of the unit owners, as their respective interests may appear, with respect to any cause of action relating to the common elements or more than one unit. Service of process on the unit owners in any action relating to the common elements or more than one unit may be made on the person designated in the declaration to receive service of process. See N.Y. Real Prop. Law Section 339-dd (Consol. 2004)

An action or special proceeding may be maintained, by the president or treasurer of an unincorporated association to recover any property, or upon any cause of action, for or upon which all the associates may maintain such an action or special proceeding, by reason of their interest or ownership therein, either jointly or in common. An action may likewise be maintained by such president or treasurer to recover from one or more members of such association his or their proportionate share of any moneys lawfully expended by such association for the benefit of such associates, or to enforce any lawful claim of such association against such member or members. See N.Y. Gen Assns Section 12 (Consol. 2004).

North Carolina

All unincorporated associations, organizations or societies, or general or limited partnerships, foreign or domestic, whether organized for profit or not, may hereafter sue or be sued under the name by which they are commonly known and called, or under which they are doing business, to the same extent as any other legal entity established by law and without naming any of the individual members composing it. Any judgments and executions against any such association, organization or society shall bind its real

and personal property in like manner as if it were incorporated. Any unincorporated association, organization, society, or general partnership bringing a suit in the name by which it is commonly known and called must allege the specific location of the recordation required by G.S. 66-68. See N.C. Gen. Stat. Section 1-69.1 (2004).

Unless the declaration expressly provides to the contrary, the association, even if unincorporated, may institute, defend, or intervene in its own name in litigation or administrative proceedings on matters affecting the condominium; make contracts and incur liabilities. See N.C. Gen. Stat. Section 47C-3-102 (2004).

Unless a master association is acting in the capacity of an association described in G.S. 47C-3-101, it may exercise the powers set forth in G.S. 47C-3-102(a)(2) only to the extent expressly permitted in the declarations of condominiums which are part of the master association or expressly described in the delegations of power from those condominiums to the master association. See N.C. Gen. Stat. Section 47C-2-120 (2004).

Unless the articles of incorporation or the declaration expressly provides to the contrary, the association [of a planned community] may institute, defend, or intervene in litigation or administrative proceedings on matters affecting the planned community; make contracts and incur liabilities. See N.C. Gen. Stat. Section 47F-3-102 (2004).

North Dakota

A [nonprofit] corporation has the powers set forth in this section, subject to any limitations provided in any other statute of this state or in its articles. A corporation may sue and be sued, complain and defend and participate as a party or otherwise in any legal, administrative, or arbitration proceeding, in its corporate name. See N.D. Cent. Code, Section 10-33-21 (2003).

Ohio

Any unincorporated association may contract or sue in behalf of those who are members and, in its own behalf, be sued as an entity under the name by which it is commonly known and called. See Ohio Rev. Code Ann. Section 1745.01 (2005).

In any action relating to the common elements or to any right, duty, or obligation possessed or imposed upon the unit owners association by statute or otherwise, the unit owners association may sue or be sued as a separate legal entity. In any action of that nature, service of summons or other process may be made upon the unit owners association by serving the process personally upon the president or other designated representative of the unit owners association named in the declaration to receive service of process, or the person named as statutory agent of the association if it is an incorporated entity, or by leaving the process at the residence or place of business of a person named in the declaration or named as statutory agent. Any action brought by or on behalf of the unit owners association shall be pursuant to authority granted by the board of directors. See Ohio Rev. Code Ann. Section 5311.20 (2005).

Unless otherwise provided in the declaration, the [condominium] unit owners association, through the board of directors, may exercise all powers of the association, including the power to do the following: Commence, defend, intervene in, settle, or compromise any civil, criminal, or administrative action or proceeding that is in the name of, or threatened against, the unit owners association, the board of directors, or the condominium property, or that involves two or more unit owners and relates to matters affecting the condominium property. See Ohio Rev. Code Ann. Section 5311.081 (2005).

Oklahoma

Except as otherwise provided by law, any person, corporation, partnership, or unincorporated association shall have capacity to sue or be sued in this state. See Okla. Stat. tit. 12, Section 2017 (2004).

Under the Unit Ownership Estate Act, actions may be brought on behalf of two or more of the unit owners, as their respective interests may appear, by the manager or board of managers, with respect to any cause of action relating to the common elements or more than one unit. Service of process on two or more unit owners in any action relating to the common elements or more than one unit may be made on the person designated in the declaration to receive service of process. See Okla. Stat. tit. 60, Section 529 (2004).

Oregon

1) Subject to subsection (2) of this section and except as otherwise provided in its declaration or bylaws, a homeowners association may:...

(e) Subject to subsection (4) of this section, initiate or intervene in litigation or administrative proceedings in its own name and without joining the individual owners in the following: ... (D) Matters relating to or affecting common property, including but not limited to actions for damage, destruction, impairment or loss of use of any common property; (E) Matters relating to or affecting the lots or interests of the owners including but not limited to damage, destruction, impairment or loss of use of a lot or portion thereof, if: (i) Resulting from a nuisance or a defect in or damage to common property; or (ii) Required to facilitate repair to any common property; and (F) Any other matter to which the association has standing under law or pursuant to the declaration or bylaws....See Or. Rev. Stat. Section 100.405 (2003).

Pennsylvania

Subject to the provisions of the declaration, the association, even if unincorporated, may institute, defend or intervene in litigation or administrative proceedings in its own name on behalf of itself or two or more unit owners on matters affecting the condominium; make contracts and incur liabilities. See 68 Pa. Cons. Stat. Section 3302 (2004).

Except as provided in subsection (b) and subject to the provisions of the declaration, the [cooperative] association may institute, defend or intervene in litigation or administrative proceedings in its own name on behalf of itself or two or more proprietary lessees on matters affecting the cooperative; make contracts and incur liabilities. See 68 Pa. Cons. Stat. Section 4302 (2004).

Except as provided in subsection (b) and subject to the provisions of the declaration and the limitations of this subpart, the [planned community] association, even if unincorporated, may institute, defend or intervene in litigation or administrative proceedings in its own name on behalf of itself or two or more unit owners on matters affecting the planned community; make contracts and incur liabilities. See 68 Pa. Cons. Stat. Section 5302 (2004).

Rhode Island

Except as provided in subsection (b), and subject to the provisions of the declaration, the association, even if unincorporated, may institute, defend, or intervene in litigation or administrative proceedings in its own name on behalf of itself or two (2) or more unit owners on matters affecting the condominium; make contracts and incur liabilities. See R.I. Gen. Laws Section 34-36.1-3.02 (2004).

South Carolina

Unless its articles of incorporation provide otherwise, every corporation has perpetual duration and succession in its corporate name and has the same powers as an individual to do all things necessary or convenient to carry out its business and affairs, including without limitation power to sue and be sued, complain, and defend in its corporate name. See S.C. Code Ann. Section 33-3-102 (2004)

South Dakota

Each corporation shall have power to sue and be sued, complain, and defend, in its corporate name. S.D. Codified Laws Section 47-2-58 (Michie 2004).

Tennessee

Unless its charter provides otherwise, every [nonprofit] corporation has perpetual duration and succession in its corporate name and has the same powers as an individual to do all things necessary or convenient to carry out its affairs, including, without limitation, power to sue and be sued, complain, and defend in its corporate name. See Tenn. Code Ann. Section 48-53-102 (2004).

Any partnership or other unincorporated association may sue and be sued in the name which it has assumed or by which it is known. [As amended July 1, 1979; and amended by order entered January 28, 2000, effective July 1, 2000.] See Tenn. Civ. Proc. Rule 17 (2004).

Texas

A nonprofit association, in its name, may institute, defend, intervene, or participate in a judicial, administrative, or other governmental proceeding or in an arbitration, mediation, or any other form of alternative dispute resolution.

A nonprofit association may assert a claim in its name on behalf of members of the nonprofit association if:
1. one or more of the nonprofit association's members have standing to assert a claim in their own right;
2. the interests the nonprofit association seeks to

protect are germane to its purposes; and
3. neither the claim asserted nor the relief requested requires the participation of a member. See Tex. Bus. Organizations Code Section 252.007 (2004).

Unless otherwise provided by the declaration, the [condominium] association, acting through its board, may institute, defend, intervene in, settle, or compromise litigation or administrative proceedings in its own name on behalf of itself or two or more unit owners on matters affecting the condominium; make contracts and incur liabilities relating to the operation of the condominium. See Tex. Prop. Code Ann. Section 82.102 (2004).

Utah

Without limiting the rights of any [condominium] unit owner, actions may be brought by the manager or management committee, in either case in the discretion of the management committee, on behalf of two or more of the unit owners, as their respective interest may appear, with respect to any cause of action relating to the common areas and facilities or more than one unit. Service of process on two or more unit owners in any action relating to the common areas and facilities or more than one unit may be made on the person designated in the declaration to receive service of process. See Utah Code Ann. Section 57-8-33 (2004).

Vermont

Except as provided in subsection (b) of this section, and subject to the provisions of the declaration, the [common interest community] association has the following powers: to initiate, defend or intervene in litigation or administrative proceedings in its name on behalf of itself or two or more unit owners on matters affecting the common interest community; to make contracts and incur liabilities. See Vt. Stat. Ann. tit. 27A Section 3-102 (2004).

Under the Condominium Ownership Act, without limiting the rights of any apartment or site owner, actions may be brought by the manager or board of directors (in either case in the discretion of the board of directors) on behalf of two or more of the apartment or site owners, as their respective interests may appear, with respect to any cause of action relating to the common areas and facilities of more than one apartment or site. Service of process on two or more apartment or site owners in any action relating to the common areas and facilities of more than one apartment or site may be made on the person designated in the declaration to receive service of process. Vt. Stat. Ann. tit. 27 Section 1327 (2004).

Virginia

All unincorporated associations or orders may sue and be sued under the name by which they are commonly known and called, or under which they do business, and judgments and executions against any such association or order shall bind its real and personal property in like manner as if it were incorporated. See Va. Code Ann. Section 8.01-15 (2004).

Washington

Without limiting the rights of any [condominium] apartment owner, actions may be brought as provided by law and by the rules of court by the manager or board of directors, in either case in the discretion of the board of directors, on behalf of two or more of the apartment owners, as their respective interests may appear, with respect to any cause of action relating to the common areas and facilities or more than one apartment. Service of process on two or more apartment owners in any action relating to the common areas and facilities or more than one apartment may be made on the person designated in the declaration to receive service of process. Actions relating to the common areas and facilities for damages arising out of tortious conduct shall be maintained only against the association of apartment owners and any judgment lien or other charge resulting therefrom shall be deemed a common expense, which judgment lien or other charge shall be removed from any apartment and its percentage of undivided interest in the common areas and facilities upon payment by the respective owner of his proportionate share thereof based on the percentage of undivided interest owned by such apartment owner. See Wash. Rev. Code Section 64.32.240 (2004).

Unless a master association is acting in the capacity of an association described in RCW 64.34.300, it may exercise the powers set forth in RCW 64.34.304(1)(b) only to the extent expressly permitted in the declarations of condominiums which are part of the master association or expressly described in the delegations of power from those condominiums to the master association. See Wash. Rev. Code Section 64.34.276 (2004).

Unless otherwise provided in the governing documents, an [homeowners'] association may institute, defend, or intervene in litigation or administrative proceedings in its own name on behalf of itself or two or more owners on matters affecting the homeowners' association, but not on behalf of owners involved in disputes that are not the responsibility of the association; make contracts and incur liabilities. See Wash. Rev. Code Section 64.38.020 (2004).

West Virginia

A nonprofit association, in its name, may institute, defend, intervene, or participate in a judicial, administrative or other governmental proceeding or in an arbitration, mediation or any other form of alternative dispute resolution.

A nonprofit association may assert a claim in its name on behalf of its members if one or more members of the nonprofit association have standing to assert a claim in their own right, the interests the nonprofit association seeks to protect are germane to its purposes, and neither the claim asserted nor the relief requested requires the participation of a member. W. Va. Code 36-11-7 (2004).

Except as provided in subsection (b), and subject to the provisions of the declaration, the [common interest community] association, even if unincorporated, may institute, defend, or intervene in litigation or administrative proceedings in its own name on behalf of itself or two or more unit owners on matters affecting the common interest community; make contracts and incur liabilities. See W. Va. Code 36B-3-102 (2004).

Wisconsin

A nonprofit association, in its name, may institute, defend, intervene or participate in a judicial, administrative or other governmental proceeding or in an arbitration, mediation or any other form of alternative dispute resolution. A nonprofit association may assert a claim in its name on behalf of its members if one or more members of the nonprofit association have standing to assert a claim in their own right, the interests that the nonprofit association seeks to protect are germane to its purposes, and neither the claim asserted nor the relief requested requires the participation of a member. See Wis. Stat. Section 184.07 (2004).

An [condominium] association has the power to sue on behalf of all unit owners. See Wis. Stat. Section 703.15 (2004).

Unless a master association is the only association for a condominium under Section 703.15 (1), it may exercise the powers set forth in Section 703.15 (3) only to the extent expressly permitted in the declarations that are associated with the master association or expressly described in the delegations of power from those condominiums to the master association. See Wis. Stat. Section 703.155 (2004).

Wyoming

A nonprofit association, in its name, may institute, defend, intervene or participate in a judicial, administrative or other governmental proceeding or in an arbitration, mediation or any other form of alternative dispute resolution.

A nonprofit association may assert a claim in its name on behalf of its members if one (1) or more members of the nonprofit association have standing to assert a claim in their own right, the interests the nonprofit association seeks to protect are germane to its purposes, and neither the claim asserted nor the relief requested requires the participation of a member. See Wyo. Stat. Ann. Section 17-22-107 (Michie 2004).

Appendix 2: Construction Defect Statutes of Limitations Laws for the 50 States and the District of Columbia

Alabama

Statute of Limitation: All civil actions in tort, contract or otherwise for recovery of damages (including personal injury and wrongful death actions) shall be commenced within two years of when action accrues or arises. See Ala. Code Section 6-5-221.

Statute of Repose: No relief for any cause of action which accrues or would have accrued more than 13 years after substantial completion. See Ala. Code Section 6-5-221.

Alaska

Statute of Limitation: A claimant may not begin an action covered under Alaska Stat. Section 09.45.881- .09.45.899 unless the notice of claim is given within 1 year after the discovery of the defect. See Alaska Stat. Section 09.10.054.

Statute of Repose: Cannot bring action for personal injury, death, or property damage unless commenced within 10 years of substantial completion or the last act alleged to have caused the injury or damage. See Alaska Stat. Section 09.10.055.

Tolling of the Statute of Limitation/Repose: Limitations imposed for an action under Alaska Stat. Section 09.45.881- .09.45.899 are tolled "between time the claimant serves notice under Alaska Stat. Section 09.45.881 and the time the claimant should reasonably understand the set-tlement under the procedures in Alaska Stat. Section 09.45.881- .09.45.899 will not succeed." See Alaska Stat. Section 09.10.054.

Arizona

Statute of Limitation: Personal injury and wrongful death actions must be brought within two years after the cause of action accrues. See Ariz. Rev. Stat. 12-542.

Statute of Repose: No action or arbitration based in contract can be initiated more than 8 years after substantial completion. If the injury occurred during the 8th year after substantial completion or was a latent defect not discovered until the 8th year, an action may be brought within one year (but not more than 9 years after substantial completion). See Ariz. Rev. Stat. 12-552.

Arkansas

Statute of Repose: No action in contract to recover damages caused by deficiency or for injury to real or personal property caused by such deficiency shall be brought more than five years after substantial completion of the improvement.

No action in tort or contract to recover damages for personal injury or wrongful death caused by any deficiency may be brought more than 4 years after substantial completion of the improvement.

In the case of personal injury or wrongful death, which injury occurred during the 3rd year after the substantial completion, and may be brought within 1 year after the date of the injury, irrespective of date of death, but not later than 5 years after substantial completion. See Ark. Code Ann. Section 16-56-112.

California

Statute of Repose: No action may be brought to recover under this title more than 10 years after substantial completion of the improvement but not later than the date of recordation of a valid notice of completion. See Cal. Civ. Code Section 941.

No action may be brought to recover damages from any person who develops real property or performs or furnishes the design or construction of an improvement to real property more than 10 years after the substantial completion of the development or improvement for any latent deficiency in the design or construction of an improvement to, or survey of, real property or injury to property, real or personal, arising out of any such latent deficiency. See Cal. Civ. Proc. Code Section 337.15.

No action shall be brought to recover damages from any person performing or furnishing the design or construction of an improvement to real property more than four years after the substantial completion of such improvement for any patent deficiency in the design or construction of an improvement to, or survey of, real property; injury to property, real or personal, arising out of any such patent deficiency; or injury to the person or for wrongful death arising out of any such patent deficiency.

If, by reason of such patent deficiency, an injury to property or the person or an injury causing wrongful death occurs during the fourth year after such substantial completion, an action in tort to recover damages for such an injury or wrongful death may be brought within one year after the date on which such injury occurred, irrespective of the date of death, but in no event may such an action be brought more than five years after the substantial completion of construction of such improvement. See Cal. Civ. Proc. Code Section 337.1.

Tolling of the Statute of Limitation/Repose: The statute of limitations is extended from the time of the claimant's original claim to 100 days after the repair is completed. If the builder fails to acknowledge the claim, elects to avoid the statutory procedure or fails to request an inspection, the time for filing an action is extended to 45 days after the time for the builder to respond to the notice of claim. See Cal. Civ. Code Section 927.

Colorado

Statute of Limitation: Tort actions, including but not limited to actions for negligence, trespass, malicious abuse of process, malicious prosecution, outrageous conduct, interference with relationships, and tortious breach of contract, all actions for strict liability, absolute liability, or failure to instruct or warn, and all actions for wrongful death shall be commenced within two years after the cause of action accrues, and not thereafter. See Colo. Rev. Stat. 13-80-102

Statute of Repose: All actions shall be brought within the time provided in section 13-80-102 after the claim for relief arises, and not thereafter, but in no case shall such an action be brought more than 6 years after the substantial completion of the improvement to the real property.

In case any such cause of action arises during the 5th or 6th year after substantial completion of the improvement to real property, said action shall be brought within two years after the date upon which said cause of action arises. See Colo. Rev. Stat. 13-80-104.

Tolling of the Statute of Limitation/Repose: If a notice of claim is sent to a construction professional in accordance with section 13-20-803.5 within the time prescribed for the filing of an action under any applicable statute of limitations or repose, then the statute of limitations or repose is tolled until sixty days after the completion of the notice of claim process described in section 13-20-803.5. See Colo. Rev. Stat. Section 13-20-805.

Connecticut

Statute of Repose: No action or arbitration in contract or tort to recover damages for any design deficiency or construction deficiency; for injury to property arising out of deficiency; for injury to person or wrongful death arising out of deficiency; or for contribution or indemnity shall be brought more than 7 years after substantial completion. If injury occurred during 7th year after substantial completion, an action in tort may be brought within 1 year after the date injury occurred, but in no event may action be brought later than 8 years after substantial completion. See Conn. Gen. Stat. Ann. Section 52-584a.

Delaware

Statute of Repose: No contract or tort action to recover damages for any deficiency (or for indemnification or contribution) shall be brought after the expiration of 6 years from whichever of the following dates shall be earlier:

1. The date of purported completion of all the work called for by the contract as provided by the contract;

2. The date when the statute of limitations commences to run in relation to the particular phase or segment of work performed pursuant to the contract in which deficiency occurred (where date included in contract);

3. The date when the statute of limitations commences to run in relation to the contract itself (where such date provided in contract);

4. The date when payment in full has been received by the person against whom the action is brought for the particular phase of such construction or phase of designing, planning etc.;

5. The date the person against whom the action is brought has received final payment in full under the contract;

6. The date when the construction of such an improvement as called for by the contract has been substantially completed;

7. The date when an improvement has been accepted by the owner;

8. For alleged personal injuries, the date upon which it is claimed that such alleged injuries were sustained; or after the period of limitations provided in the contract, if the contract provides such a period and if such period expires prior to the expiration of 2 years from whichever of the foregoing dates is earliest. See Del. Code Ann. tit. 10, Section 8127.

District of Columbia

Statute of Repose: Any action to recover damages for personal injury, injury to real or personal property, or wrongful death, resulting from the defective or unsafe condition of an improvement to real property, and for contribution or indemnity which is brought as a result of such injury or death, shall be barred unless in the case where injury is the basis of such action, such injury occurs within the 10-year period beginning on the date the improvement was substantially completed, or in the case where death is the basis of such action, either such death or the injury resulting in such death occurs within such 10-year period. See D.C. Code Ann. Section 12-310.

Florida

Statute of Repose: Within four years, an action must be filed that is founded on the design, planning, or construction of an improvement to real property, with the time running from

1. The date of actual possession by the owner,
2. The date of the issuance of a certificate of occupancy,
3. The date of abandonment of construction if not completed,
4. Or the date of completion or termination of the contract between the professional engineer, registered architect, or licensed contractor and his or her employer, whichever date is latest.

When the action involves a latent defect, the time runs from the time the defect is discovered or should have been discovered with the exercise of due diligence. In any event, the action must be commenced within 15 years after

1. The date of actual possession by the owner,
2. The date of the issuance of a certificate of occupancy,
3. The date of abandonment of construction if not completed,
4. Or the date of completion or termination of the contract between the professional engineer, registered architect, or licensed contractor and his or her employer, whichever date is lat-

est. See Fla. Stat. ch. 95.11.

Tolling of the Statute of Limitation/Repose: A claimant's mailing of the written notice of claim tolls the applicable statute of limitations relating to any person covered by this chapter and any bond surety until the later of: 90 days, or 120 days, as applicable, after receipt of the notice of claim or 30 days after the end of the repair period or payment period stated in the offer, if the claimant has accepted the offer. By stipulation of the parties, the period may be extended and the statute of limitations is tolled during the extension. See Fla. Stat. ch. 558.004.

Georgia

Statute of Repose: No action to recover damages for any deficiency or construction of an improvement to real property; for injury to property, real or personal, arising out of any such deficiency; or for injury to the person or for wrongful death arising out of any such deficiency shall be brought against any person more than eight years after substantial completion of the improvement.

In the case of such an injury to property or the person or such an injury causing wrongful death, which injury occurred during the 7th or 8th year after such substantial completion, an action in tort to recover damages for such an injury or wrongful death may be brought within two years after the date on which such injury occurred, irrespective of the date of death, but in no event may such an action be brought more than 10 years after the substantial completion of construction of such an improvement. See Ga. Code Ann. Section 9-3-51.

Tolling of the Statute of Limitation/Repose: If, during the notice, inspection, offer, acceptance, or repair process, an applicable limitations period would otherwise expire, the claimant may file an action against the contractor, but such action shall be immediately stayed until completion of the notice of claim process described in this part. This subsection shall not be construed to revive a statute of limitations period that has expired prior to the date on which a claimant's written notice of claim is served; or extend any applicable statute of repose. See Ga. Code Ann. 8-2-38.

Hawaii

Statute of Repose: No action to recover damages for any injury to property, real or personal, or for bodily injury or wrongful death, arising

191

out of any deficiency or neglect in the construction of an improvement to real property shall be commenced more than two years after the cause of action has accrued, but in any event not more than 10 years after the date of completion of the improvement. See Haw. Rev. Stat. Section 657-8.

Idaho

Statute of Limitation: Actions will be deemed to have accrued and the statute of limitations shall begin to run as to actions against any person by reason of his having performed or furnished the design, planning, supervision or construction of an improvement to real property, as follows: tort actions, if not previously accrued, shall accrue and the applicable limitation statute shall begin to run six years after the final completion of construction of such an improvement.

Contract actions shall accrue and the applicable limitation statute shall begin to run at the time of final completion of construction of such an improvement. See Idaho Code Section 5-241.

Within two years, an action must be filed to recover damages for professional malpractice, or for an injury to the person, or for the death of one caused by the wrongful act or neglect of another, including any such action arising from breach of an implied warranty or implied covenant. See Idaho Code Section 5-219.

Tolling of the Statute of Limitation/Repose: If a written notice of claim is served under this section within the time prescribed for the filing of an action under this chapter, the statute of limitations for construction-related claims is tolled until 60 days after the period of time during which the filing of an action is barred. See Idaho Code Section 6-2503.

Illinois

Statute of Repose: Actions based upon tort, contract or otherwise against any person for an act or omission of such person in the design or construction of an improvement to real property shall be commenced within four years from the time the person bringing an action, or his or her privity, knew or should reasonably have known of such act or omission.

No action based upon tort, contract or otherwise may be brought against any person for an act or omission of such person in the design or construction of an improvement to real property after 10 years have elapsed from the time of such act or omission. Any person who discovers

such act or omission prior to expiration of 10 years from the time of such act or omission shall in no event have less than four years to bring an action. See 735 Ill. Comp. Stat. 5/13-214.

Indiana

Statute of Repose. An action to recover damages, whether based upon contract, tort, nuisance, or another legal remedy, for a deficiency or an alleged deficiency in the design or construction of an improvement to real property; an injury to real or personal property arising out of a deficiency; or an injury or wrongful death of a person arising out of a deficiency may not be brought against any person who designs or constructs an improvement to the real property unless the action is commenced within the earlier of 10 years after the date of substantial completion of the improvement or 12 years after the completion and submission of plans and specifications to the owner if the action is for a deficiency in the design of the improvement. See Ind. Code Section 32-30-1-5.

If an injury to or wrongful death of a person occurs during the ninth or tenth year after substantial completion of an improvement to real property, an action in tort to recover damages for the injury or wrongful death may be brought within two years after the date on which the injury occurred, irrespective of the date of death. However, an action may not be brought more than 12 years after the substantial completion of construction of the improvement; or 14 years after the completion and submission of plans and specifications to the owner, if the action is for a deficiency in design, whichever comes first. See Ind. Code Section 32-30-1-6.

Tolling of the Statute of Limitation/Repose: If a written notice of claim is served under section 2 of this chapter within the time prescribed for the filing of an action against a construction professional based on an alleged construction defect, the applicable statute of limitations for construction related claims is tolled with respect to the alleged construction defect described in the notice of claim from the day on which the notice of claim is served until 60 days after the period of time during which the filing of an action is barred under this chapter. See Ind. Code Section 32-27-3-14.

Iowa

Statute of Repose: An action arising out of the unsafe or defective condition of an improvement to real property based on tort and implied warranty and for contribution and indemnity, and founded on injury to property, real or personal, or injury to the person or wrongful death, shall not be brought more than 15 years after the date on which occurred the act or omission of the defendant alleged in the action to have been the cause of the injury or death. See Iowa Code Section 614.1.

Kansas

Statute of Limitation: Within two years, actions for the following must be brought: an action for taking, detaining or injuring personal property, including actions for the specific recovery thereof; an action for injury to the rights of another, not arising on contract, and not herein enumerated; and an action for wrongful death.

The causes of action above shall not be deemed to have accrued until the act giving rise to the cause of action first causes substantial injury, or, if the fact of injury is not reasonably ascertainable until some time after the initial act, then the period of limitation shall not commence until the fact of injury becomes reasonably ascertainable to the injured party, but in no event shall an action be commenced more than 10 years beyond the time of the act giving rise to the cause of action. See Kan. Stat. Ann. Section 60-513.

Tolling of the Statute of Limitation/Repose: If the statute of limitations would expire during the time period necessary to allow the parties to comply with the provisions of this act, the statute of limitations shall be tolled if the claimant gives notice of the claim to the contractor within 90 days of entry of the order of dismissal of the action without prejudice pursuant to the notice requirements under Kan. Stat. Ann. Section 60-4702(a).

If the statute of limitations would expire during the time period necessary to allow the parties to comply with the provisions of this act, the claimant's notice of claim shall serve to toll the statute of limitations for 180 days after the latest of the following three dates: (1) The date the claimant personally serves or mails the notice of claim; (2) the date agreed upon for the contractor to make payment under subsection (c)(3) or (g)(2) of K.S.A. 2003 Supp. 60-4704, and amendments thereto; or (3) the date agreed upon for the contractor to completely remedy the construction defect under subsection (c)(2) or (g)(1) of K.S.A. 2003 Supp. 60-4704, and amendments thereto. See Kan. Stat. Ann. Section 60-4702.

Kentucky

Statute of Repose: An action for personal injuries suffered by any person against the builder of a home or other improvements actions shall be commenced within five (5) years after the cause of action accrued. This cause of action shall be deemed to accrue at the time of original occupancy of the improvements which the builder caused to be erected. See Ky. Rev. Stat. Ann. Section 413.120.

No action to recover damages, whether based upon contract or sounding in tort, resulting from or arising out of any deficiency in the construction components, design or construction of any improvement to real property, or for any injury to property, either real or personal, arising out of such deficiency, or for injury to the person or for wrongful death arising out of any such deficiency, shall be brought against any person after the expiration of seven (7) years following the substantial completion of such improvement.

In the case of such an injury to property or the person or wrongful death resulting from such injury, which injury occurred during the seventh year following substantial completion of such improvement, an action to recover damages for such injury or wrongful death may only be brought within one (1) year from the date upon which such injury occurred (irrespective of the date of death), but in no event may such an action be brought more than eight (8) years after the substantial completion of construction of such improvement. See Ky. Rev. Stat. Ann. 413.135.

Tolling of the Statute of Limitation/Repose: If a written notice of claim is served under KRS 411.258, then the statute of limitation for the underlying action is tolled until seventy-five (75) days after the expiration of the time frame agreed to by the parties as permitted in KRS 411.258(2), or the date established for inspection pursuant to KRS 411.258(2)(a), or the expiration of the time frame contained in KRS 411.258(4)(b), whichever occurs later. See Ky. Rev. Stat. Ann. Section 411.264.

Louisiana

Statute of Repose: An action against a contractor or an architect on account of defects of construction, renovation, or repair of buildings and other works is subject to a liberative prescription of ten years. See La. Civ. Code Ann. art. 3500.

No action, whether *ex contractu, ex delicto,* or otherwise, including but not limited to an action for failure to warn, to recover on a contract, or to recover damages, or otherwise arising out of an engagement of planning, construction, design, or building immovable or movable property which may include, without limitation, consultation, planning, designs or construction, demolition, or work, shall be brought against any person performing or furnishing land surveying services, as such term is defined in R.S. 37:682, including but not limited to those services preparatory to construction, or against any person performing or furnishing the design, planning, supervision, inspection, or observation of construction or the construction of immovables, or improvement to immovable property, including but not limited to a residential building contractor as defined in R.S. 37:2150.1(9):

1. More than five years after the date of registry in the mortgage office of acceptance of the work by owner.

2. If no such acceptance is recorded within six months from the date the owner has occupied or taken possession of the improvement, in whole or in part, more than five years after the improvement has been thus occupied by the owner.

If the person performing or furnishing the land surveying services, as such term is defined in R.S. 37:682, does not render the services preparatory to construction, or if the person furnishing such services or the design and planning preparatory to construction does not perform any inspection of the work, more than five years after he has completed the surveying or the design and planning with regard to actions against that person. See La. Rev. Stat. Ann. Section 9:2772.

Maine

Statute of Limitation: All civil actions shall be commenced within 6 years after the cause of action accrues and not afterwards, except actions on a judgment or decree of any court of record of the United States, or of any state or of a justice of the peace in this State, and except as otherwise specially provided. See Me. Rev. Stat. Ann. tit. 14, Section 752.

Statute of Repose: All civil actions for malpractice or professional negligence against architects or engineers duly licensed or registered under Title 32 shall be commenced within 4 years after

such malpractice or negligence is discovered, but in no event shall any such action be commenced more than 10 years after the substantial completion of the construction contract or the substantial completion of the services provided, if a construction contract is not involved. See Me. Rev. Stat. tit. 14, Section 752-A.

Maryland

Statute of Limitation: A civil action at law shall be filed within three years from the date it accrues unless another provision of the Code provides a different period of time within which an action shall be commenced. See Md. Code. Ann., Cts. & Jud. Proc. Section 5-101.

Statute of Repose: No cause of action for damages accrues and a person may not seek contribution or indemnity for damages incurred when wrongful death, personal injury, or injury to real or personal property resulting from the defective and unsafe condition of an improvement to real property occurs more than 20 years after the date the entire improvement first becomes available for its intended use. A cause of action for damages does not accrue and a person may not seek contribution or indemnity from any architect, professional engineer, or contractor for damages incurred when wrongful death, personal injury, or injury to real or personal property, resulting from the defective and unsafe condition of an improvement to real property, occurs more than 10 years after the date the entire improvement first became available for its intended use.

Upon accrual of a cause of action referred to above, an action shall be filed within three years. Section 5-108 does not apply if in a cause of action for damages for injury to real property that results from a defective and unsafe condition of an improvement to real property:

1. The defendant is a manufacturer of a product that contains asbestos;

2. The damages to an improvement to real property are caused by asbestos or a product that contains asbestos;

3. The improvement first became available for its intended use after July 1, 1953;

4. The improvement:

A. Is owned by a governmental entity and used for a public purpose; or

B. Is a public or private institution of elementary, secondary, or higher education; and

5. The complaint is filed by July 1, 1993.

A cause of action for an injury described in

Section 5-108 accrues when the injury or damage occurs. See Md. Code Ann., Cts. & Jud. Proc. Section 5-108.

Massachusetts

Statute of Repose: Action of tort for damages arising out of any deficiency or neglect in the design, planning, construction or general administration of an improvement to real property, other than that of a public agency shall be commenced only within three years next after the cause of action accrues; provided, however, that in no event shall such actions be commenced more than six years after the earlier of the dates of: (1) the opening of the improvement to use; or (2) substantial completion of the improvement and the taking of possession for occupancy by the owner. See Mass. Gen. Laws Ann. ch. 260, Section 2B.

Michigan

Statute of Repose: No person may maintain any action to recover damages for any injury to property, real or personal, or for bodily injury or wrongful death, arising out of the defective and unsafe condition of an improvement to real property, nor any action for contribution or indemnity for damages sustained as a result of such injury, against any state licensed architect or professional engineer performing or furnishing the design or supervision of construction of the improvement, or against any contractor making the improvement, more than six years after the time of occupancy of the completed improvement, use, or acceptance of the improvement, or 1 year after the defect is discovered or should have been discovered, provided that the defect constitutes the proximate cause of the injury or damage for which the action is brought and is the result of gross negligence on the part of the contractor or licensed architect or professional engineer. However, no such action shall be maintained more than 10 years after the time of occupancy of the completed improvement, use, or acceptance of the improvement. See Mich. Comp. Laws Section 600.5839.

Minnesota

Statute of Repose: No action by any person in contract, tort, or otherwise to recover damages for any injury to property, real or personal, or for bodily injury or wrongful death, arising out of the defective and unsafe condition of an improvement to real property, nor any action for contribution or indemnity for damages sustained on account of the injury, shall be brought against any person performing or furnishing the design, planning, supervision, materials, or observation of construction or construction of the improvement to real property or against the owner of the real property more than two years after discovery of the injury or, in the case of an action for contribution or indemnity, accrual of the cause of action, nor, in any event shall such a cause of action accrue more than ten years after substantial completion of the construction.

In the case of an action which accrues during the ninth or tenth year after substantial completion of the construction, an action to recover damages may be brought within two years after the date on which the action accrued, but in no event may an action be brought more than 12 years after substantial completion of the construction. See Minn. Stat. Ann. Section 541.051

Mississippi

Statute of Limitation: All actions for which no other period of limitation is prescribed shall be commenced within three (3) years next after the cause of such action accrued, and not after. See Miss. Code Ann. Section 15-1-49.

Statute of Repose: No action may be brought to recover damages for injury to property, real or personal, or for an injury to the person, arising out of any deficiency in the design, planning, supervision or observation of construction, or construction of an improvement to real property, and no action may be brought for contribution or indemnity for damages sustained on account of such injury except by prior written agreement providing for such contribution or indemnity, against any person, firm or corporation performing or furnishing the design, planning, supervision of construction or construction of such improvement to real property more than six (6) years after the written acceptance or actual occupancy or use, whichever occurs first, of such improvement by the owner thereof. This limitation shall apply to actions against persons, firms and corporations performing or furnishing the design, planning, supervision of construction or construction of such improvement to real property for the State of Mississippi or any agency, department, institution or political subdivision thereof as well as for any private or nongovernmental entity. See Miss. Code Ann. Section 15-1-41.

Missouri

Statute of Repose: Any action to recover damages for economic loss, personal injury, property damage or wrongful death arising out of a defective or unsafe condition of any improvement to real property, including any action for contribution or indemnity for damages sustained on account of the defect or unsafe condition, shall be commenced within ten years of the date on which such improvement is completed. See Mo. Ann. Stat. Section 516.97.

Montana

Statute of Repose: An action to recover damages (other than an action upon any contract, obligation, or liability founded upon an instrument in writing) resulting from or arising out of the design& construction, or observation of construction of any improvement to real property or resulting from or arising out of land surveying of real property may not be commenced more than 10 years after completion of the improvement or land surveying.

An action for damages for an injury that occurred during the 10th year after the completion of the improvement or land surveying may be commenced within 1 year after the occurrence of the injury. See Mont. Code Ann. Section 27-2-208.

Tolling of the Statute of Limitation/Repose: Prior to commencing an action against a construction professional for a construction defect, the claimant shall serve written notice of claim on the construction professional. The notice of claim must state that the claimant asserts a construction defect claim against the construction professional and must describe the claim in reasonable detail sufficient to determine the general nature of the defect. If a written notice of claim is served under this section within the time prescribed for the filing of an action under 27-2-208, the statute of limitations for construction defect claims is tolled.

If the construction professional disputes the claim or does not respond to the notice, the claimant may initiate an action. If the construction professional inspects the residence but does not proceed further to remedy the alleged defect, the claimant may initiate an action. If the claimant receives an offer from the construction professional and rejects it, the claimant may initiate an action. See Mont. Code Ann. Section 70-19-427.

Nebraska

Statute of Limitation: Any action to recover damages based on any alleged breach of warranty on improvements to real property or based on any alleged deficiency in the design or construction of an improvement to real property shall be commenced within four years after any alleged act or omission constituting such breach of warranty or deficiency. See Neb. Rev. Stat. Section 25-223.

Statute of Repose: If such cause of action to recover damages based on any alleged breach of warranty on improvements to real property or based on any alleged deficiency in the design or construction of an improvement to real property is not discovered and could not be reasonably discovered within such four-year period, or within one year preceding the expiration of such four-year period, then the cause of action may be commenced within two years from the date of such discovery or from the date of discovery of facts which would reasonably lead to such discovery, whichever is earlier.

In no event may any action be commenced to recover damages for an alleged breach of warranty on improvements to real property or deficiency in the design, planning, supervision, or observation of construction, or construction of an improvement to real property more than ten years beyond the time of the act giving rise to the cause of action. See Neb. Rev. Stat. Section 25-223.

Nevada

Statute of Limitation: An action for damages for injury or wrongful death caused by a deficiency (resulting from willful misconduct and fraudulently concealed deficiencies) in construction of improvements to real property may be commenced against the owner, occupier or any person performing or furnishing the design, planning, supervision or observation of construction, or the construction of an improvement to real property at any time after the substantial completion of such an improvement, for the recovery of damages for:

a. Any deficiency in the design, planning, supervision or observation of construction or the construction of such an improvement which is the result of his willful misconduct or which he fraudulently concealed;

b. Injury to real or personal property caused by any such deficiency; or

c. Injury to or the wrongful death of a person

caused by any such deficiency. See Nev. Rev. Stat. 11.202.

Statute of Repose: Except as otherwise provided in NRS 11.202 and 11.206, no action may be commenced against the owner, occupier or any person performing or furnishing the design, planning, supervision or observation of construction, or the construction of an improvement to real property more than 10 years after the substantial completion of such an improvement, for the recovery of damages for:

a. Any deficiency in the design, planning, supervision or observation of construction or the construction of such an improvement which is known or through the use of reasonable diligence should have been known to him;

b. Injury to real or personal property caused by any such deficiency; or

c. Injury to or the wrongful death of a person caused by any such deficiency.

If an injury occurs in the 10th year after the substantial completion of such an improvement, an action for damages for injury to property or person, damages for wrongful death resulting from such injury or damages for breach of contract may be commenced within two years after the date of such injury, irrespective of the date of death, but in no event may an action be commenced more than 12 years after the substantial completion of the improvement. See Nev. Rev. Stat. 11.203.

No action may be commenced against the owner, occupier or any person performing or furnishing the design, planning, supervision or observation of construction, or the construction, of an improvement to real property more than 8 years after the substantial completion of such an improvement, for the recovery of damages for:

a. Any latent deficiency in the design, planning, supervision or observation of construction or the construction of such an improvement;

b. Injury to real or personal property caused by any such deficiency; or

c. Injury to or the wrongful death of a person caused by any such deficiency.

If an injury occurs in the eighth year after the substantial completion of such an improvement, an action for damages for injury to property or person, damages for wrongful death resulting from such injury or damages for breach of contract may be commenced within two years after the date of such injury, irrespective of the date of death, but in no event may an action be commenced more than 10 years after the substantial

completion of the improvement. See Nev. Rev. Stat 11.204.

No action may be commenced against the owner, occupier or any person performing or furnishing the design, planning, supervision or observation of construction, or the construction of an improvement to real property more than six years after the substantial completion of such an improvement, for the recovery of damages for:

a. Any patent deficiency in the design, planning, supervision or observation of construction or the construction of such an improvement;

b. Injury to real or personal property caused by any such deficiency; or

c. Injury to or the wrongful death of a person caused by any such deficiency.

If an injury occurs in the sixth year after the substantial completion of such an improvement, an action for damages for injury to property or person, damages for wrongful death resulting from such injury or damages for breach of contract may be commenced within two years after the date of such injury, irrespective of the date of death, but in no event may an action be commenced more than eight years after the substantial completion of the improvement. See Nev. Rev. Stat. 11.205.

Tolling of the Statute of Limitation/Repose: Before a claimant commences an action or amends a complaint to add a cause of action for a constructional defect against a contractor, subcontractor, supplier or design professional the claimant must give notice to the contractor (or subcontractor if certain conditions apply). See Nev. Rev. Stat. 40.645.

Statutes of limitation or repose applicable to a claim based on a constructional defect governed by NRS 40.600 to 40.695, inclusive, are tolled from the time notice of the claim is given, until 30 days after mediation is concluded or waived in writing pursuant to NRS 40.680. See Nev. Rev. Stat. 40.695.

New Hampshire

Statute of Limitation: Except as otherwise provided by law, all personal actions, except actions for slander or libel, may be brought only within three years of the act or omission complained of, except that when the injury and its causal relationship to the act or omission were not discovered and could not reasonably have been discovered at the time of the act or omission, the action shall be commenced within three years of the time the plaintiff discovers, or in the exercise of reasonable diligence should have discovered, the injury and its causal relationship to the act or omission complained of. N.H. Rev. Stat. Ann. Section 508:4.

Statute of Repose: All actions to recover damages for injury to property, injury to the person, wrongful death or economic loss arising out of any deficiency in the creation of an improvement to real property, including without limitation the design, labor, materials, engineering, planning, surveying, construction, observation, supervision or inspection of that improvement, shall be brought within eight years from the date of substantial completion of the improvement, and not thereafter. N.H. Rev. Stat. Ann. Section 508:4b.

New Jersey

Statute of Repose: No action, whether in contract, in tort, or otherwise, to recover damages for any deficiency in the design or construction of an improvement to real property, or for any injury to property, real or personal, or for an injury to the person, or for bodily injury or wrongful death, arising out of the defective and unsafe condition of an improvement to real property, nor any action for contribution or indemnity for damages sustained on account of such injury, shall be brought against any person performing or furnishing the design or construction of such improvement to real property, more than 10 years after the performance or furnishing of such services and construction. See N.J. Stat. Ann. Section 2A:14-1.1.

New Mexico

Statute of Repose: No action to recover damages for any injury to property, real or personal, or for injury to the person, or for bodily injury or wrongful death, arising out of the defective or unsafe condition of a physical improvement to real property, nor any action for contribution or indemnity for damages so sustained, against any person performing or furnishing the construction or the design, planning, supervision, inspection or administration of construction of such improvement to real property, and on account of such activity, shall be brought after ten years from the date of substantial completion of such improvement; provided this limitation shall not apply to any action based on a contract, warranty or guarantee which contains express terms inconsistent herewith. N.M. Stat. Ann. 1978, Section 37-1-27.

New York

Statute of Repose: No claim for personal injury, or wrongful death or property damage, or a cross or third-party claim for contribution or indemnification arising out of an action for personal injury, wrongful death or property damage may be asserted against a licensed architect, engineer arising out of conduct by such licensed architect, engineer, land surveyor or landscape architect or such firm occurring more than ten years prior to the accrual of such claim shall be commenced or interposed against any such licensed architect, engineer, land surveyor or landscape architect or such firm unless it shall appear by and as an allegation in the complaint or necessary moving papers that the claimant has complied with the requirements of this section. N.Y. C.P.L.R. Section 214-d (Consolidated 2004).

Tolling of the Statute of Limitation/Repose: Any person asserting a claim for personal injury, wrongful death or property damage, or a cross or third-party claim for contribution or indemnification arising out of an action for personal injury, wrongful death or property damage, against a licensed architect, engineer shall give written notice of such claim to each such architect, engineer, land surveyor or landscape architect or such firm at least ninety days before the commencement of any action or proceeding against such licensed architect, engineer, land surveyor or landscape architect or such firm including any cross or third-party action or claim.

Service of a notice as provided in N.Y. C.P.L.R. Section 214-d shall toll the applicable statute of limitations to and including a period of one hundred twenty days following such service.

After the expiration of ninety days from service of the notice provided in subdivision one of this section, the claimant may commence or interpose an action, proceeding or cross or third-party claim against such licensed architect, engineer, land surveyor or landscape architect or such firm. The action shall proceed in every respect as if the action were one brought on account of conduct occurring less than ten years prior to the claim described in said action, unless the defendant architect, engineer, land surveyor or landscape architect or such firm shall have made a motion under rule three thousand two hundred eleven or three thousand two hundred twelve of this chapter, in which event the action shall be stayed pending determination of the motion. Such motion shall be granted upon a showing that such claimant has failed to comply with the notice of claim requirements of this section or for the reasons set forth in subdivision (h) of rule three thousand two hundred eleven or subdivision (i) of rule three thousand two hundred twelve of this chapter; provided, however, such motion shall not be granted if the moving party is in default of any disclosure obligation as set forth in subdivision four of this section. See N.Y. C.P.L.R. Section 214-d (Consolidated 2004).

North Carolina

Statute of Limitation: Except where otherwise provided by statute, a cause of action for malpractice arising out of the performance of or failure to perform professional services shall be deemed to accrue at the time of the occurrence of the last act of the defendant giving rise to the cause of action: Provided that whenever there is bodily injury to the person, economic or monetary loss, or a defect in or damage to property which originates under circumstances making the injury, loss, defect or damage not readily apparent to the claimant at the time of its origin, and the injury, loss, defect or damage is discovered or should reasonably be discovered by the claimant two or more years after the occurrence of the last act of the defendant giving rise to the cause of action, suit must be commenced within one year from the date discovery is made: Provided nothing herein shall be construed to reduce the statute of limitation in any such case below three years. Provided further, that in no event shall an action be commenced more than four years from the last act of the defendant giving rise to the cause of action: Provided further, that where damages are sought by reason of a foreign object, which has no therapeutic or diagnostic purpose or effect, having been left in the body, a person seeking damages for malpractice may commence an action therefore within one year after discovery thereof as hereinabove provided, but in no event may the action be commenced more than 10 years from the last act of the defendant giving rise to the cause of action. See N.C. Gen. Stat. Section 1-15(c) (2004).

Within three years, unless otherwise provided by statute, an action must be brought for personal injury or physical damage to claimant's property, the cause of action, except in causes of actions referred to in G.S. 1-15(c), shall not accrue until bodily harm to the claimant or physical damage to his property becomes appar-

ent or ought reasonably to have become apparent to the claimant, whichever event first occurs. Provided that no cause of action shall accrue more than 10 years from the last act or omission of the defendant giving rise to the cause of action. See N.C. Gen. Stat. Section 1-52 (2004).

Within two years, actions for damages on account of the death of a person caused by the wrongful act, neglect or fault of another under G.S. 28A-18-2 must be brought; the cause of action shall not accrue until the date of death. Provided that, whenever the decedent would have been barred, had he lived, from bringing an action for bodily harm because of the provisions of G.S. 1-15(c) or 1-52(16), no action for his death may be brought. See N.C. Gen. Stat. Section 1-53 (2004).

Statute of Repose: No action to recover damages based upon or arising out of the defective or unsafe condition of an improvement to real property shall be brought more than six years from the later of the specific last act or omission of the defendant giving rise to the cause of action or substantial completion of the improvement.

An action based upon or arising out of the defective or unsafe condition of an improvement to real property includes:

1. Actions to recover damages for breach of a contract to construct or repair an improvement to real property;

2. Actions to recover damages for the negligent construction or repair of an improvement to real property;

3. Actions to recover damages for personal injury, death or damage to property;

4. Actions to recover damages for economic or monetary loss;

5. Actions in contract or in tort or otherwise;

6. Actions for contribution indemnification for damages sustained on account of an action described in this subdivision;

7. Actions against a surety or guarantor of a defendant described in this subdivision;

8. Actions brought against any current or prior owner of the real property or improvement, or against any other person having a current or prior interest therein;

9. Actions against any person furnishing materials, or against any person who develops real property or who performs or furnishes the design, plans, specifications, surveying, supervision, testing or observation of construction, or construction of an improvement to real property,

or a repair to an improvement to real property.

This subdivision prescribes an outside limitation of six years from the later of the specific last act or omission or substantial completion, within which the limitations prescribed by G.S. 1-52 and 1-53 continue to run. For purposes of the three-year limitation prescribed by G.S. 1-52, a cause of action based upon or arising out of the defective or unsafe condition of an improvement to real property shall not accrue until the injury, loss, defect or damage becomes apparent or ought reasonably to have become apparent to the claimant. However, as provided in this subdivision, no action may be brought more than six years from the later of the specific last act or omission or substantial completion. N.C. Gen. Stat. Section 1-50 (2004).

North Dakota

Statute of Repose: No action, whether in contract, oral or written, in tort or otherwise, to recover damages:

a. For any deficiency in the design, planning, supervision, or observation of construction or construction of an improvement to real property;

b. For injury to property, real or personal, arising out of any such deficiency; or

c. For injury to the person or for wrongful death arising out of any such deficiency, may be brought against any person performing or furnishing the design, planning, supervision, or observation of construction, or construction of such an improvement more than ten years after substantial completion of such an improvement. In the case of such an injury to property or the person or such an injury causing wrongful death, which injury occurred during the tenth year after such substantial completion, an action in tort to recover damages for such an injury or wrongful death may be brought within two years after the date on which such injury occurred, irrespective of the date of death, but in no event may such an action be brought more than twelve years after the substantial completion of construction of such an improvement. Nothing in this section may be construed as extending the period prescribed by the laws of this state for the bringing of any action. See N.D. Cent. Code Section 28-01-44 (2004).

Ohio

Statute of Limitation: An action for an injury to the rights of the plaintiff not arising on contract nor enumerated in sections 1304.35, 2305.10 to 2305.12, and 2305.14 of the Revised Code shall be brought within four years after the cause thereof accrued. See Ohio Rev. Code Ann. Section 2305.09(D) (2004).

Oklahoma

Statute of Repose: No action in tort to recover damages

i. for any deficiency in the design, planning, supervision or observation of construction or construction of an improvement to real property,

ii. for injury to property, real or personal, arising out of any such deficiency, or

iii. for injury to the person or for wrongful death arising out of any such deficiency, shall be brought against any person owning, leasing, or in possession of such an improvement or performing or furnishing the design, planning, supervision or observation of construction or construction of such an improvement more than ten (10) years after substantial completion of such an improvement. See Okla. Stat. 12 Section 109 (2004).

In the case of such an injury to property or the person or such an injury causing wrongful death, which injury occurred during the fifth year after such substantial completion, an action in tort to recover damages for such an injury or wrongful death may be brought within two (2) years after the date on which such injury occurred (irrespective of the date of death) but in no event may such an action be brought more than seven (7) years after the substantial completion of construction of such an improvement. See Okla. Stat. 12 Section 110 (2004).

Oregon

Statute of Repose: An action against a person, whether in contract, tort or otherwise, arising from such person having performed the construction, alteration or repair of any improvement to real property & shall be commenced within the applicable period of limitation otherwise established by law; but in any event such action shall be commenced within 10 years from substantial completion or abandonment of such construction, alteration or repair of the improvement to real property.

An action against a person for the practice of architecture, as defined in ORS 671.010, the practice of landscape architecture, as defined in ORS 671.310, or the practice of engineering, as defined in ORS 672.005, to recover damages for injury to a person, property or to any interest in property, including damages for delay or economic loss, regardless of legal theory, arising from the construction, alteration or repair of any improvement to real property shall be commenced within two years from the date the injury or damage is first discovered or in the exercise of reasonable care should have been discovered; but in any event the action shall be commenced within 10 years from substantial completion or abandonment of the construction, alteration or repair. See Or. Rev. Stat. Section 12.135 (2004).

Tolling of the Statute of Limitation/Repose: If an owner sends a contractor, subcontractor or supplier a notice of defect within the time allowed for the owner to commence a court action against that contractor, subcontractor or supplier for a claim described in ORS 701.565, the time for the owner to commence the action shall be extended, notwithstanding any statute of limitation or statute of ultimate repose, until the later of:

a. One hundred and twenty days after the owner receives a written response from the contractor, subcontractor or supplier that received the notice of defect if the written response does not contain a written offer to perform remediation or pay monetary compensation for one or more of the defects or incidental damage described in the notice of defect;

b. One hundred and twenty days after the owner rejects a written offer by any contractor, subcontractor or supplier to perform remediation or pay monetary compensation for one or more of the defects or incidental damage described in the notice of defect; or

c. Thirty days after the date specified in an accepted written offer by which the offering contractor, subcontractor or supplier is to complete the remediation or complete payment of monetary compensation for one or more of the defects and any incidental damage described in the notice of defect. See Or. Rev. Stat. Section 701.585 (2003).

Pennsylvania

Statute of Repose: A civil action or proceeding brought against any person lawfully performing or furnishing the design or construction of any improvement to real property must be commenced within 12 years after completion of construction of such improvement to recover damages for:

1. Any deficiency in the design, planning,

supervision or observation of construction or construction of the improvement.

2. Injury to property, real or personal, arising out of any such deficiency.

3. Injury to the person or for wrongful death arising out of any such deficiency.

4. Contribution or indemnity for damages sustained on account of any injury mentioned in paragraph (2) or (3).

If an injury or wrongful death shall occur more than ten and within 12 years after completion of the improvement a civil action or proceeding within the scope of subsection (a) may be commenced within the time otherwise limited by this subchapter, but not later than 14 years after completion of construction of such improvement. See Pa. Cons. Stat. Ann. Section 5536 (2004).

Tolling of the Statute of Limitation/Repose: In an action relating to residential construction defects, the claimant must provide notice of a claim to the contractor at least 120 days before filing suit.

Service under this act shall toll all applicable statutes of limitations until 120 days after the receipt of the notice of claim. H.B. 2761, 187th Gen. Assem., Reg. Sess. (2003).

Rhode Island

Statute of Repose: No action (including arbitration proceedings) in tort to recover damages shall be brought against any architect or professional engineer who designed, planned, or supervised to any extent the construction of improvements to real property, or against any contractor or subcontractor who constructed the improvements to real property, or material suppliers who furnished materials for the construction of the improvements, on account of any deficiency in the design or construction of any such improvements or in the materials furnished for the improvements:

1. For injury to property, real or personal, arising out of any such deficiency;

2. For injury to the person or for wrongful death arising out of any such deficiency; or

3. For contribution or indemnity for damages sustained on account of any injury mentioned in subdivisions (1) and (2) hereof more than ten (10) years after substantial completion of such an improvement; provided, however, that this shall not be construed to extend the time in which actions may otherwise be brought under Section 9-1-13 and 9-1-14. See R.I. Gen. Laws Section 9-1-29 (2004).

South Carolina

Statute of Repose: No actions to recover damages based upon or arising out of the defective or unsafe condition of an improvement to real property may be brought more than thirteen years after substantial completion of such an improvement. For purposes of this section, an action based upon or arising out of the defective or unsafe condition of an improvement to real property includes:

1. An action to recover damages for breach of a contract to construct or repair an improvement to real property;

2. An action to recover damages for the negligent construction or repair of an improvement to real property;

3. An action to recover damages for personal injury, death, or damage to property;

4. An action to recover damages for economic or monetary loss;

5. An action in contract or in tort or otherwise;

6. An action for contribution or indemnification for damages sustained on account of an action described in this subdivision;

7. An action against a surety or guarantor of a defendant described in this section;

8. An action brought against any current or prior owner of the real property or improvement, or against any other person having a current or prior interest in the real property or improvement;

9. An action against owners or manufacturers of components, or against any person furnishing materials, or against any person who develops real property, or who performs or furnishes the design, plans, specifications, surveying, planning, supervision, testing, or observation of construction, or construction of an improvement to real property, or a repair to an improvement to real property. See S.C. Code Ann. Section 15-3-640 (2003).

Tolling of the Statute of Limitation/Repose: If the claimant files an action in court before first complying with the requirements of this article, on motion of a party to the action, the court shall stay the action until the claimant has complied with the requirements of this article. See S.C. Code Ann. Section 40-59-830 (2004).

South Dakota

Statute of Repose: No action to recover damages for any injury to real or personal property, for personal injury or death arising out of any deficiency in the design or construction, of an improvement to real property, nor any action for contribution or indemnity for damages sustained on account of such injury or death, may be brought against any person performing or furnishing the design, planning, supervision, inspection and observation of construction, or construction, of such an improvement more than ten years after substantial completion of such construction. The date of substantial completion shall be determined by the date when construction is sufficiently completed so that the owner or his representative can occupy or use the improvement for the use it was intended. See S.D. Codified Laws Section 15-2A-3 (2004).

In the case of such an injury to property or the person or such an injury causing death, which injury occurred during the tenth year after the substantial completion of such construction, an action to recover damages for such an injury or death may be brought within one year after the date on which such injury occurred, irrespective of the date of death; but in no event may such an action be brought more than eleven years after the substantial completion of construction of such an improvement. See S.D. Codified Laws Section 15-2A-5 (2004).

Tennessee

Statute of Repose: All actions to recover damages for any deficiency in the design or construction of an improvement to real property, for injury to property, real or personal, arising out of any such deficiency, or for injury to the person or for wrongful death arising out of any such deficiency, shall be brought against any person performing or furnishing the design, planning, supervision, observation of construction, construction of, or land surveying in connection with, such an improvement within four (4) years after substantial completion of such an improvement. See Tenn. Code Ann. Section 28-3-202 (2004).

In the case of such an injury to property or person or such injury causing wrongful death, which injury occurred during the fourth year after such substantial completion, an action in court to recover damages for such injury or wrongful death shall be brought within one (1) year after the date on which such injury occurred, without respect to the date of death of such injured person. Such action shall, in all events, be brought within five (5) years after the substantial completion of such an improvement.

See Tenn. Code Ann. Section 28-3-203 (2004).
Tolling of the Statute of Limitation/Repose: In actions brought against a contractor, subcontractor, supplier, or design professional related to an alleged construction defect, the claimant shall, before filing an action, serve written notice of claim on the contractor, subcontractor, supplier, or design professional, as applicable.

A claimant's written notice of claim tolls the applicable statute of limitations until the later of:

1. One hundred eighty (180) days after the contractor, subcontractor, supplier, or design professional receives the notice; or

2. Ninety (90) days after the end of the correction or repair period stated in the offer, if the claimant has accepted the offer. By stipulation of the parties, the period may be extended and the statute of limitations is tolled during the extension.

3. The procedures in this section apply to each alleged construction defect. However, a claimant may include multiple defects in one (1) notice of claim. See Tenn. Code Ann. Section 66-36-103 (2004).

Texas

Statute of Repose: A person must bring suit for damages for: injury, damage, or loss to real or personal property; personal injury; wrongful death; contribution; or indemnity against a registered or licensed architect, engineer, interior designer, or landscape architect in this state, who designs, plans, or inspects the construction of an improvement to real property or equipment attached to real property, not later than 10 years after the substantial completion of the improvement or the beginning of operation of the equipment in an action arising out of a defective or unsafe condition of the real property, the improvement, or the equipment.

If the claimant presents a written claim for damages, contribution, or indemnity to the architect, engineer, interior designer, or landscape architect within the 10-year limitations period, the period is extended for two years from the day the claim is presented. See Tex. Civ. Prac. & Rem. Code Ann. Section 16.008 (2004).

A claimant must bring suit for damages for: injury, damage, or loss to real or personal property; personal injury; wrongful death; contribution; or indemnity against a person who constructs or repairs an improvement to real property not later than 10 years after the substantial completion of the improvement in an action arising out of a defective or unsafe condition of

the real property or a deficiency in the construction or repair of the improvement.

If the claimant presents a written claim for damages, contribution, or indemnity to the person performing or furnishing the construction or repair work during the 10-year limitations period, the period is extended for two years from the date the claim is presented.

If the damage, injury, or death occurs during the 10th year of the limitations period, the claimant may bring suit not later than two years after the day the cause of action accrues. See Tex. Civ. Prac. & Rem. Code Ann. Section 16.009 (2004).

Tolling of the Statute of Limitation/Repose: This chapter does not create a cause of action or derivative liability or extend a limitations period. See Tex. Prop. Code Section 27.005 (2004).

Utah

Statute of Repose: An action by or against a provider based in contract or warranty shall be commenced within six years of the date of completion of the improvement or abandonment of construction. Where an express contract or warranty establishes a different period of limitations, the action shall be initiated within that limitations period.

All other actions by or against a provider shall be commenced within two years from the earlier of the date of discovery of a cause of action or the date upon which a cause of action should have been discovered through reasonable diligence. If the cause of action is discovered or discoverable before completion of the improvement or abandonment of construction, the two-year period begins to run upon completion or abandonment.

An action may not be commenced against a provider more than nine years after completion of the improvement or abandonment of construction. In the event the cause of action is discovered or discoverable in the eighth or ninth year of the nine-year period, the injured person shall have two additional years from that date to commence an action.

This section applies to all causes of action that accrue after May 3, 2003, notwithstanding that the improvement was completed or abandoned before May 3, 2004. See Utah Code Ann. Section 78-12-21.5 (2004).

Vermont

Statute of Limitation: A civil action, except one brought upon the judgment or decree of a court of record of the United States or of this or some other state, and except as otherwise provided, shall be commenced within six years after the cause of action accrues and not thereafter. See Vt. Stat. Ann. tit. 12 Section 511 (2004).

When a person entitled to bring a personal action is prevented from so doing by the fraudulent concealment of the cause of such action by the person against whom it lies, the period prior to the discovery of such cause of action shall be excluded in determining the time limited for the commencement thereof. See Vt. Stat. Ann. tit. 12 Section 555 (2004).

Virginia

Statute of Repose: No action to recover for any injury to property, real or personal, or for bodily injury or wrongful death, arising out of the defective and unsafe condition of an improvement to real property, nor any action for contribution or indemnity for damages sustained as a result of such injury, shall be brought against any person performing or furnishing the design, planning, surveying, supervision of construction, or construction of such improvement to real property more than five years after the performance or furnishing of such services and construction. See Va. Code Ann. Section 8.01-250 (2004).

Washington

Statute of Repose: All claims or causes of action as set forth in RCW 4.16.300 shall accrue, and the applicable statute of limitation shall begin to run only during the period within six years after substantial completion of construction, or during the period within six years after the termination of the services enumerated in RCW 4.16.300, whichever is later.

Any cause of action which has not accrued within six years after such substantial completion of construction, or within six years after such termination of services, whichever is later, shall be barred: provided that this limitation shall not be asserted as a defense by any owner, tenant or other person in possession and control of the improvement at the time such cause of action accrues. The limitations prescribed in this section apply to all claims or causes of action as set forth in RCW 4.16.300 brought in the name or for the benefit of the state which are made or commenced after June 11, 1986. See Wash. Rev. Code Section 4.16.310 (2004).

Tolling of the Statute of Limitation/Repose: If a written notice is filed under RCW 64.50.020 within the time prescribed for the filing of an action under this chapter, the period of time during which the filing of an action is barred under RCW 64.50.020 plus sixty days shall not be a part of the period limited for the commencement of an action, nor for the application of this section.

If a written notice of claim is served under RCW 64.50.020 within the time prescribed for the filing of an action under this chapter, the statutes of limitations for construction-related claims are tolled until sixty days after the period of time during which the filing of an action is barred under RCW 64.50.020. Wash. Rev. Stat. Section 4.16.325 (2004).

West Virginia

Statute of Repose: No action, whether in contract or in tort, for indemnity or otherwise, nor any action for contribution or indemnity to recover damages for any deficiency in the planning, design, surveying, observation or supervision of any construction or the actual construction of any improvement to real property, or, to recover damages for any injury to real or personal property, or, for an injury to a person or for bodily injury or wrongful death arising out of the defective or unsafe condition of any improvement to real property, may be brought more than ten years after the performance or furnishing of such services or construction: Provided, That the above period shall be tolled according to the provisions of section twenty-one [Section 55-2-21] of this article. The period of limitation provided in this section shall not commence until the improvement to the real property in question has been occupied or accepted by the owner of real property, whichever occurs first. See W. Va. Code Section 55-2-6a (2004).

Tolling of the Statute of Limitation/Repose: During negotiations under this article, if the running of the applicable statute of limitations would otherwise become a bar to a civil action, service of a claimant's written notice of claim pursuant to this article tolls the applicable statute of limitations until six months after the termination of negotiations under this article. See W. Va. Code Section 21-11a-10 (2004).

Wisconsin

Statute of Repose: No cause of action may accrue and no action may be commenced, including an action for contribution or indemnity, against the owner or occupier of the property or against any person involved in the improvement to real property after the end of the exposure period, to recover damages for any injury to property, for any injury to the person, or for wrongful death, arising out of any deficiency or defect in the design the construction of, or the furnishing of materials for, the improvement to real property. This subsection does not affect the rights of any person injured as the result of any defect in any material used in an improvement to real property to commence an action for damages against the manufacturer or producer of the material.

If a person sustains damages as the result of a deficiency or defect in an improvement to real property, and the statute of limitations applicable to the damages bars commencement of the cause of action before the end of the exposure period, the statute of limitations applicable to the damages applies.

If, as the result of a deficiency or defect in an improvement to real property, a person sustains damages during the period beginning on the first day of the 8th year and ending on the last day of the 10th year after the substantial completion of the improvement to real property, the time for commencing the action for the damages is extended for three years after the date on which the damages occurred. See Wis. Stat. Section 893.89 (2004).

Wyoming

Statute of Repose: Unless the parties to the contract agree otherwise, no action to recover damages, whether in tort, contract, indemnity or otherwise, shall be brought more than ten (10) years after substantial completion of an improvement to real property, against any person constructing, altering or repairing the improvement, manufacturing or furnishing materials incorporated in the improvement, or performing or furnishing services in the design or administration of construction contracts for:

i. Any deficiency in the design, planning, supervision, construction, surveying, manufacturing or supplying of materials or observation or management of construction;

ii. Injury to any property arising out of any deficiency listed in paragraph (i) of this subsection; or

iii. Injury to the person or wrongful death arising out of any deficiency listed in paragraph (i) of this subsection.

If an injury to property or person or an injury causing wrongful death occurs during the ninth year after substantial completion of the improvement to real property, an action to recover damages for the injury or wrongful death may be brought within one (1) year after the date on which the injury occurs. See Wyo. Stat. Ann. Section 1-3-111 (2004).

Appendix 3: Commercial General Liability Insurance Triggers of Coverage

This appendix is a state survey of triggers of coverage in reported cases, which have been applied in a continuous-loss, construction-defect setting. Where no such reported cases exist, a scenario most resembling a continuing loss is included for arguable analogy. For example, some sates have reported cases dealing with similar latent exposures such as environmental, asbestos, or other toxic tort fact pattern. Splits in authority have been noted.

The reader should use caution in applying the following information, bearing in mind that the trigger of coverage analysis should start by reviewing the specific policy language, followed by reviewing specific facts of a given claim to determine if the trigger of coverage is appropriate. Simply because a trigger has been applied in one type of case does not ensure that a different trigger will apply under a different fact pattern, or that the same trigger will be applied in the same type of case with slight variations in policy language or operative facts.

Alabama

Type of case: Asbestos bodily injury.
Facts: Insured sought coverage for asbestos bodily injury claims.
Finding: Exposure.
Comment: Court found that undisputed medical evidence supported the exposure theory.
Citation: Commercial Union Ins. Co. v. Sepco Corp., 765 F.2d 1543 (11th Circuit 1985).

Alaska

Type of case: Environmental property damage.
Facts: Insured sought coverage for groundwater pollution resulting from the release of crude oil from a petroleum refinery.
Finding: Exposure.
Comment: Coverage is triggered by exposure to contaminants rather than by manifestation of the damage.
Citation: Mapco Alaska Petroleum, Inc., v. Central National Insurance Co. of Omaha 795 F. Sup. 941 (D.Alaska 1991).

California

Type of case: Asbestos bodily injury.
Facts: Insured sought coverage for asbestos building claims.
Finding: Injury-in-fact.
Comment: Coverage is triggered if any part of the underlying property damage (installation, release, or re-entrainment) took place during a policy period.
Citation: Armstrong World Indus., Inc. v. Aetna Casualty & Surety Co. 45 Cal.App.4th 1, 52 Cal.Rptr.2d 690 (1966).

Type of case: Asbestos bodily injury.
Facts: Insured sought coverage for asbestos building claims.
Finding: Continuous.
Comment: All policies in effect from first exposure to asbestos until the date of death or date of claim, whichever occurs first are triggered.
Citation: Armstrong World Indus., Inc. v. Aetna Casualty & Surety Co. 45 Cal.App.4th 1, 52 Cal.Rptr.2d 690 (1966).

Type of case: Environmental property damage.
Facts: Insured sought a defense to various lawsuits which involved pollution arising from the insured's disposal of waste at various landfills.
Finding: Continuous.
Comment: Bodily injury and property damage that is continuous or progressively deteriorating throughout several policy periods is potentially covered by all policies in effect during those periods.
Citation: Montrose Chem. Corp. v. Admiral Ins. Co. 10th Cal.4th 645, 913 P.2d 878, 42 Cal.Rptr.2d 324 (1995).

Colorado

Type of case: Environmental property damage.
Facts: Insured sought coverage for pollution arising out of its operation of a wood cleaning and preservation manufacturing facility.
Finding: Injury-in-fact.
Comment: Where coverage is triggered by an occurrence during the policy period, the occurrence was the continuous and repeated leakage

of TCA from the insured's storage tanks into the soil and ultimately the groundwater.
Citation: Scott's Liquid Gold, Inc. v. Lexington Ins. Co. No. 97-B-107 (D. Colo. May 27, 1998), reprinted in 12 Mealey's Ins. Litig. Rep. No. 31 Section G (June 23, 1998).

Type of case: Construction Damage.
Facts: Insured sought coverage for claim of property damage caused by construction defects brought by subsequent purchaser of its motel.
Finding: Injury-in-fact.
Comment: Where the claimant does not sustain property damage during the policy period, even though property damage took place during the policy period, there is no occurrence that would trigger coverage.
Citation: Browder v. United States Fid. & Guar. Co. 893 P.2d 132 (Colo. 1995).

Connecticut
Type of case: DES (diethylstilbestrol) bodily injury.
Facts: Insured sought coverage for DES bodily injury claims.
Finding: Injury-in-fact.
Comment: Coverage is triggered for DES-related injuries upon occurrence of injury-in-fact during the policy period.
Citation: Aetna Cas. & Sur. Co. v. Abbott Labs., Inc. 636 F. Supp. 546 (D. Conn. 1986).

Delaware
Type of case: Environmental property damage.
Facts: Insured sought coverage for pollution arising out of a chemical manufacturing plant.
Finding: Continuous.
Comment: A continuous trigger applies to continuous damage, and each insurer as well as the insured for self-insured periods is liable for a pro-rata share of damages.
Citation: Hercules, Inc. v. Aetna Cas. & Sure. Co. 1998 WL 962089 (Del. Super. 1995).

Type of case: Environmental property damage.
Facts: Insured sought coverage for pollution arising out of its operation of various manufacturing facilities.
Finding: Continuous.
Comment: Where the process of containment had been ongoing for decades, the continuous trigger should apply, and each insurer is liable in proportion to the amount of time it provided

insurance.
Citation: E.I. du Pont de Nemours & Co. v. Admiral Ins. Co. 1995 WL 654020 (Del. Super. 1995).

District of Columbia
Type of case: Asbestos bodily injury.
Facts: Insured sought coverage for asbestos bodily injury claims.
Finding: Continuous.
Comment: Court found bodily injury means any part of the single injurious process from exposure through exposure in residence to manifestation. All policies on risk are jointly and severally liable in full, and insured entitled to select the policy to cover the loss.
Citation: Keene Corp. v. Insurance Co. Of N. Am 667 F.2d 1034 (D.C. Cir. 1981), cert. denied, 445 U.S. 1007 (1982).

Florida
Type of case: Bodily injury.
Facts: Insured sought coverage for claims asserted by two victims of shooting in restaurant lobby.
Finding: Multiple occurrence.
Comment: Where the insured is sued for negligent failure to provide security, "occurrence" is defined by immediate injury producing act (gunshots) and not by the underlying tortious omission (failure to provide security).
Citation: Koikos v. Travelers Ins. Co. 849 So. 2d 263 (Fla. 2003).

Type of case: Property Damage.
Facts: Insured sought coverage for damage to buildings caused by a defective water sealant product.
Finding: Manifestation.
Comment: Coverage is triggered only at the time that damage manifests itself.
Citation: Harris Spec. Chems. Inc. v. United States Fire Ins. Co., No. 3-98-CV-351 (M.D. Fla July 7, 2000) reprinted in 14 Mealey's Ins. Litig. Rep. No. 39, Section F (August 15, 2000).

Type of case: Construction defect.
Facts: Insured was accused of negligent construction of the roof of a shopping mall.
Finding: Injury-in-fact.
Comment: Court held that actual damage must occur during the policy period for there to be coverage.
Citation: Trizec Props., Inc. v. Biltmore Constr. Co., 767 F.2d 810 (11th Cir. 1985).

Georgia

Type of case: Environmental property damage.
Facts: Insured sought coverage for pollution damage resulting from discharges of untreated waste water into unlined surface impoundments.
Finding: Exposure.
Comment: The court finds that the "exposure" trigger of coverage is applicable.
Citation: Briggs & Stratton Corp. v. Royal Globe Ins. Co., 64 F. Sup.2d 1346 (M.D. Ga. 1999).

Type of case: Environmental property damage.
Facts: Insured sought a defense to state agency letters requesting cleanup of ground petroleum contamination at two gasoline stations.
Finding: Exposure.
Comment: Exposure during the dates of coverage to conditions that result in property damage constitutes an occurrence.
Citation: Boardman Petroleum, Inc. v. Federated Mutual Ins. Co., 926 F. Suppl. 1566 (S.D. Ga. 1995) rev'd on other grounds 150 F.3d 1327 (11th Cir. 1998).

Type of case: Environ property damage.
Facts: Insured sought coverage for cleanup costs incurred in complying with an administrative order.
Finding: Injury-in-fact.
Comment: Where both the exposure to pollutants and the discovery of contamination took place prior to the inception of the policy, no coverage was available.
Citation: South Carolina Ins. Co. v. Coody, 813 F. Supp. 1570 (M.D. Ga. 1993).

Hawaii

Type of case: Construction damage.
Facts: Insured sought coverage for claim involving water infiltration damage to an apartment complex.
Finding: Injury-in-fact.
Comment: Where injury-in-fact occurs continuously over a period covered by different insurers or policies, a continuous trigger may be employed to equitable apportion liability among insurers.
Citation: Sentinel Ins. Co. v. First Ins. Co. of Haw., Ltd., 76 Haw. 277, 875 P.2d894 (1994).

Illinois

Type of case: Property damage.
Facts: Insured sought coverage for claims involving defective polybutylene pipes.
Finding: Injury-in-fact.

Comment: Under the unambiguous terms of the policy, no "physical injury to tangible property" occurred when the plumbing system was installed in homes that did not experience leaks.
Citation: Travelers Ins. Co. v. Eljer Mfg., Inc. 757 N.E.2d 481 (Ill. 2001).

Type of case: Employment discrimination.
Facts: Insured sought coverage for the costs of settlement of a class action involving discriminatory hiring practices.
Finding: Injury-in-fact.
Comment: The damages will be deemed to have occurred during the policy in which the representation of the futile employment application took place.
Citation: Illinois Cent. R.R. v. Accident & Cas. Co. of Winterthur, 317 Ill.App.3d 737, 739 N.E.2d 1049 (Ill.App.2000).

Type of case: Environmental property damage.
Facts: Insured sought coverage for pollution damage resulting from the disposal of waste oil at a landfill.
Finding: Continuous.
Comment: Damage resulting from the discharge of pollutants is a continuing process and does not stop and start in discrete time periods.
Citation: Benoy Motor Sales, Inc. v. Universal Underwriters Inc. Co. 287 Ill.App.3d 942,679 N.E.2d 414 (1997).

Type of case: Environ property damage.
Facts: Insured sought coverage for PCB contamination of Waukegan Harbor.
Finding: Continuous.
Comment: All policies in effect during the time of release of pollutants are triggered and each policy, of the insured for uninsured years, is responsible for a pro-rata, time-on-the-risk allocation.
Citation: Outboard Marine Corp. v. Liberty Mut. Ins. Co. 283 Ill.Aaa.3d 630, 670 N.E.2d 740 (1996).

Type of case: Asbestos.
Facts: Insured sought coverage for asbestos building claims.
Finding: Continuous.
Comment: All polices from the exposure to, or installation of, asbestos to manifestation or discovery of damage are triggered.
Citation: United States Gypsum Co. v. Admiral Ins. Co., 268 Ill.App3d 598, 643 N.E.2d 1226 (1994).

Type of case: Asbestos bodily injury.
Facts: Insured sought coverage for asbestos building claims.
Finding: Injury-in-fact.
Comment: Court found that injury-in-fact occurred during the period of asbestos exposure as well as at the time of the date of diagnosis.
Citation: Zurich Inc. Co. v. Raymark Indus., Inc., 118 Il.2d 23, 514 N.E.2d 150 (1997).

Indiana

Type of case: Environ property damage.
Facts: Insured sought coverage for numerous pollution claims.
Finding: Injury-in-fact.
Comment: An actual injury must occur during the time the policy is in effect in order to be indemnifiable, and each triggered policy is liable only for the portion of the damage that resulted during that particular policy period, and the insured is responsible for uninsured periods.
Citation: Dana Corp. v. Hartford Accident & Indem. Co., No. 49D01-9301-CP-0026 (Ind. Super. September 10, 1996) reprinted in 10 Mealey's Ins. Litig. Rep. No. 43, Section A (September 17, 1996).

Type of case: DES (diethylstilbestrol) bodily injury.
Facts: Insured sought coverage for DES bodily injury claims.
Finding: Continuous.
Comment: Coverage is triggered for any policy in effect from date of ingestion of the drug through date of manifestation.
Citation: Eli Lily & Co. v. Home Ins. Co., 482 N.E.2d 467 (Ind. 1985), cert. Denied, 479 U.S. 1060 (1987).

Kansas

Type of case: Hearing loss bodily injury.
Facts: Insured sought coverage for numerous noise induced hearing loss claims.
Finding: Continuous.
Comment: All policies are triggered from the commencement of exposure to excessive noise until implementation by the insured of a hearing conservation program.
Citation: Atchison, Topeka & Santa Fe Ry. v. Stonewall Inc. Co., No. 94-CV-1464 (Kan. Dist. Ct. Jul. 24, 2000) reprinted in 14 Mealey's Ins. Litig. Rep. No. 47 Section A (October 17, 2000).

Type of case: Environmental property damage.
Facts: Insured sought coverage for groundwater contamination resulting from releases from its manufacturing facility.
Finding: Injury-in-fact.
Comment: Injury occurs when damage actually takes place, not at the time of manifestation.
Citation: Cessna Aircraft Co. v. Hartford Accident & Indem. Co. 900 F. Sup. 1489 (D. Kan. 1995).

Louisiana

Type of case: Property damage.
Facts: Insured sought coverage for termite damage to condominium.
Finding: Manifestation.
Comment: The manifestation theory if applicable and the effects of the termite infestation in the condominiums did not become "damage" until the homeowner discovered it.
Citation: James Pets Control, Inc. v. Scottsdale Ins. Co. 785 So.2d 485 (La. Ct. App 2000).

Type of case: Property damage.
Facts: Insured sought coverage for fire damage caused by the faulty installation of an air-conditioning system.
Finding: Manifestation.
Comment: The date when negligence manifests itself by causing actual damage is generally the time of occurrence.
Citation: St. Paul Fire & Marine Ins. Co. v. Valentine, 665 (La.).

Maine

Type of case: Product liability.
Facts: Insured manufactured a dryer which had problems with welds in 1975 and which sustained cracks in 1977.
Finding: Manifestation.
Comment: Court found that an occurrence happens when the injurious effects of the occurrence become apparent or manifest themselves.
Citation: Honeycomb Sys., Inc. v. Admiral Ins. Co., 567 F. Supp. 1400 (D. Me 1983).

Maryland

Type of case: Asbestos property damage.
Facts: Insured sought coverage for asbestos-in-building claims.
Finding: Continuous.
Comment: A continuous trigger of coverage is applicable for long term and continuing damage posted by the installation and continued presence of asbestos in buildings.

CONSTRUCTION DEFECT LITIGATION

Citation: *Mayor & City Council of Baltimore v. Utica Mut. Ins. Co.*, 145 Md. App. 256, 802 A.2d 1070 (2002).

Type of case: Lead bodily injury.
Facts: Insured sought coverage for bodily injuries resulting from the ingestion of lead paint chips.
Finding: Exposure.
Comment: Coverage is triggered during any policy period in which a claimant ingested lead paint.
Citation: *Chantel Assoc. v. Mount Vernon Fire Ins. Co.*, 338 Md. 131, 656 A.2d 779 (1995).

Type of case: Property damage.
Facts: Insured sought coverage for claims arising out of defective cement incorporated into concrete railroad ties.
Finding: Injury-in-fact.
Comment: Because the underlying complaint alleged that deterioration of railroad ties began immediately upon installation, complaint alleged damage during the policy.
Citation: *Nationwide Mut. Ins. Co. v. Lafarge Corp.*, 1994 WL 706538 (D. Md. 1994).

Type of case: Environmental property damage.
Facts: County sought coverage for pollution at various landfills which it operated.
Finding: Injury-in-fact.
Comment: Manifestation is not the sole trigger of coverage, and coverage may be triggered earlier upon proof of detectable property damage during a policy period.
Citation: *Harford County v. Harford Mut. Ins. Co.*, 327 Md. 418, 610 A.2 286 (1992).

Massachusetts
Type of case: Environmental property damage.
Facts: Insured sought coverage for pollution resulting from leaking underground storage tanks.
Finding: Continuous.
Comment: Coverage is triggered under all policies in effect when the property was being continuously contaminated by oil, and each triggered policy is jointly and severally liable for the entire claim.
Citation: *Rubenstein v. Royal Ins. Co. of Am.* 44 Mass. App. Ct. 842, 694 N.E.2d 381 (1998).

Type of case: Lead bodily injury.
Facts: Insured sought coverage for bodily injury

claims resulting from the ingestion of lead paint.
Finding: Exposure.
Comment: Coverage is triggered at the time of exposure where the claimant suffered new and further injuries during the policy period.
Citation: *United States Liab. Ins. Co. v. Selman*, 70 F.3d 684 (1st Cir. 1995).

Type of case: Asbestos.
Facts: Insured sought coverage for occupational disease claims arising out of asbestos.
Finding: Manifestation.
Comment: Coverage for occupational disease claims falls upon the last insurer on the date of disability, as determined by the date of decreased earning capacity.
Citation: *Liberty Mut. Ins. Co. v. Commercial Union Ins. Co.*, 978 F.2 750 (1st Cir. 1992).

Michigan
Type of case: Environmental property damage.
Facts: Insured sought coverage for groundwater contamination arising out of its operation of a manufacturing facility.
Finding: Injury-in-fact.
Comment: Each insurer is only responsible for coverage during its policy period based on a time-on-the-risk approach.
Citation: *Arco. Indus. Corp. v. American Motorist Ins. Co.*, 232 Mich. App. 146 594 N.W.2d 330 (Mich. 2000).

Type of case: Environmental property damage.
Facts: Insured sought coverage for chemical contamination at its manufacturing plant.
Finding: Injury-in-fact.
Comment: An actual injury must occur during the time that the policy is in effect in order for coverage to be triggered.
Citation: *Gelman Sciences, Inc. v. Fidelity & Cas. Co. of N.Y.*, 456 Mich. 305, 572 N.W.2d 617 (1998).

Minnesota
Type of case: Environmental property damage.
Facts: Insured sought coverage for pollution arising out of the insured's operation of a tar refining plant.
Finding: Continuous.
Comment: Each insurer is liable only for that period of time it was on the risk compared to the entire period during which damages occurred.
Citation: *Domtar, Inc. v. Niagara Fire Ins. Co.*, 563 N.W.2d 724 (Minn. 1997).

Type of case: Environmental property damage.
Facts: Insured sought coverage for pollution damage after it received an information request from state pollution control agency.
Finding: Injury-in-fact.
Comment: Where the fact-finder concludes that property damage arose in a single year, from a sudden and accidental occurrence, and concludes that the damage was not divisible, only policies in effect in the year the property damage arose are triggered.
Citation: SCSC Corp. v. Allied Mut Ins. Co., 536 N.W.2d 305 (Minn. 1995).

Type of case: Environmental property damage.
Facts: Insured sought coverage for pollution arising out of contamination resulting from its operation of a coal-tar gasification plant.
Finding: Injury-in-fact.
Comment: Each insurer is liable only for those damages that occur during its policy period, and damages should be apportioned on a pro-rata basis.
Citation: Northern States Power Co. v. Fidelity & Cas. Co. of N.Y., 523 N.W.2d 657 (Minn. 1994).

Mississippi

Type of case: Asbestos property damage.
Facts: Insured sought coverage for settlement of asbestos building claims.
Finding: Continuous.
Comment: Damage to building from asbestos products are in place and the damage continues as long as the building contains the products.
Citation: W. R. Grace Co. v. Maryland Cas. Co., No. 89-5138 (Miss. Cir. 1991).

Missouri

Type of case: Environmental property damage.
Facts: Insured sought coverage for pollution arising out of its long-term use of aircraft maintenance facilities.
Finding: Exposure.
Comment: All policies on the risk during the period when hazardous substances were released are triggered and are reliable for pro-rata share of damages.
Citation: Trans World Airlines, Inc. v. Associated Aviation Underwriters, No. 942-01848 (Mo. Cir. Oct. 20 1998), reprinted in 13 Mealey's Ins. Litig. Rep. No.7, Section G (Dec. 15, 1998).

Type of case: Environmental bodily injury and property damage.

Facts: Insured sought coverage for various bodily injury and property damage claims arising out of the release of contaminants.
Finding: Injury-in-fact.
Comment: Coverage is triggered by a showing of actual injury or damage during the policy period, not the negligent act.
Citation: Monsanto Co. v. Aetna Cas. & Sur. Co., 1994 WL 161953 (Del. Super.), rev'd on other grounds, 652 A.2d 30 (Del. 1994).

New Jersey

Type of case: Environmental property damage.
Facts: Insured sought coverage for pollution resulting from the disposal of hazardous waste into a landfill.
Finding: Continuous.
Comment: Exposure relating to Borough's initial depositing of toxic waste into a landfill is the first trigger of coverage under the continuous trigger theory.
Citation: Quincy Mut. Fire ins. v. Borough of Bellmawr, 172 N.J. 409, 799 A.2d 499 (2002).

Type of case: Environmental property damage.
Facts: Insured sought coverage for pollution arising out of its disposal of waste at a landfill.
Finding: Continuous.
Comment: Damages should be allocated among years based upon the amount of risk assumed by the insured and insurers in each year and then allocated vertically among policies in each year based upon full policy limits.
Citation: Carter-Wallace, Inc. v. Admiral Ins. Co., 154 N.J. 312, 712 A.2d 116 (1998).

Type of case: Asbestos bodily injury and property damage.
Facts: Insured sought coverage for asbestos bodily injury and asbestos building claims.
Finding: Continuous.
Comment: Each insurer on the risk between exposure to asbestos (installation in a building) and manifestation of disease (discovery or remediation) is liable for defense and indemnity.
Citation: Owens-Illinois, Inc. v. United Ins. Co., 138 N.J. 437, 650 A.2d 974 (1994).

Type of case: Dioxin bodily injury.
Facts: Insured sought coverage for its settlement of the Agent Orange case.
Finding: Injury-in-fact.
Comment: Court found that the simple exposure to dioxin is injury-in-fact. Coverage was

therefore triggered four months after delivery of a given shipment of Agent Orange to the military.
Citation: Diamond Shamrock Chems. Co. v. Aetna Cas. & Sur. Co., 258 N.J. Super. 167, 609 A.2d 440 (1992), cert. denied, 134 N.J. 481, 634 A .2d 528 (1998).

New York
Type of case: Property damage.
Facts: Insured sought coverage for claims involving defective polybutylene pipes.
Finding: Injury-in-fact.
Comment: If installation of potentially defective plumbing system caused a diminution of value of home greater than the value of the plumbing system itself, injury to tangible property occurred under policies governed by New York law.
Citation: Travelers Ins. Co. v. Eljer Mfg., Inc., 757 N.E.2d 481(Ill. 2001).

Type of case: DES (diethylstilbestrol) bodily injury.
Facts: Insured sought coverage for bodily injury claims asserted by women who ingested DES, the children of women who ingested DES, and the grandchildren of women who ingested DES.
Finding: Injury-in-fact.
Comment: For second-generation claimants, injury-in-fact includes predisposition to illness or disability as a result of cell maturation caused by DES. For third-generation claimants, injury-in-fact includes casual consequence of injuries-in-fact to the reproductive system of second generation claimants that took place during the period of coverage.
Citation: E.R. Squibb & Sons, Inc. v. Lloyd's & Cos., 241 F.3d 154 (2d Cir. 2001).

Type of case: Asbestos bodily injury.
Facts: Insured sought coverage for asbestos bodily injury claims.
Finding: Injury-in-fact.
Comment: The insured has the right to demand that a policy pay full coverage for each insurance claim in which the underlying claimant suffered asbestos exposure and therefore asbestos injury during the policy period.
Citation: In re Prudential Lines, Inc., 158 F.3d 65 (2d Cir. 1998).

Type of case: Asbestos bodily injury.
Facts: Insured sought coverage for asbestos bodily injury claims.

Finding: Continuous.
Comment: Coverage is triggered under all policies in effect from the date of the first exposure to manifestation and all policies, and the insured for uninsured periods, are liable for a pro-rata share of damages.
Citation: Stonewall Ins. Co. v. Asbestos Claims Mgmt. Corp., 73 F.3d 65 (2d Cir. 1995), modified, 85 F3d 49 (1996).

Type of case: Asbestos property damage.
Facts: Insured sought coverage for asbestos building claims.
Finding: Injury-in-fact.
Comment: Property damage in fact occurs upon installation of products containing asbestos into a building, and exists regardless of whether it had been discovered by building owners; this injury to property does not continue after that event.
Citation: Maryland Cas. Co. v. W.R. Grace & Co., 23 F.3d 617 (2d Cir. 1993), cert. denied, 513 U.S. 1052 (1994).

North Carolina
Type of case: Property damage.
Facts: Insured sought coverage for underlying claims that a diagnostic dye was contaminated due to a leak in a pressure vessel.
Finding: Injury-in-fact.
Comment: The property damage occurred on a single date when the pressure vessel ruptured and a single policy period is triggered even though the contamination continued until it was discovered in a subsequent policy period.
Citation: Gaston County Dyeing Mach. Co. v. Northfield Ins. Co., 351 N.C. 293, 524 S.E.2d 558 (2000).

Type of case: Environmental property damage.
Facts: Insured sought coverage for pollution arising out of its operation of a polyester manufacturing plant.
Finding: Manifestation.
Comment: Property damage occurs when it is manifested or discovered.
Citation: Home Indem. Co. v. Hoechst Callanese Corp. 128 N.C. App. 189, 494 S.E.2d 774 (1998).

Type of case: Asbestos bodily injury.
Facts: Insured sought coverage for asbestos bodily injury claims.
Finding: Exposure.
Comment: The date on which coverage is trig-

gered is the date on which the first exposure to injury-causing condition occurred.

Citation: Imperial Cas. & Indem. Co. v. Radiator Specialty Co., 962 R. Supp. 1437 (E.D. N.C. 1994), aff'd 67 F.3d 534 (4th Cir. 1995).

North Dakota

Type of case: Property damage.
Facts: Insured sought coverage for claim based on progressive damage to grain storage bin.
Finding: Injury-in-fact.
Comment: Appropriate trigger of coverage for progressive property damage was whether real but undiscovered loss or damage could be proved in retrospect to have commenced during policy period, regardless of when loss of damage became manifest.
Citation: Kief Farmers Co-Op Elevator Co. v. Farmland Mut. Ins. Co., 534 N.W.2d 28 (N.D. 1995).

Ohio

Type of case: Welding rod bodily injury.
Facts: Insured sought coverage for numerous welding rod bodily injury claims.
Finding: Continuous.
Comment: A duty to defend and pay all defense costs is triggered under any policy in effect from the time of the claimant's initial exposure to welding fumes until diagnosis of injury.
Citation: Lincoln Elec. Co. v. St. Paul Fire & Maine Ins. Co., 10 F. Supp.2 856 (N.D. Ohio 1998), aff'd in part & rev'd in part, 210 F.3d 672 (6th Cir. 2000).

Type of case: Asbestos.
Facts: Insured sought coverage for asbestos bodily injury claims.
Finding: Continuous.
Comment: All policies in effect from initial exposure until diagnosis or death are triggered, and each triggered policy is obligated to pay the claim in full, subject to policy limits.
Citation: Owen-Corning Fiberglass Corp. v. American Centennial Ins. Co., 74 Ohio Misc. 2d 183, 660 N.E.2d 770 (Ohio Comp. Pleas 1995).

Type of case: Asbestos bodily injury.
Facts: Insured sought coverage for asbestos bodily injury claims.
Finding: Manifestation.
Comment: Court held that injury occurs when the asbestos disease becomes reasonably capable of medical diagnosis. In the asbestos context, the date of diagnosis was held to be the date six years prior to the date of diagnosis or death.

Citation: Eagle-Picher Indus., Inc. v. Liberty Mut. Ins. Co., 682 F.2d 12 (1st Cir. 1982), cert. denied, 460 U.S. 1028 (1983).

Oregon

Type of case: Environmental property damage.
Facts: Insured sought coverage for pollution arising out of its operation of several wood treatment plants.
Finding: Injury-in-fact.
Comment: If property is injured during the policy period, coverage is triggered regardless of when the property damage is discovered or when the insured's liability becomes fixed.
Citation: St. Paul Fire & Marine Ins. Co. v. McCormick & Baxter Creosoting Co., 324 Or. 184, 923 P.2d 1200 (1996).

Pennsylvania

Type of case: Environmental bodily injury and property damage.
Facts: Insured sought coverage for bodily injury and property damage caused by radioactive emissions from the insured's facility.
Finding: Manifestation.
Comment: The date of manifestation of injury is the appropriate date for determining the applicable policy and coverage limits.
Citation: Babcock & Wilcox Co. v. American Nuclear Insurers, 2002 WI 31749119 (Pa. Super. 2002).

Type of case: Environmental property damage.
Facts: Insured sought coverage for pollution at a former manufacturing facility.
Finding: Injury-in-fact.
Comment: A policy is triggered at the time that the act causing the environmental injury occurs.
Citation: General Elec. Co. v. Travelers Indem. Co., No. L-4931-81 (N.J. Super. July 15, 2001), reprinted in 15 Mealey's Ins. Litig. Rep. No. 37, Section A (Aug. 7, 2001).

Type of case: Property damage.
Facts: Insured sought coverages for structural property damage caused by its mining operations.
Finding: Manifestation.
Comment: An occurrence happens for purposes of insurance when the injurious effects of the negligence act first manifest.
Citation: Rockwood Cas. Ins. Co. v. American Mining Ins. Co., No. G.D. 98-5324 (Pa. Com. Pleas Aug. 6, 1999), reprinted in 13 Mealey's Ins. Litig. Rep. No. 40, Section D (Aug 24, 1999).

Rhode Island

Type of case: Environmental property damage.
Facts: Insured sought coverage for pollution damage resulting from its storage and transportation of hazardous waste to a landfill.
Finding: Manifestation.
Comment: There is no occurrence under the policy without property damage that becomes apparent during the policy period.
Citation: *Truk-Away of R.I., Inc. v. Aetna Cas. & Sur. Co.,* 723 A.2d 309 (R.I. 1999).

Type of case: Environmental property damage.
Facts: Insured sought coverage for pollution arising out of its operation of a manufacturing facility.
Finding: Manifestation.
Comment: Coverage is triggered by an occurrence that takes place when the property damage, which includes property loss, manifests or is discovered in the exercise of reasonable diligence.
Citation: *CPC Int'l., Inc. v. Northbrook Excess & Surplus Ins. Co.* 668 A.2d 647 (R.I. 1995).

South Carolina

Type of case: Property damage.
Facts: Insured sought coverage for construction defect claims involving defective buildings.
Finding: Continuous.
Comment: Coverage is triggered by all policies in effects from the time the complaint was actually damaged and continuously thereafter until the end of the progressive damage, even if damage continues after discovery.
Citation: *Stonehenge Eng'g Corp. v. Employers Ins. of Wausau,* 201 F.3d 269 (4th Cir. 2000).

Type of case: Environmental property damage.
Facts: Insured sought coverage for pollution damage resulting from a leaking underground gasoline storage system.
Finding: Injury-in-fact.
Comment: Damage to the property of the underlying claimant must occur during the policy period and, in cases of continuous damage, all policies and the insured (in cases of no coverage) are responsible for a pro rata share of damages.
Citation: *Spartan Petroleum Co. v. Federated Mut. Ins. Co.,* 162 F.3d 805 (4th Cir. 1998).

Type of case: Construction damage.
Facts: Insured sought coverage for progressive property damage caused by defective construction.
Finding: Injury-in-fact.
Comment: Coverage is triggered at the time of an injury-in-fact and continuously thereafter to allow coverage under all policies in effect from the time of injury in-fact throughout the entire time of the progressive damage.
Citation: *Joe Harden Builders, Inc. v. Aetna Cas. & Sur. Co.,* 326 S.C. 231, 486 S.E.2d 89 (1997).

Texas

Type of case: Asbestos bodily injury.
Facts: Insured sought coverage for numerous asbestos bodily injury claims.
Finding: Exposure.
Comment: Injury takes place at the time of exposure to or inhalation of asbestos fibers.
Citation: *Guaranty Nat'l Ins. Co. v. Azrock Indus., Inc.* 211 F.3d 289 (5th Cir. 2000).

Type of case: Environmental property damage.
Facts: Insured sought coverage for various environmental claims.
Finding: Injury-in-fact.
Comment: Coverage is triggered by the occurrence of actual personal injury or property damage during the policy period, regardless of whether such injury or damage is manifested, discovered or known during the policy period.
Citation: *Union Pac. Res Co. v. Continental Ins. Co.,* No. 249_23-98 (Tex. Dist., Dec. 17, 1998), reprinted in 13 Mealey's Ins. Litig. Rep. No. 11, Section A (Jan. 19, 1999).

Type of case: Property damage.
Facts: Insured sought coverage for damage resulting from contaminated fuel that had to be replaced.
Finding: Manifestation.
Comment: The time of the occurrence is when the complaining party actually was damaged, not the time that the wrongful act was committed; a party sustains damage that is readily apparent.
Citation: *America Home Assurance Co. v. Unitramp Ltd.,* 146 F.3d 311 (5th Cir. 1998).

Type of case: Breast implants.
Facts: Insured sought coverage for numerous breast implant claims filed against it.
Finding: Continuous.
Comment: Damage injury in the case of toxic or harmful substances, begins with the first

exposure and continues up to and through the manifestation of illness.

Citation: *Bristol-Myers Squibb Co. v. AUI Ins. Co.,* 1995 WL 861100 (Tex. Dist. 1995).

Type of case: Environmental bodily injury.

Facts: Insured sought coverage for bodily injury claims arising out of exposure to chemicals used in a steel mill

Finding: Continuous.

Comment: All insurers and the insured must share equally in the defense until there can be adjustments for the defense as to each claimant based on a pro-rata sharing between the insurers and the insured.

Citation: *Gulf Chem. & Metallurgical Corp. v. Associated Metals & Minerals,* 1 F.3d 365 (5th Cir. 1993).

Utah

Type of case: Environmental property damage.

Facts: Insured received a PRP letter and sought coverage for pollution arising out of its disposal of waste oil at a waste oil recycling facility.

Finding: Injury-in-fact.

Comment: Coverage is triggered each time hazardous waste such as waste oil was discharged onto the property.

Citation: *Quaker State Minit-Lube, Inc. v. Fireman's Fund Ins. Co.,* 886 F. Supp 1278 (D Utah 1994), aff'd, 52 F.3d 1522 (10th Cir 1995).

Vermont

Type of case: Environmental property damage.

Facts: Insured sought coverage for environmental cleanup damage sought from it in an administrative proceeding.

Finding: Injury-in-fact.

Comment: Where there is no evidence of damage from the date of discharge of pollutants in 1950s and the discovery of pollution in the 1990s, a continuous trigger does not apply.

Citation: *State of Vermont v. CNA Ins. Cos.,* 172 Vt. 318, 79 A.2d 662 (2201).

Type of case: Environmental property damage.

Facts: Insured sought coverage for pollution arising out of its disposal of waste at a landfill.

Finding: Exposure.

Comment: Where multiple exposures occur over several years, multiple policies may be triggered.

Citation: *Vermont Am. Corp. v. American Employers' Ins. Co.,* No. 330-6-95 (Vt. Super. Nov. 24, 1997)

reprinted in 12 Mealey's Ins. Litig. Rep. No.2 Section F (December 2, 1997).

Washington

Type of case: Asbestos bodily injury.

Facts: Insured sought coverage for asbestos bodily injury claims under a marine insurance policy.

Finding: Continuous.

Comment: Every policy throughout the injury-causing process is triggered for the entire amount of the covered loss.

Citation: *Skinner Corp. v. Fireman's Fund Ins. Co.,* 1996 WL 376657 (W.D. Wash. 1996).

Type of case: Environmental property damage.

Facts: Insured sought coverage for its liability arising out of the disposal of flue dust over a ten year period.

Finding: Exposure pro rata.

Comment: Where damage was caused by a series of acts over several years, the damage should be allocated over the time period where a quantification of the damage can be made based on yearly deliveries to the site.

Citation: *Northwest Steel Rolling Mills Liquidation Trust v. Fireman's Funds Ins. Co.,* 1991 WL 639662 (W.D. Wash. 1991).

Type of case: Environmental property damage.

Facts: Insured was sued for contamination arising out of its operation of an oil recycling facility.

Finding: Continuous.

Comment: Court noted that the parties had agreed that Washington had adopted continuous damage theory.

Citation: *Time Oil Co. v. Cigna Prop. & Cas. Ins. Co.* 743 F. Supp. 1400 (W.D. Wash 1990).

Wisconsin

Type of case: Environmental property damage.

Facts: Insured sought coverage for costs of cleaning up contamination at the town dump.

Finding: Continuous.

Comment: All policies in effect while the occurrence was ongoing are triggered for their full limits.

Citation: *Society Ins. v. Town of Franklin,* 223 Wis. 2d 207, 607 N.W.2d 342 (Wis. App. 2000).

Type of case: Negligence property damage.

Facts: Insured sought coverage for injuries to dairy cows due to stray voltage from an improper power supply which took place over a 12 year period.

Finding: Continuous.

Comment: The occurrence triggering coverage began with the installation of the power supply in 1970 and continued uninterrupted until the problem was resolved in 1982.

Citation: Wisconsin Elec. Power Co. v. California Union Ins. Co. 141 Wis. 2d 673, 419 N.W.2d 255 (Wis. App. 1987).

Type of case: DES (diethylstilbestrol) bodily injury.

Facts: Insured sought coverage for DES bodily injury claims.

Finding: Exposure.

Comment: Court held that ingestion of drug during the policy period triggered coverage even though the injury manifested years later.

Citation: Kremers-Urban Co. v. American Employers Ins. Co., 119 Wis. 2d 772, 351 N.W.2d 156 (1984).

Appendix 4: Reconstruction Contract Term Definitions

Association boards and managers need to be familiar with the terms that are common in the stipulated-sum agreements they will enter into with a reconstruction contractor. A good example of these terms can be found in the American Institute of Architects document A107-1977, which is the basis for the following descriptions.

1. Parties to the Agreement: The parties to a reconstruction contract are the owner (either a homeowners association or a group of individual homeowners) and the contractor performing the reconstruction services. Although they are not parties to the agreement, other members of the association's reconstruction team—the architect, reconstruction consultant, or other designated project manager—are mentioned throughout the typical reconstruction agreement because of the key roles they play.

2. The Work of the Contract: The agreement spells out the work to be accomplished by the contractor during the reconstruction, and the association should ensure that it does so in great detail so that disputes do not arise once work gets underway.

3. Dates of Commencement and Substantial Completion: The agreement must define the date that the work will begin, the contract time, and the date of substantial completion. The date when work begins is frequently fixed in a document called a Notice to Proceed issued by either the owner or the contractor. The contract time is the date between the date of commencement and the date of substantial completion. The contract time is generally defined as a specified number of calendar days. In a typical reconstruction contract involving a common interest development with more than 100 units, it isn't unusual for the contract time to run several months, or even more than a year.

4. Contract Sum: The contract sum is the total amount the contractor will be paid for accomplishing the work specified in the contract. In virtually every reconstruction project, changes in the scope of the work are required along the way, therefore agreements provide for additions and deletions to the contract sum as specified by change orders. Change orders must always be approved by the architect or other project manager. The contractor's hourly rates, overhead, and profit for change orders should be spelled out in the agreement.

5. Payments: Payments under a typical reconstruction contract fall into two categories: progress payments and a final payment. The contractor makes applications for progress payments to the architect or other project manager. The agreement will specify the period covered by each application, which is generally one calendar month. The agreement will also specify when monthly applications are to be submitted and when payment will be made—assuming the monthly application is received on time. The owner makes the final payment when the contractor has fully performed the contract and the architect or other project manager has issued a final certificate of payment. The agreement will specify how soon after the certificate of payment is received the final payment must be made.

6. Description of Contract Documents: Contract documents are used to define the scope of work under the contract and typically include the reconstruction agreement itself, the architect's plans and specifications, the scope-of-repair used for bidding, and expert reports generated during litigation. Ensuring that all contract documents are accurate and fully describe the work is extremely important.

7. General Conditions: General conditions describe many details of the relationship between the parties, including defining contract documents and the work, as well as specifying ownership and use of the architect's drawings and specifications.

8. Information and Services Required of the Owner: This paragraph lays out information that the owner must supply, such as surveys and legal descriptions, and spells out the owner's responsibility to secure and pay for necessary

approvals from governmental agencies like permits and easements. This paragraph also spells out the owner's right to stop the work if the contractor fails to correct work that's not in accordance with the agreement.

9. Information and Services Required of the Contractor: These provisions spell out the contractor's obligations to review and compare the contract documents before beginning work and to report errors, omissions, or inconsistencies to the architect. They also spell out the contractor's responsibility to supervise and direct the work using the contractor's best skill and attention. The contractor is required to have sole responsibility for and control over the construction methods, techniques, sequences, and procedures, and for coordinating all aspects of the work. Furthermore, the contractor is required to install materials in accordance with manufacturers' instructions.

10. Warranty: The warranty provisions should be closely scrutinized by the association or homeowners for completeness. In standard form AIA contracts, the contractor's warranty is quite limited. Associations or owners should consider asking the association's attorney to expand the warranty language. Furthermore, the agreement should provide that the contractor is to comply with all laws, ordinances, rules, and regulations in effect at the time the work is performed.

11. Taxes and Fees: The agreement needs to spell out who is responsible for paying taxes, permits, and fees. Generally speaking, the cost of taxes, permits, and fees are part of the contractor's bid, and therefore should be included in the stipulated sum of the agreement.

12. Indemnification: The indemnification provisions of the agreement should be closely scrutinized by the association's attorney for appropriate scope. Standard form AIA agreements provide that the contractor shall indemnify and hold harmless the owner, architect, and the agents and employees of the owner and architect from and against claims, damages, loss, and expenses, including but not limited to attorneys' fees, arising out of or resulting from the performance of the work, but only to the extent caused by the negligent acts or omissions of the contractor, subcontractor, or anyone employed by the contractor or a subcontractor.

13. Administration of the Contract: The agreement should spell out the role of the architect or other project manager in the administering the reconstruction agreement. This includes keeping the owner informed of progress and quality, guarding against defects, and determining whether the completed work will comply with the contract. This doesn't make the architect responsible for the contractor's work or in control of it. Further administrative responsibilities of the architect or other project manager include reviewing applications for progress payments and certifying the amounts that are due.

14. Claims and Disputes: The reconstruction agreement should spell out the manner by which claims and disputes between the owner and contractor will be resolved. Standard form AIA agreements provide that mediation will be used first and, failing that, by binding arbitration. Many of the binding arbitration procedures are spelled out in the agreement.

15. Subcontractors: A subcontractor is defined as a person or entity that has a direct contract with the contractor to perform a portion of the work. Reconstruction contracts typically require contractors to submit a list of all subcontractors and their scope of work to the owner. Usually, the agreement requires that the contractor is bound, to the extent of the work to be performed by the subcontractor, to the terms of the master agreement between the owner and the contractor.

16. Change Orders: The agreement will provide that the owner, without invalidating the agreement, may order changes within the general scope of the agreement consisting of additions, deletions, or other revisions, with the contract sum and the contract time being adjusted accordingly. Changes require a written change order signed by the owner, contractor, and architect or other project manager. The resulting cost or credit to the owner is mutually agreed on using the contractor's labor costs, overhead, and profit.

17. Payments and Completion: The agreement will spell out the mechanics for payments. Typically, the contractor submits monthly certificates for payment to the architect. The architect issues a certificate of payment for amounts he or she believes are due. The architect's certificate for payment indicates to the owner that the

work is in accordance with the contract documents. The architect may withhold a certificate for payment if he or she finds the work unacceptable or incomplete. Final payment is made after the architect approves the work and the contractor has obtained release of any liens.

18. Protection of Persons and Property: The contractor is responsible for safety and must immediately stop work in any area containing hazardous materials and remove it at the contractor's expense.

19. Insurance: The agreement should specify the limits of the contractor's commercial general liability, vehicular, and workers' compensation insurance and require that certificates of insurance be provided to the owner. While not required in a standard form AIA agreement, the owner should insert provisions requiring that the contractor requires its subcontractors to carry workers compensation, vehicular, and comprehensive general liability insurance with specified limits.

20. Correction of Work: The contractor must promptly correct work rejected by the architect. Additionally, under a standard form AIA contract, if, within a year of substantial completion,

any of the work is not in accordance with the standard documents, the contractor must correct the work promptly after the owner has notified the contractor in writing to do so. In effect, the standard form AIA agreement incorporates a one year warranty by the contractor.

21. Termination of the Contract: The circumstances under which the agreement may be terminated either by the contractor or the owner are spelled out in the standard form AIA agreement. Generally, if the architect fails to recommend payment for a specified time through no fault of the contractor, or if the owner fails to make payment within the time required by the agreement, the contractor may terminate the contract upon written notice and recover from the owner payment for work executed and for proven loss of materials, equipment, and labor, including reasonable overhead and profit. On the other hand, the owner may terminate the contractor if the contractor: (1) repeatedly refuses to supply enough properly skilled workers or proper materials for the job; (2) fails to make payment to subcontractors for materials or labor; (3) persistently disregards laws, ordinances, rules, or regulations of public authorities; or (4) otherwise is guilty of substantial breach of the reconstruction agreement.

Appendix 5: Investigating and Remediating Mold

Concern about indoor exposure to mold has been increasing as the public becomes aware that exposure to mold can cause a variety of health effects and symptoms, including allergic reactions. Mold is of particular concern to community managers, board members, and others involved in managing common-interest developments because mold can be expensive to investigate and remediate. The business judgment rule can come into play as well: boards must conduct appropriate investigations and make informed decisions. Otherwise they are vulnerable to claims by owners who have suffered personal injuries or property damage from exposure to mold. According to the U.S. Environmental Protection Agency (EPA):

Molds can be found almost anywhere; they can grow on virtually any organic substance, as long as moisture and oxygen are present. Molds can grow on wood, paper, carpet, and insulation. When excessive moisture accumulates on buildings or on building materials, mold growth will often occur, particularly if the moisture problem remains undiscovered or is not addressed. It is impossible to eliminate all molds and mold spores in the indoor environment. However, mold growth can be controlled indoors by controlling moisture indoors.[1]

Molds reproduce by making spores that usually cannot be seen without magnification. Mold spores [circulate] through the indoor and outdoor air continually. When mold spores land on a damp spot indoors, they may begin growing, and digesting whatever they are growing on in order to survive. Molds gradually destroy the things they grow on. Many types of molds exist. All molds have the potential to affect health. Molds can produce allergens that can trigger allergic reactions or asthma in people allergic to mold. Others are known to produce potent toxins or irritants. Potential health concerns are an important reason to prevent mold growth and to clean up any existing indoor mold growth.[2]

Since mold requires moisture to grow, it is important to prevent moisture problems in buildings. Moisture problems can have many causes, including water intrusion and uncontrolled humidity. Some moisture problems in buildings have been linked to changes in building construction practices [in recent decades]. Some of these changes have resulted in buildings that are tightly sealed, but lack adequate ventilation, potentially leading to moisture buildup. Building materials, such as drywall, may not allow moisture to escape easily. Moisture problems [also may stem from] roof leaks and landscaping or gutters that direct water into or under the building. Unvented combustion appliances such as furnaces may increase moisture content. Delayed maintenance or insufficient maintenance are also associated with many moisture problems.[3]

Mold Prevention

Community managers should work with boards and companies charged with maintaining a common areas to develop a program to solve mold problems before they damage structures and adversely affect residents' health. The key to mold control is moisture control. The EPA recommends that a mold prevention program include the following:[4]

1. Locate and repair water intrusion in the building as soon as possible.

2. Locate and repair plumbing leaks, HVAC leaks, and fire sprinkler leaks as soon as possible.

3. Watch for condensation and wet spots; [repair] sources of moisture problems as soon as possible.

4. Prevent condensation by increasing surface temperatures or reducing the humidity in the air. Temperature can be increased by heating, insulating, or increasing air circulation. The moisture level of air can be reduced by repairing water leaks, increasing ventilation—if outside air is cold and dry—or by dehumidifying air, if outdoor air is warm and humid.

5. Keep HVAC drip pans clean, flowing properly, and unobstructed.

6. Vent moisture-generating appliances such as dryers to the outside.

7. Maintain low indoor humidity below 60 percent.

8. Perform regular building /HVAC inspections and maintenance.

9. Clean and dry wet or damp spots as soon as possible.

10. Do not let foundations stay wet. Provide drainage, and slope ground away from foundations.

11. Maintain adequate ventilation in crawl spaces.

Common Sites for and Sources of Mold Growth

Common sites for indoor mold growth include bathroom tile, basement walls, wall cavities where water intrusion has occurred, areas around windows where moisture condenses, and near leaky plumbing fixtures. Common causes of water intrusion or moisture leading to mold growth include roof leaks, deck leaks, leaks through or around windows and sliding glass doors, condensation associated with high humidity or cold spots, localized flooding due to plumbing leaks or heavy rains, slow leaks in pipes and plumbing fixtures, and malfunction or poor design of humidification systems. Uncontrolled humidity can also be a source of moisture leading to mold growth particularly in hot, humid climates.[5]

Mold can be detected in a home by sight, or by an earthy or musty odor. Visible mold growth can be found around or under water damaged surfaces. Mold often results in discolored and cracked ceilings, walls, and floors. Moisture and mold are especially attracted to carpeting, carpet padding, and products containing paper such as drywall and insulation.

Health Effects and Symptoms of Mold Exposure

When mold growth occurs in buildings, adverse health problems may be reported by some building occupants, particularly those with allergies or respiratory problems. Mold does not always present a health problem; however, for those who are sensitive, mold spores can lead to allergic and other symptoms such as:[6] 1. respiratory problems—wheezing and difficulty breathing; 2. nasal and sinus congestion; 3. burning and watering eyes; 4. dry, hacking cough; 5. sore throat; 6. nose and throat irritation; 7. shortness of breath; 8. skin irritation; 9. difficulty swallowing, choking, vomiting; 10. burning in throat and lungs; 11. bladder, liver, spleen or kidney pain; 12. memo-

ry loss or slurred speech; 13. vision problems; 14. swollen lymph nodes; 15. thyroid irregularities; 16. headaches; 17. night sweats and hot flashes; and 18. generalized fatigue.

Residents with any of these symptoms should immediately seek medical attention.

Potential Signs of Mold Growth

Signs of mold growth include:[7]

1. Stained ceilings, walls, and floors.

2. Musty, earthy, or urine-scented odor.

3. Black, brown, orange, pink, or green speckled walls or plumbing, grout, or tile.

4. Delaminating siding, resulting in inadequate building coverage and water intrusion.

5. Lumber that is not protected from weather in lumber yards—frequently called lumberyard mold.

6. Cracked wood trim leading to water intrusion.

7. Swollen or crumbling walls or buckling floorboards.

8. Sewer backup leading to water damage.

9. Roof leaks.

10. Improperly installed flashing.

11. Flood or hurricane damage.

12. Water intrusion through windows and doors.

13. Washing machine leaks and over flow.

14. Leaking toilet seals.

15. Leaking bathtub drains.

16. Lack of ventilation.

17. Relative humidity above 55 percent.

18. Damp basements.

19. Broken window and door seals.

20. Plumbing leaks.

21. Water damage following fires.

22. Faulty heating or air conditioning systems.

23. Clogged vents or air ducts.

24. Disconnected downspouts.

Mold Testing

Once mold is detected in a common-interest development, the board, acting on advice from the community manager, needs to decide whether to test. This is a very important decision, in which the board must weigh the costs of testing—mold testing can be very expensive—against the costs of not testing. If the board fails to test, and it turns out residents are becoming ill and structures are being damaged because of mold, the board is open to legal action.

Many construction companies that perform maintenance and repair at common-interest developments have experience evaluating mold. Experienced contractors can give an opinion whether an indoor air quality professional, industrial hygienist, or toxicologist should conduct tests. A rule of thumb adopted by the EPA is that if a moldy area is less than 10 square feet, professionals need not be employed to conduct a clean-up.[8] It follows that small areas of mold growth may not merit the expense of professional testing by indoor air quality professionals. If the board is uncertain whether to test—hire professionals.

The most important first step to identify a possible mold problem is to visually inspect various components for signs of water damage. Pay particular attention to absorbent materials like ceiling tiles, drywall, cardboard, or paper for water stains. Also check ventilation systems for damp filters and overall cleanliness. If any of these components show signs of water intrusion, consider contacting an indoor air-quality professional to determine the extent of moisture in building materials.[9]

If the inspection reveals significant mold growth or residents are experiencing health problems associated with exposure to mold, the association should hire a qualified industrial hygienist or toxicologist to test affected areas. Bulk, or surface sampling, and air sampling are the two most common tests, and they should only be performed by a trained professional. Bulk samples are collected from moldy surfaces by scraping or cutting, and surface samples are collected by wiping or stripping. Clearly, surface sampling is less destructive than bulk sampling.[10]

Air sampling is generally reserved for specific situations: residents are complaining of symptoms associated with fungal exposure, the ventilation systems may be contaminated, or the exact location of mold is unknown—such as within walls. Air samples are collected in various indoor and outdoor locations at the same time using specialized equipment and compared.[11]

Following inspection and testing, the industrial hygienist or toxicologist (and the defect attorney, if he or she is involved) should provide a written report to the board. A typical report contains a description of the inspection and testing methodology, the results of the inspections and testing, recommendations for remediation and further testing, and conclusions.

Mold Remediation

One part of the report mentioned above is the recommendations for remediation—or clean up—of the mold. Before cleaning up, make sure the cause of the water intrusion or accumulation has been corrected.[12] Otherwise, remediation is a waste of time and money.

There are five generally recognized levels of mold remediation or abatement[13], and each requires different personnel and techniques:[14]

Level I: This level of remediation is directed at small, isolated areas of mold limited to 10 square feet or less—ceiling tiles or small wall areas. Building maintenance personnel can undertake the remediation—if they've been trained in proper clean-up methods, how to protect themselves, and how to avoid potential health hazards. Containment of the area isn't necessary; however the work area should be unoccupied, and materials that can't be cleaned should be sealed in plastic bags and removed. Mold should be removed with a damp cloth and detergent and allowed to dry free from contamination and debris.

Level II is defined as mid-sized, isolated areas of 10–30 square feet. Again, regular building maintenance personnel can conduct the remediation, and they should wear dust masks, gloves, and goggles. The work area should be unoccupied, sealed with plastic sheets and tape, and misted to suppress dust. Materials should be removed in sealed plastic bags. All areas—including where workers entered—should be vacuumed with high-efficiency, particulate air (HEPA) filtering equipment then cleaned with a damp cloth and detergent and left to dry free from contamination and debris.

Level III consists of large, isolated areas of 30–100 square feet. For this level, an indoor air-quality professional should establish the remediation method, oversee the cleanup, and test the area when remediation is complete. Only people trained to handle hazardous materials and use disposable respirators should perform the work. Precautions for Level III are all the same as Level II; however, not only the work area should be unoccupied, but adjacent areas as well.

Level IV involves extensive contamination in an area greater than 100 square feet. Only trained personnel should conduct the cleanup and they should be equipped with HEPA full-face respirators, gloves, and disposable protective clothing that covers head and shoes. Efforts to seal the area are also extensive—plastic sheeting and tape, air locks, decontamination rooms, negative pressure, and HEPA-filtered exhaust fans. Vacating the area is obviously required. Not only are contaminated materials removed in sealed plastic bags, but the outside of the bags are decontaminated before leaving the building. Before the area can be reoccupied, the air must be tested be air-quality professional.

Level V is limited to remediation of HVAC system components. Many of the parameters described for Levels I–IV apply, depending on the size of the contaminated components. The HVAC system should be shut down prior to any remedial activities.

Communications during Mold Investigation, Testing, and Remediation

When mold is discovered, residents may become very concerned since the dangers of mold have been exaggerated by the media. On the other hand, it's important for community managers and boards to investigate potential mold problems thoroughly and to make informed decisions on how to deal with mold. The key to making informed decisions is using experienced indoor air-quality professionals.

When mold is found, the most important action the manager and board can take is to communicate effectively with owners and residents. Notify occupants of the affected areas immediately. Explain the remediation plan, describe the cleanup measures, and provide a time table for completion. If several units must be cleaned, it may be effective to convene a group meeting of all involved residents to discuss the remediation process. Usually, only a few rooms or areas have to be sealed off; but in extreme cases, resident may have to relocate during remediation. They'll need advance notice to plan for these inconveniences.[15]

Advise residents to see their doctors if they appear to have health problems related to mold. Provide them with copies of all inspection reports to give to their doctors.

And, finally, before authorizing final payment to the contractors who did the cleanup, the manager will, of course, want to ensure that the unit has been restored to its pre-contamination condition.

Endnotes

1. U.S. Environmental Protection Agency, Mold Remediation in Schools and Commercial Buildings, www.epa.gov/iaq/molds, Introduction at page 1.
2. *Ibid.*
3. *Id.,* Introduction at page 2.
4. *Id.,* Prevention at page 1.
5. *Id.,* Appendix B, Introduction to Molds, at pages 1-2.
6. *Id.,* Appendix B, Introduction to Molds, at pages 2-3; U.S. Environmental Protection Agency, A Brief Guide to Mold, Moisture, and Your Home, www.epa.gov./iaq, at pages 2-3.
7. California Department of Health Services, Indoor Air Quality Info Sheet, Mold in My Home: What Do I Do? (revised June 2004), http://www.cal-iaq.org/mold0107.htm page 1.
8. U.S. Environmental Protection Agency, A Brief Guide to Mold, Moisture, and Your Home, supra, Who Should do the Cleanup, at page 1.
9. New York City Department of Health and Mental Hygiene, Environmental & Occupational Disease Epidemiology, Guidelines on Assessment and Remediation of Fungi in Indoor Environments (1993), www.ci.nyc.us/html/doh/html/epi/mol-drpt1.shtml, page 5.
10. *Ibid.*
11. *Id.* at page 6.
12. *Ibid.*
13. *Ibid.*
14. *Id.* at pages 7-8.
15. *Id.* at pages 9-10.

Index

Aas v. Superior Court of San Diego County, 94

Alternate living accommodations (*see relocation*)

Alternative dispute resolution, 127ff

American Arbitration Association, 15

American Institute of Architects, 41, 160

American rule, 151

Anchor Center, 172

Appraiser(s), 39

Arbitration, 135ff

Architect(s), 37, 159-60, 164

Association, 83ff

Attorney, construction defect, 33ff

Attorney/client privilege, 16, 23, 25, 75-6

Attorneys' reports, 15, 41

Avner v. Longridge Estates, 100

Bank loans, 144

Becker v. IRM Corp., 100

Benton-Robb, 172

BOSA Development Corporation, 172

Breach of duty, 103-105

Breach of warranty, 96-97, 150

Builder's right to repair, 59ff, 69ff, 130

Building code(s), 7

Business judgment rule, 6, 104

Calderon process, 9, 78

Calloway v The City of Reno, 95

Carpenter v. Donohoe, 96

Case management
  meeting, 79
  order(s), 12, 112ff, 131, 174
  schedule, 122

Caveat emptor, 106

CC&Rs, 23, 31, 54, 74, 103, 137-37, 151

Claims (*see complaints*)

Class action(s), 85ff

Columbia Western Corp. v. Vela, 96

Comparative fault, 153

Complaints, 9, 12, 111

Confidentiality, 130

Contractor(s)
  general, 39
  response to claims, 61-2

Contribution, 62, 112, 132, 146

Cost of repair, 55, 77, 119, 158

Costs, allocating, 119 (*see also expenses*)

Crescent Heights, 171

Damages, 149ff

Davis-Sterling CID Act, 59

Deceit, 106

Defense Research Institute, 41

Del Mar Beach Club, 7

Depositions, 120

Design professionals, 101

Diminution, property value, 159

Disclosure statement(s), 16-17, 166

Discovery, 113-114

Dispute resolution, 78-79

Document(s), 10, 31, 69, 73-74, 114

Economic-loss rule, 94-95, 151

Edgewater Condo, 172

Eichler Homes, Inc. v Anderson, 96

Electrical systems, 49

Emotional distress, 153

Engineer(s), 38, 40, 47ff

English rule, 151

Environmental Protection Agency, 220

Esplanade Place, 172

Evidence gathering, 9

Executive session(s), 24

Expense(s), 143ff

Expert(s), 11, 37ff, 119, 152

Federal Arbitration Act, 136

Fibermesh, 86

Final completion (*see substantial completion*)

Final Subdivision Public Report, 103

Financial institutions, 101

Fire protection/safety, 39, 48, 69

Flyers, 20

Fraud, 106

Frequently asked questions, 20

Grande at Santa Fe Place, 172

Greenman v. Yuba Power Products, 99

Hawaiki Tower, 172

Hicks v. Kaufman and Broad Homecorp, 86

High-rise buildings, 171ff

Hilton Hotels Corp., 173

Horizons project, 172

Indemnity, 112

Individual unit, (*see separate interest*)

Industrial hygiene consultant, 39, 47

Industry standards, 7, 45ff

Inspection(s), 70, 117, 174

Insurance, 78, 146ff, 176, 206ff

Investment account(s), 146

Issue release, 76

Jimenez v. Superior Court of San Diego County, 100

Judicial reference, 136

Kalia Tower, 173

Krielgler v. Eichler Homes, 99

La Jolla Village v. Superior Court,
100-101
Lamden v. La Jolla Shores, 104
Landlords, 100
Landscape architect, 38, 51
Landscaping, 9, 157
Lesser-of rule, 150
Licensed general contractor,
39, 161
Life-safety issues, 18, 157, 158,
159
Limited liability corporations,
74, 112
Litigation, traditional, 112
Loan(s), 145
Loss of use, 152

Materials suppliers, 100
Mediation, 120-21, 127ff,
Mediator(s), 113-114, 131
Meeting(s), 16, 17, 18, 24, 162
Mold, 173, 220ff

National Association of Home
Builders, 60
National Electrical Code, 49
Negligence, 91ff, 150
Newsletters, 20
Notice, 18, 61, 69-70, 78
Nuisance, 104-106, 150

*Occidental Land, Inc. v Superior
Court,* 86
Offset, 153
Orders to show cause, 145

Pennsylvania's Residential
Construction Dispute
Resolution Act (PRCDRA),
59ff
Persons most knowledgeable
(PMKs), 120-21
Plumbing and sewer, 49
*Pollard v. Saxe & Yolles
Development Co.,* 97
Pre-litigation, 11
mediation, 131
requirements, 78
Pretrial conferences, 12, 121
Private judges, 135, 138
Privity of contract, 97, 98

*P.S. Farrington v. Casa Solana
Condominium Assn,* 6
Punch list, 55, 146, 165

Quality control, 166

*Raven's Cove Townhomes, Inc.
v Knuppe,* 105, 151
Reconstruction, 13, 157ff,
217ff
Recoverable damages, *(see
damages)*
Recovery theories, 91ff
Regatta Seaside, 171, 172
Relocation, 152
Repairs, 43, 69-71, 118, 145
Requests for proposals, 34
Reserves, 143
Responsible parties, 10, 73
Responsive pleadings, 112
Restatement (Second) of Torts, 98
Risk control programs, 43
Roofing specialist/consultant,
39, 46, 51, 121
Rowland v. Christian, 91

Sabella v Whistler, 92
Safety, 42, 49, 153
Scope of repair, 158
Securities and Exchange
Commission, 75
Separate interest, 83
Settlement(s), 19, 64, 75, 79,
119, 121, 133, 145-46
Show and tell, 118
Soils & soils issues, 39, 48, 157
Special assessments, 144
Special verdict procedure, 123
Standing to sue, 83-85, 173,
178ff
Statistical consultant, 39
Statute of limitations, 29ff, 63,
189ff
Statutory causes of action, 101
Strict liability, 98
Structural issues, 47-48
Stucco consultant(s), 39-40, 47
Subcontractors *(see also, experts),*
101
Substantial completion, 165
Surveys, homeowners, 11, 16

Tavares v. Horstman, 30
Tempe Town Lake, 172
Testing, 53ff, 118-19
Trial, 19, 121-23
Trust account(s), 145
Turnberry One, 172-73
Type V construction, 172

Uniform Building Code, 7
Uniform Commercial Code,
96
Uniform Common Interest
Ownership Act, 84

Vaughn v Dame Construction Co.,
87

Walk through, 10, 21
Warranties, 96, 102
Water intrusion, 45-6, 157
Waterproofing specialist,
39, 47
William Lyon Company, 94
Window consultant, 39
Work product privilege, 10, 24

About the Authors

Ronald L. Perl, ESQ.

Ronald L. Perl is a partner of Hill Wallack, Attorneys at Law. He is partner-in-charge of the firm's Community Association Law Practice Group and is a member of the Government Affairs Practice Group. He concentrates his practice in the areas of community association law, transactional real estate, eminent domain, and tax appeals. He is also a mediator for construction, real estate, and community association disputes.

Mr. Perl is nationally recognized for his work in the field of community association law and is a member and former governor of the prestigious national College of Community Association Lawyers. In 2005, he was named a Super Lawyer by *Law & Politics* and *New Jersey Monthly*. He is an adjunct professor at Seton Hall Law School in Newark and has served on the faculties of the Community Association Law Seminar and CAI's Professional Management Development Program (PMDP). As a PMDP instructor, Mr. Perl taught community association law to professional managers who were candidates for the Professional Community Association Manager (PCAM) designation. He is a frequent lecturer on all aspects of community law.

Mr. Perl is national president elect of Community Associations Institute and will serve as its president in 2007. He is past president of the New Jersey chapter and past president of its political action committee.

Ross W. Feinberg, ESQ.

Ross W. Feinberg is a member of the California, Nevada and Colorado bars. He is the senior partner of the law firm of Feinberg, Grant, Mayfield, Kaneda & Litt, LLP and has received an AV rating from Martindale-Hubbell on behalf of himself and the entire firm indicating very high to pre-eminent legal ability and very high ethical standards. Mr. Feinberg has the privilege of serving as a member of the national board of trustees and national faculty for Community Associations Institute (CAI) and serves as the Institute's 2006 national president.

He serves as an author and faculty member for the California Association of Community Managers (CACM), co-chair of numerous national seminars on behalf of Mealeys Lexis-Nexis, and is a member of the speakers and topics committee for the annual West Coast Casualty Conference on Construction Defects.

Additionally, Mr. Feinberg has the distinguished honor of being a member of the College of Community Association Lawyers of CAI. He has received numerous industry related awards both from the community association field and the construction defect bar including being the only plaintiff attorney to be awarded the prestigious Jerrold S. Oliver Award of Excellence at the 2003 West Coast Casualty Conference.

Mr. Feinberg received his preparatory education at the University of Southern California where he graduated with a Bachelors of Science degree in Business Administration cum laude in 1981. He received his law degree from the University of San Diego School of Law in 1984. He is a frequent speaker at local, national, and international seminars relative to construction defect litigation, community association law, and consumer class actions, and he is the author of books and articles relative to laws affecting community associations and construction defects.

Most recently, he had the honor of serving as a panelist for the Judicial Symposium on Construction Defect Litigation on behalf of the AEI-Brookings Institute Joint Center for Regulatory Studies in Washington D.C.

About CAI and Community Associations Press

Founded in 1973 as a multidisciplinary, nonprofit alliance serving all stakeholders in community associations, Community Associations Institute is America's leading advocate for responsible communities. CAI is the only national organization dedicated to fostering vibrant, responsible, competent community associations. Our mission is to assist community associations in promoting harmony, community, and responsible leadership.

CAI has more than 25,000 members in 55 chapters throughout the United States. To find out more about CAI, visit www.caionline.org or call CAI Direct at (888) 224-4321 (M–F, 9–6:30 ET).

Community Associations Press, the publishing division of Community Associations Institute (CAI), is dedicated solely to publishing the very best resources available for community associations. It publishes the largest collection of books and guides on community associations available today. Visit our bookstore online at www.caionline.org/bookstore.cfm

Praise for Construction Defect Litigation

"This is not just an excellent and informative publication, it's the first book that adequately explains the legal and procedural aspects of construction defects— a must read for any party in a construction defect case." —Benjamin Dutton, RS

"This book is great. The author's have done an excellent job of bringing this complex subject to the industry in a clear, concise, and comprehensive format." —Scott B. Carpenter, ESQ.

"A must read for every homeowner association board considering construction deficiencies." —Nico March, CFM

"This book will help developers and their attorneys refine their strategies for avoiding litigation in connection with construction defects." —G. Douglass White, P.E.

"As a manager that has just started working with developers, this book had a lot to offer as far as correcting the defects and tracking issues." —Lauren Lee, CMCA, AMS

"As the board president of a high rise-luxury condominium in Hawaii recently involved in constructions defect litigation, I wish we'd had a book like this to guide us through the initial phases. Our success was due to consistent and constant communication, but the process would have been even easier had this text been available." —Patty Kawakami

"This book should be required reading for anyone facing construction defect litigation." —Judge Louis Cardenas, Retired

Date Due

	AUG 1 0 2007		
JUL 0 4 2011			

BRODART, CO.   Cat. No. 23-233-003   Printed in U.S.A.